Anonymous

Epworth hymnal

Containing standard hymns of the church, songs for the Sunday-school, songs for

social services

Anonymous

Epworth hymnal
Containing standard hymns of the church, songs for the Sunday-school, songs for social services

ISBN/EAN: 9783337264765

Printed in Europe, USA, Canada, Australia, Japan

Cover: Foto ©Thomas Meinert / pixelio.de

More available books at **www.hansebooks.com**

THE EPWORTH HYMNAL,

CONTAINING

STANDARD HYMNS OF THE CHURCH,

SONGS FOR THE SUNDAY-SCHOOL,

SONGS FOR SOCIAL SERVICES,

SONGS FOR THE HOME CIRCLE,

SONGS FOR SPECIAL OCCASIONS.

NEW YORK: | CINCINNATI:
PHILLIPS & HUNT. | CRANSTON & STOWE.

Copyright, 1885, by PHILLIPS & HUNT, New York.

PREFACE.

IN the old parish of Epworth, in Lincolnshire, England, lived the earnest, eccentric, and scholarly father, and the gifted, wise, and consecrated mother, of the illustrious John and Charles Wesley.

The story of Samuel Wesley's ministry at Epworth, extending over a period of thirty-nine years—from 1696 to 1735—is alive with interest. The people whom he served were, for the most part, poor, ignorant, coarse, and cruel. Those were days of political strife, when missiles and firebrands were used as arguments. The godly rector, unflinching in his devotion to conviction, paid the price of his fidelity.

In poverty most oppressive; in conflicts most bitter; in labors most abundant, did the old rectory of Epworth hold and train the remarkable family from which were to come forth two of the most widely-known and most successful workers in the Church of God—the one a preacher and bishop, the other a writer of sacred hymns. By sermon and song, they two went forth to make known to the world the exceeding glory and the saving power of the Lord Jesus; to defend by Scripture the great doctrines of redemption, and by persuasive song to win the hearts of men from sin to righteousness, from self to Christ.

However grand the work and its results, we must not forget that the beginnings and the most valuable preparations were at Epworth, where Samuel Wesley studied and prayed and served, and where Susannah Wesley trained her children, counseled her husband, instructed their parishioners, and walked with God. Before Oxford was Epworth. Before Bristol and City Road Chapel was Epworth.

The poetic fire burned in Samuel Wesley. It reached white heat in the soul of his son Charles, "who was a poet by nature and habit," and of whose productions a distinguished critic says: "There are no hymns in the world of such 'spontaneous devotion;' none so loftily spiritual; none so unmistakably genuine and intensely earnest, as the best-known and largely-used of Wesley's." *

John Wesley was also a writer of hymns, a lover of poetry, and a firm believer in the service of song as a means of grace for saints, and of awakening for sinners. He urged all the people to sing. He gave wise directions concerning the spirit and manner of singing, and his followers in all parts of the world have been famous for the ardor and power with which they have sung the praises of the Lord.

All this carries us back to Epworth, where, in addition to the songs of the rectory at family worship, we hear from the church the songs of the people as the faithful rector taught them to sing. The biographer of "The Mother of the Wesleys" says: "Samuel Wesley regarded psalmody as 'the most elevated part of public worship.' Notwithstanding his love for 'anthems and cathedral music,' he was willing to forego his own preferences for the sake of his uneducated flock, and allowed 'the novel way of parochial singing.' . . . Discarding the lazy and inharmonious drawlings of a choir of ignorant and self-important rustics, he resolutely set himself to teach the congregation and children the divine art of sacred song. His efforts were so successful that he declares 'they did sing well after it had cost a pretty deal to teach them.'"

Thus from the Epworth church and parsonage rang out strains of music that have attracted the attention of the world; filled chapel, cathedral, and tented grove with melody; lifted the cry of penitence and the shout of triumph to the heavens; filled

* The Rev. Frederic M. Bird, in "Bibliotheca Sacra." 1864.

PREFACE.

the mouths of children with praise, the hearts of believers with joy, the chamber of death with the pæans of victory.

The Committee appointed in pursuance of the action of the General Conference to prepare this book, has done well in calling it THE EPWORTH HYMNAL. Besides a certain euphony in the title, there come with it reverent and grateful thoughts concerning the character and services of the most excellent father of the Wesleys, and that modern Monica, whose strength and loveliness, whose piety and scholarship, are so manifest in the sons whom generations honor. There come also with the title—THE EPWORTH HYMNAL—memories of family prayer and family songs, of neighbors gathered by the devout Susannah on Sunday afternoons for special services of prayer, praise, and admonition, and of the meetings in Epworth church for the training of all the people, old and young, to sing the songs of the sanctuary.

The Committee, to which the work of compiling THE EPWORTH HYMNAL was assigned, is as follows: Rev. J. H. VINCENT, Rev. J. S. CHADWICK, JAMES M'GEE, JOHN E. SEARLES, JR., A. S. NEWMAN, JOHN J. MATTHIAS.

The editorial work of this book has been performed by Mr. JOHN E. SEARLES, JR., by appointment of the Committee.

The greatest care has been taken by the Committee to meet the demands of the diverse constituency at whose request the book has been prepared, and to serve the variety of purposes involved in the terms of the appointment. Here are hymns of the ages that can never grow old or drop out of use. Here are more recent hymns which have already become standards, and which are to be hymns for the ages. Here are songs full of strength and sweetness, favorites of the devout, and attractive also to youth and childhood. Here are "popular songs" which hold much truth rhythmically told. The severest criticisms might point out slight defects in them which, although sufficient to exclude them from the classic lists, do not justify their omission in a book "for the people." Here are new songs—experiments of poetry and music—which the Committee has approved, but which must be tested by the leaders and the led in the service of song.

THE EPWORTH HYMNAL is designed for use in the family, the social meeting, and the Sunday-school. Its selections will tend to promote congregational singing in the sanctuary, by making youth and adults familiar with the words and music which already are, or certainly ought to be, rendered at the public service.

The Committee urges upon all pastors the importance of commending THE EPWORTH HYMNAL to the homes of our people. Back of the public activity of the Church we find the family. No religious training can become a substitute for home influence and instruction. In this day there is especial need of renewed endeavor in this direction. Shall THE EPWORTH HYMNAL be a delightful reminder of the old Epworth rectory in Lincolnshire? and by the power of music open the doors of neglectful homes to the sweet ministries of religion?

Sweet home of Epworth, where reverent scholarship presided; where parents governed and children obeyed; where the Holy Scriptures were continually quoted and habitually followed; where songs rose from grateful hearts to the listening heavens; where the voice of prayer was scarcely ever silent; where neighbors were collected for worship and counsel; where each child was brought into sacred conference with its mother concerning the soul, the law of God, the grace of Christ, and the home in heaven!

May our homes be full of law and liberty, of grace and gladness; and from them may there come into Sunday-school, social meeting, and public service those who are well prepared to study the word of God diligently, pray reverently, sing heartily, listen attentively, and live consistently!

J. H. VINCENT.

RESPONSIVE SERVICES.
FOR THE SUNDAY-SCHOOL AND SOCIAL MEETINGS.

OPENING SERVICE FOR THE SUNDAY-SCHOOL.

Leader. Grace be to you, and peace from God our Father and from the Lord Jesus Christ.

School. Blessed be God, even the Father of our Lord Jesus Christ, the Father of mercies and the God of all comfort.

L. Give unto the Lord the glory due unto his name: worship the Lord in the beauty o' holiness.

S. Unto thee, O God, do we give thanks unto thee do we give thanks: for that thy name is near thy wondrous works declare.

L. It is a good thing to give thanks unto the Lord, and to sing praises unto thy name, O Most High.

S. To show forth thy loving kindness in the morning, and thy faithfulness every night.

L. Sing praise to the Lord, which dwelleth in Zion; declare among the people his doings.

S. O Lord, open thou my lips; and my mouth shall show forth thy praise.

L. Blessed are they that dwell in thy house; they will be still praising thee.

S. Praise waiteth for thee, O God, in Zion: and unto thee shall the vow be performed.

L. O come, let us sing unto the Lord; let us make a joyful noise to the Rock of our Salvation.

S. Let us come before his presence with thanksgiving, and make a joyful noise unto him with psalms.

Singing. A hymn of praise. See Index, p. 226.
PRAYER.

CLOSING SERVICE.

Leader. Let the word of Christ dwell in you richly in all wisdom.

School. We ought to give the more earnest heed to the things which we have heard, lest at any time we should let them slip.

L. The Lord bless thee, and keep thee:

S. The Lord make his face shine upon thee, and be gracious unto thee:

L. The Lord lift up his countenance upon thee, and give thee peace.

S. Amen.

Singing. Gloria Patri, No. 1; or a closing hymn. See Index, p. 226.

OPENING SERVICE FOR THE PRAYER-MEETING.

Leader. I was glad when they said unto me, Let us go into the house of the Lord.

Congregation. We will go into his tabernacle; we will worship at his footstool.

L. Enter into his gates with thanksgiving and into his courts with praise.

C. It is good to sing praises unto our God: for it is pleasant, and praise is comely.

Singing. A hymn of praise. See Index, p. 226.

L. They that wait upon the Lord shall renew their strength; they shall mount up with wings as eagles;

C. They shall run, and not be weary; they shall walk, and not faint.

L. Blessed are they which do hunger and thirst after righteousness: for they shall be filled.

C. I am the living bread which came down from heaven: if any man eat of this bread he shall live forever.

Singing. Break Thou the Bread of Life. No. 90.

L. If any man sin, we have an advocate with the Father, Jesus Christ the righteous.

C. Wherefore he is able to save them to the uttermost, that come unto God by him,

L. If any man will do his will, he shall know of the doctrine.

C. And ye shall know the truth, and the truth shall make you free.

L. Continue in prayer, and watch in the same with thanksgiving.

C. Now we know that God heareth not sinners; but if any man be a worshiper of God, and doeth his will, him he heareth.

L. Draw nigh to God, and he will draw nigh to you.

C. Verily, verily, I say unto you, whatsoever ye shall ask the Father in my name, he will give it you.

L. Seeing then that we have a great high-priest, that is passed into the heavens, Jesus the Son of God,

C. Let us therefore come boldly unto the throne of grace, that we may obtain mercy, and find grace to help in time of need.

PRAYER.

RESPONSIVE SERVICES.

VESPER SERVICE.

Leader. Behold now the day draweth toward evening.
Congregation. Behold the day groweth to an end.
L. The day goeth away.
C. For the shadows of evening are stretched out.

    Sing: "Softly now the light of day."
                No. 18, first verse.

Leader. And thou shalt make an altar to burn incense upon: . . . when Aaron lighteth the lamps at even, he shall burn incense upon it.
Congregation. Let my prayer be set forth before thee as incense, and the lifting up of my hands as the evening sacrifice.
PRAYER.
L. And it came to pass at the time of the offering of the evening sacrifice, that Elijah the prophet came near, and prayed. . . . Then the fire of the Lord fell, and consumed the burnt sacrifice.
C. Evening, and morning, and noon will I pray and cry aloud, and he shall hear my voice.

    Sing: "Again as evening's shadow falls."
                No. 17, three verses.

Leader. From the rising of the sun unto the going down of the same the Lord's name is to be praised.
Congregation. Praise waiteth for thee, O God, in Zion: and unto thee shall the vow be performed.
L. Sing praises to God, sing praises. For God is the king of all the earth; sing ye praises with understanding.
C. To him that made great lights: the sun to rule by day; the moon and stars to rule by night.
L. It is a good thing to give thanks unto the Lord, and to sing praises unto thy name, O Most High.
C. O God, thou God of my salvation, my tongue shall sing aloud of thy righteousness.
L. To show forth thy loving-kindness in the morning, and thy faithfulness every night.
C. And to stand every morning to thank and to praise the Lord, and likewise at even.
L. Behold, bless ye the Lord all ye servants of the Lord, which by night stand in the house of the Lord.

C. I will bless the Lord at all times: his praise shall continually be in my mouth.

    Sing: "Glory to thee, my God, this night."
                No. 19, three verses.

Leader. O taste and see that the Lord is good:
Congregation. Blessed is the man that trusteth in him.
L. Thou shalt not be afraid for the terror by night.
C. Whoso putteth his trust in the Lord shall be safe.
L. Nor for the arrow that flieth by day.
C. He is a shield for them that put their trust in him.
L. Nor for the pestilence that walketh in darkness.
C. He that trusteth in the Lord, mercy shall compass him about.
L. Nor for the destruction that wasteth at noonday.
C. The name of the Lord is a strong tower; the righteous runneth into it, and is safe.
L. O Lord of hosts, blessed is the man that trusteth in thee.
C. Let thy mercy, O Lord, be upon us, according as we hope in thee.

    Sing: "When all thy mercies, O my God."
                No. 42, three verses.

Leader. Thou makest the outgoings of the morning and evening to rejoice.
Congregation. The Lord will command his loving-kindness in the day-time, and in the night his song shall be with me.
L. At midnight Paul and Silas prayed and sang praises unto God.
C. God, my Maker, who giveth songs in the night.
L. If I say, Surely the darkness shall cover me; even the night shall be light about me.
C. It shall come to pass that at evening time it shall be light.
L. Yea, the darkness hideth not from thee, but the night shineth as the day: the darkness and the light are both alike to thee.
C. I will both lay me down and sleep, for thou, Lord, makest me to dwell in safety.

    Sing: "Sun of my soul, thou Saviour dear."
                No. 23, verses 1, 2, 3, and 6.

Leader. And when he had sent the multitudes away, he went up into a mountain apart to pray.

RESPONSIVE SERVICES.

Congregation. And when even was now come, his disciples went down unto the sea, and entered into a ship, and went over the sea toward Capernaum.

L. And in the fourth watch of the night Jesus went unto them, walking on the sea.

C. And when the disciples saw him walking on the sea they were troubled, saying, It is a spirit; and they cried out for fear.

L. But straightway Jesus spake unto them, saying, Be of good cheer; it is I, be not afraid.

C. And when they were come into the ship the wind ceased.

Sing: "If on a quiet sea."
No. 301, verses 1, 2, 4.

Leader. Our days on the earth are as a shadow, and there is none abiding.

Congregation. So teach us to number our days that we may apply our hearts unto wisdom.

L. For here we have no continuing city, but we seek one to come.

C. A building of God, a house not made with hands, eternal in the heavens.

L. There shall be no night there.

C. And there shall be no more death, neither sorrow nor crying, neither shall there be any more pain.

L. Therefore, my beloved brethren, be ye steadfast, unmovable, always abounding in the work of the Lord.

C. Thanks be to God, who giveth us the victory through our Lord Jesus Christ.

Sing: "Saviour, again to thy dear Name we raise."
No. 29.

THE SABBATH.

Leader. Remember the Sabbath-day to keep it holy.

School. This is the day which the Lord hath made; we will rejoice and be glad in it.

L. Ye shall keep my Sabbaths, and reverence my sanctuary: I am the Lord.

S. Six days may work be done; but in the seventh is the Sabbath of rest, holy to the Lord.

L. If thou turn away thy foot from the Sabbath, from doing thy pleasure on my holy day: and call the Sabbath a delight, the holy of the Lord, honorable; and shalt honor him, not doing thine own ways, nor finding thine own pleasure, nor speaking thine own words; then shalt thou delight thyself in the Lord.

S. We will go into his tabernacle; we will worship at his footstool.

L. Exalt ye the Lord our God, and worship at his footstool, for he is holy.

S. Thy way, O God, is in the sanctuary: who is so great a God as our God?

THE WORD OF GOD.

Leader. Come hither, and hear the word of the Lord your God.

School. Open thou mine eyes, that I may behold wondrous things out of thy law.

L. Be ye mindful always of his covenant; the word which he commanded to a thousand generations.

S. The statutes of the Lord are right, rejoicing the heart: the commandment of the Lord is pure, enlightening the eyes.

L. Blessed are they that hear the word of God and keep it.

S. I will hear what God the Lord will speak: for he will speak peace unto his people and to his saints.

L. Search the Scriptures; for in them ye think ye have eternal life: and they are they which testify of me.

S. All Scripture is given by inspiration of God, and is profitable for doctrine, for reproof, for correction, for instruction in righteousness.

L. These are written that ye might believe that Jesus is the Christ, the Son of God: and that believing ye might have life through his name.

S. The grass withereth, the flower fadeth; but the word of God shall stand forever.

THE LORD'S PRAYER.

Our Father who art in heaven, hallowed be thy name. Thy kingdom come. Thy will be done in earth as it is in heaven. Give us this day our daily bread; and forgive us our trespasses, as we forgive them that trespass against us. And lead us not into temptation: but deliver us from evil: for thine is the kingdom, and the power, and the glory, forever. *Amen.*

RESPONSIVE SERVICES.

THE BEATITUDES.

BLESSED are the poor in spirit: for theirs is the kingdom of heaven.

Blessed are they that mourn: for they shall be comforted.

Blessed are the meek: for they shall inherit the earth.

Blessed are they which do hunger and thirst after righteousness: for they shall be filled.

Blessed are the merciful: for they shall obtain mercy.

Blessed are the pure in heart: for they shall see God.

Blessed are the peace-makers: for they shall be called the children of God.

Blessed are they which are persecuted for righteousness' sake: for theirs is the kingdom of heaven.

Blessed are ye, when men shall revile you, and persecute you, and shall say all manner of evil against you falsely, for my sake.

Rejoice, and be exceeding glad: for great is your reward in heaven: for so persecuted they the prophets which were before you.

THE TEN COMMANDMENTS.

And God spake all these words, saying,

I. THOU shalt have no other gods before me.

II. Thou shalt not make unto thee any graven image, or any likeness of any thing that is in heaven above, or that is in the earth beneath, or that is in the water under the earth: thou shalt not bow down thyself to them, nor serve them: for I the Lord thy God am a jealous God, visiting the iniquity of the fathers upon the children unto the third and fourth generation of them that hate me; and showing mercy unto thousands of them that love me, and keep my commandments.

III. Thou shalt not take the name of the Lord thy God in vain: for the Lord will not hold him guiltless that taketh his name in vain.

IV. Remember the Sabbath-day, to keep it holy. Six days shalt thou labor, and do all thy work: but the seventh day is the Sabbath of the Lord thy God: in it thou shalt not do any work, thou, nor thy son, nor thy daughter, thy man-servant, nor thy maid-servant, nor thy cattle, nor thy stranger that is within thy gates: for in six days the Lord made heaven and earth, the sea, and all that in them is, and rested the seventh day: wherefore the Lord blessed the Sabbath-day, and hallowed it.

V. Honor thy father and thy mother: that thy days may be long upon the land which the Lord thy God giveth thee.

VI. Thou shalt not kill.

VII. Thou shalt not commit adultery.

VIII. Thou shalt not steal.

IX. Thou shalt not bear false witness against thy neighbor.

X. Thou shalt not covet thy neighbor's house, thou shalt not covet thy neighbor's wife, nor his man-servant, nor his maid-servant, nor his ox, nor his ass, nor any thing that is thy neighbor's.

BAPTISMAL COVENANT.

I RENOUNCE the devil and all his works, the vain pomp and glory of the world, with all covetous desires of the same, and the carnal desires of the flesh, so that I will not follow nor be led by them.

THE APOSTLES' CREED.

I BELIEVE in God the Father Almighty, Maker of heaven and earth; and in Jesus Christ his only Son our Lord; who was conceived by the Holy Ghost, born of the Virgin Mary, suffered under Pontius Pilate; was crucified, dead, and buried; the third day he rose from the dead; he ascended into heaven, and sitteth on the right hand of God the Father Almighty; from thence he shall come to judge the quick and the dead.

I believe in the Holy Ghost; the Holy Catholic Church,* the communion of saints: the forgiveness of sins; the resurrection of the body, and the life everlasting. *Amen.*

Having been baptized in this faith, I will obediently keep God's holy will and commandments, and walk in the same all the days of my life, God being my helper.

* By the Holy Catholic Church is meant the Church of God in general.

ORDER OF ARRANGEMENT.

	HYMNS
SONGS OF WORSHIP.................................Nos.	1–30
SONGS OF THE SABBATH............................	31–36
SONGS OF GOD......................................	37–47
SONGS OF CHRIST....................................	48–84
SONGS OF THE HOLY SPIRIT.......................	85–88
SONGS OF THE SCRIPTURES.......................	89–92
SONGS OF SALVATION...............................	93–132
SONGS OF THE CHRISTIAN LIFE..................	133–239
SONGS OF THE CHURCH............................	240–260
SONGS OF HEAVEN...................................	261–278
SONGS FOR THE LITTLE ONES.....................	279–292
SONGS—MISCELLANEOUS............................	293–306
CHANTS...	307–319
TOPICAL INDEX..............................Page	226
INDEX: TITLES AND FIRST LINES.................	227

THE EPWORTH HYMNAL

FOR

Sunday-Schools and Social Services.

OLD HUNDRED. L. M.   Louis Bourgeois.

1. All peo - ple that on earth do dwell, Sing to the Lord with cheer - ful voice; Him serve with mirth, his praise forth tell, Come ye be - fore him, and re - joice.

1   *Invitation to worship*, Psalm 108.
2 Know that the Lord is God indeed,
    Without our aid he did us make :
    We are his flock, he doth us feed,
    And for his sheep he doth us take.
3 O enter then his gates with praise,
    Approach with joy his courts unto :
    Praise, laud, and bless his name always,
    For it is seemly so to do.

4 For why? the Lord our God is good,
    His mercy is forever sure ;
    His truth at all times firmly stood,
    And shall from age to age endure.
                              Wm. Kethe.

DOXOLOGY. L. M.
Praise God, from whom all blessings flow;
Praise him, all creatures here below;
Praise him above, ye heavenly host;
Praise Father, Son, and Holy Ghost.
                              Bp. Thomas Ken.

GLORIA PATRI.

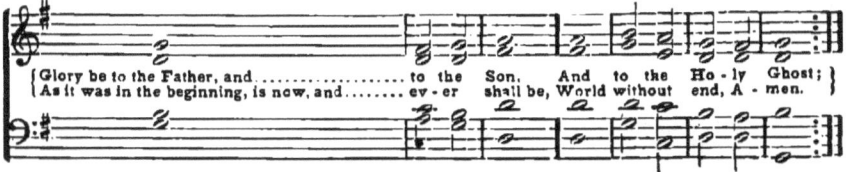

{ Glory be to the Father, and.............. to the Son. And to the Ho - ly Ghost; }
{ As it was in the beginning, is now, and........ ev - er shall be, World without end, A - men. }

SONGS OF WORSHIP.

AZMON. C. M. — Carl Gotthelf Glaser.

1. O for a thousand tongues, to sing My great Redeemer's praise; The glories of my God and King, The triumphs of his grace!

Exultant praise to the Redeemer.

2 My gracious Master and my God,
 Assist me to proclaim,
To spread through all the earth abroad,
 The honors of thy name.

3 Jesus! the name that charms our fears,
 That bids our sorrows cease;
'Tis music in the sinner's ears,
 'Tis life, and health, and peace.

4 He breaks the power of canceled sin,
 He sets the prisoner free;
His blood can make the foulest clean;
 His blood availed for me.

5 Hear him, ye deaf; his praise, ye dumb,
 Your loosened tongues employ;
Ye blind, behold your Saviour come;
 And leap, ye lame, for joy.

Charles Wesley.

PETERBORO'. C. M. — Ralph Harrison.

1. Come, let us join our cheerful songs With angels round the throne; Ten thousand thousand are their tongues, But all their joys are one.

Worshiping the Lamb.

1 Come, let us join our cheerful songs
 With angels round the throne;
Ten thousand thousand are their tongues,
 But all their joys are one.

2 "Worthy the Lamb that died," they cry,
 "To be exalted thus!"
"Worthy the Lamb!" our hearts reply,
 "For he was slain for us."

3 Jesus is worthy to receive
 Honor and power divine;
And blessings more than we can give,
 Be, Lord, forever thine.

4 The whole creation join in one,
 To bless the sacred name
Of him that sits upon the throne,
 And to adore the Lamb.

Isaac Watts.

SONGS OF WORSHIP.

4   *The Rock of Salvation.*
1 Praise the Rock of our salvation,
   Praise the mighty God above;
Come before his sacred presence
   With a grateful song of love.
Cho.—Hallelujah! Hallelujah!
     He is God, and he alone;
   Wake the song of adoration,
     Come with joy before his throne.
2 Jesus' blood so freely offered,
   Jesus' blood avails for sin;
Jesus at the door of mercy,
   Waits to let the wanderer in.

Cho.—Hallelujah! Hallelujah!
   He is God, and he alone;
Wake the song of adoration,
   Come with joy before his throne.

3 Praise the Rock of our salvation;
   Catch from yonder radiant clime,
Strains by everlasting ages,
   Echoed back in tones sublime.
Cho.—Hallelujah! Hallelujah?
   He is God, and he alone;
Wake the song of adoration,
   Come with joy before his throne.
                            Fanny J. Crosby.

SONGS OF WORSHIP.

DUKE STREET. L. M.
JOHN HATTON.

1. From all that dwell be-low the skies, Let the Cre-a-tor's praise a-rise; Let the Re-deem-er's name be sung, Through every land, by every tongue.

5 *General invitation to praise God.*

2 Eternal are thy mercies, Lord;
Eternal truth attends thy word:
Thy praise shall sound from shore to shore,
Till suns shall rise and set no more.

3 Your lofty themes, ye mortals, bring;
In songs of praise divinely sing;
The great salvation loud proclaim,
And shout for joy the Saviour's name.

4 In every land begin the song;
To every land the strains belong:
In cheerful sounds all voices raise,
And fill the world with loudest praise.
Isaac Watts.

LUTHER. S. M.
THOMAS HASTINGS.

1. A-wake, and sing the song Of Mo-ses and the Lamb; Wake, ev-ery heart and ev-ery tongue, To praise the Saviour's name, To praise the Saviour's name.

6 *Song of Moses and the Lamb.*

2 Sing of his dying love;
  Sing of his rising power;
Sing how he intercedes above
  For those whose sins he bore.

3 Sing on your heavenly way,
  Ye ransomed sinners, sing;
Sing on, rejoicing every day
  In Christ, the eternal King.

4 Then shall each raptured tongue
  His endless praise proclaim;
And sweeter voices tune the song
  Of Moses and the Lamb.
William Hammond, alt.

SONGS OF WORSHIP.

COME AND WORSHIP.

MRS. JOSEPH F. KNAPP.

1. An-gel voic-es breath-ing ev-er, Songs of praise to God on high,
Thro' the gates of light and glo-ry, Call us now from yon-der sky.

CHORUS.
Come and wor-ship, Come and wor-ship, Wor-ship Christ our Lord and King;
Come and wor-ship, Come and wor-ship, Wor-ship Christ our Lord and King.

Copyright, 1884, by Joseph F. Knapp.

7 *Call to worship.*

2 O'er the lovely realm of nature,
By her sparkling fountains clear,
Thro' the forest and the valley,
Still the earnest call we hear,
  Come and worship, etc.

3 When the morning in its beauty
Wakes the earth from sleep profound,
In the music of the song bird
We can hear the grateful sound,
  Come and worship, etc.

4 In the whisper of the twilight,
When the zephyrs murmur low,
In the sighing of the leaflet,
We can hear where'er we go,
  Come and worship, etc.

5 Come and worship our Creator,
Him whose mercy we adore;
Come and worship our Redeemer,
Sing and praise him evermore;
  Come and worship, etc.

Fanny J. Crosby.

SONGS OF WORSHIP.

ITALIAN HYMN. 6, 4. — Felice Giardini

1. Come, thou al-migh-ty King, Help us thy name to sing, Help us to praise: Father all-glo-ri-ous, O'er all vic-to-ri-ous, Come, and reign over us, Ancient of days!

8 *Invocation of the Trinity.*

2 Come, thou incarnate Word,
Gird on thy mighty sword,
  Our prayer attend;
Come, and thy people bless,
And give thy word success:
Spirit of holiness,
  On us descend!

3 Come, holy Comforter,
Thy sacred witness bear
  In this glad hour:
Thou who almighty art,
Now rule in every heart,
And ne'er from us depart,
  Spirit of power!

4 To thee, great One and Three,
Eternal praises be,
  Hence evermore:
Thy sovereign majesty
May we in glory see,
And to eternity
  Love and adore!
Charles Wesley.

HENDON. 7. — Abraham Henri Cæsar Malan.

1 Lord, we come be-fore thee now, At thy feet we hum-bly bow; O do not our suit dis-dain; Shall we seek thee, Lord, in vain? Shall we seek thee, Lord, in vain?

9 *Blessings implored.*

2 Lord, on thee our souls depend;
In compassion now descend;
Fill our hearts with thy rich grace,
Tune our lips to sing thy praise.

3 In thine own appointed way,
Now we seek thee, here we stay;
Lord, we know not how to go,
Till a blessing thou bestow.

4 Send some message from thy word,
That may joy and peace afford;
Let thy Spirit now impart
Full salvation to each heart
William Hammond.

SONGS OF WORSHIP.

HEAVENLY FATHER WE ADORE THEE.

E. D. BEDDALL.

1. Heavenly Father we adore thee, And thy gracious name we praise, Take, O take our hearts we pray thee, While our songs to thee we raise,

CHORUS.
When to heav-en we as-cend, We thy prais-es ne'er shall end, We will sing re-deem-ing love, With the shin-ing host a-bove.

When to heav-en, when to heav-en we as-cend, We thy prais-es, we thy prais-es ne'er shall end, We will sing, yes we will sing re-deem-ing love.

Copyright, 1885, by Phillips & Hunt.

10 *Joyful adoration.*

2 Gentle Shepherd be thou near us,
   While we journey here below.
Guide our footsteps with thy mercy,
   Show us all the way to go.
    CHO.—When to heaven, &c,

3 Keep, O keep us from all evil,
   May we each from sin be free,
Guide us safely on our journey,
   Till in heaven thy face we see.
    CHO.—When to heaven, &c.

4 Then with angels we'll adore thee,
   High our voices then we'll raise,
With the bloodwashed throng in glory,
   Sing aloud thy glorious praise.
    CHO.—When to heaven, &c.

E. D. Beddall.

SONGS OF WORSHIP.

MALVERN. L. M.   LOWELL MASON.

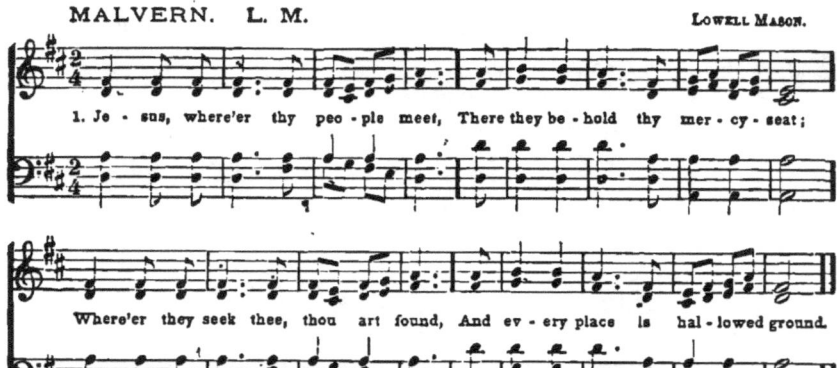

1. Jesus, where'er thy people meet, There they behold thy mercy-seat;
Where'er they seek thee, thou art found, And every place is hallowed ground.

11   *The great Shepherd with his flock.*

2 For thou, within no walls confined,
Dost dwell with those of humble mind;
Such ever bring thee where they come,
And, going, take thee to their home.

3 Great Shepherd of thy chosen few,
Thy former mercies here renew;
Here, to our waiting hearts, proclaim
The sweetness of thy saving name.

4 Here may we prove the power of prayer
To strengthen faith and sweeten care;
To teach our faint desires to rise,
And bring all heaven before our eyes.
                         William Cowper.

GRATEFUL PRAISE. 7.

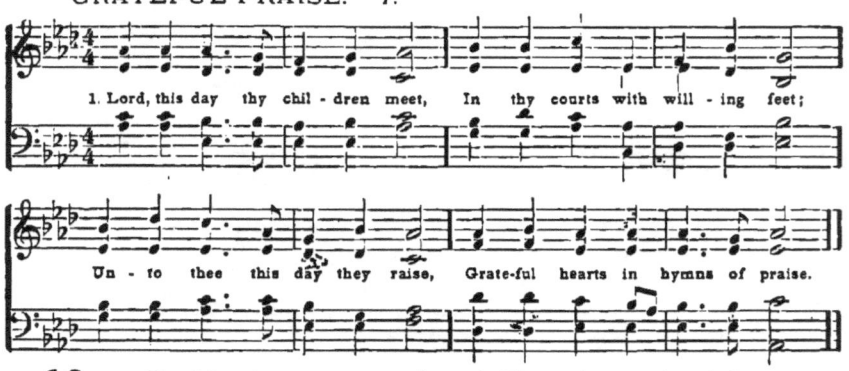

1. Lord, this day thy children meet, In thy courts with willing feet;
Unto thee this day they raise, Grateful hearts in hymns of praise.

12   *Cheerful service.*

2 Not alone the day of rest
With thy worship shall be blest;
In our pleasure and our glee,
Lord, we would remember thee.

3 Help us unto thee to pray,
Hallowing our happy day;
From thy presence thus to win
Hearts all pure and free from sin.

4 All our pleasures here below,
Saviour, from thy mercy flow.
Little children thou dost love;
Draw our hearts to thee above.

5 Make, O Lord, our childhood shine,
With all lowly grace, like thine;
Then, through all eternity,
We shall live in heaven with thee.
                       W. Walsham How.

SONGS OF WORSHIP.

BLESSED HOUR OF PRAYER. — W. H. DOANE.

1. 'Tis the bless-ed hour of prayer, when our hearts low-ly bend, And we gath-er to Je-sus, our Saviour and Friend; If we come to Him in faith, His pro-tec-tion to share,

CHORUS. What a balm for the weary! O how sweet to be there! Blessed hour of pray'r, Blessed hour of pray'r;

D.S.—What a balm for the weary! O how sweet to be there!

Copyright, 1880, by Biglow & Main.

13   *Blessed hour.*

2 'Tis the blessed hour of prayer, when the Saviour draws near,
With a tender compassion his children to hear;
When he tells us we may cast at his feet every care, What a balm, etc.—CHO.

3 'Tis the blessed hour of prayer, when the tempted and tried
To the Saviour who loves them their sorrow confide;
With a sympathizing heart he removes every care; What a balm, etc.—CHO.

4 At the blessed hour of prayer, trusting him we believe
That the blessing we're needing we'll surely receive,
In the fullness of this trust we shall lose every care; What a balm, etc.—CHO.

                                                           Fanny J. Crosby.

SUPPLICATION. — T. R. MATTHEWS.

1. Je-sus, high in glo-ry, Lend a listening ear, When we bow before thee, Children's praises hear.

14   *The hearer of prayer.*

2 Though thou art so holy,
   Heaven's almighty king,
Thou wilt stoop to listen,
   When thy praise we sing.

3 Save us, Lord, from sinning,
   Watch us day by day;

Help us now to love thee;
   Take our sins away:

4 Then, when Jesus calls us
   To our heavenly home,
We would gladly answer,
   "Saviour, Lord, we come."

                              Anon, 1847.

SONGS OF WORSHIP.

15 *Heavenly joy anticipated.*

1 IN thy name, O Lord, assembling,
  We, thy people, now draw near:
Teach us to rejoice with trembling;
  Speak, and let thy servants hear:
    Hear with meekness,
  Hear thy word with godly fear.

2 While our days on earth are lengthened,
  May we give them, Lord, to thee:
Cheered by hope, and daily strengthened,
  May we run, nor weary be,
    Till thy glory
  Without cloud in heaven we see.

3 There, in worship purer, sweeter,
  All thy people shall adore;
Sharing then in rapture greater
  Than they could conceive before:
    Full enjoyment,
  Full and pure, for evermore.
              Thomas Kelly.

16 *For the fullness of peace and joy.*

1 LORD, dismiss us with thy blessing,
  Fill our hearts with joy and peace;
Let us each, thy love possessing,
  Triumph in redeeming grace;
    O refresh us,
  Traveling through this wilderness.

2 Thanks we give, and adoration,
  For thy gospel's joyful sound;
May the fruits of thy salvation
  In our hearts and lives abound;
    May thy presence
  With us evermore be found.

3 So, whene'er the signal's given
  Us from earth to call away,
Borne on angels' wings to heaven,
  Glad the summons to obey,
    May we ever
  Reign with Christ in endless day.
              John Fawcett.

SONGS OF WORSHIP.

ZEPHYR. L. M.   WILLIAM B. BRADBURY.

1. Again as evening's shadow falls, We gather in these hallowed walls; And vesper hymn and vesper prayer Rise mingling on the holy air.

17   *Evening prayer.*

2 May struggling hearts that seek release
Here find the rest of God's own peace;
And, strengthened here by hymn and prayer;
Lay down the burden and the care.

3 O God, our light! to thee we bow;
Within all shadows standest thou:
Give deeper calm than night can bring;
Give sweeter songs than lips can sing.

4 Life's tumult we must meet again,
We cannot at the shrine remain;
But in the Spirit's secret cell
May hymn and prayer forever dwell.

Samuel Longfellow.

GOTTSCHALK. 7.   LOUIS MOREAU GOTTSCHALK. ARR BY E. P. PARKER.

1. Softly now the light of day Fades upon our sight away; Free from care, from labor free, Lord, we would commune with thee.

18   *Communion with God.*

2 Thou, whose all-pervading eye
  Naught escapes, without, within,
Pardon each infirmity,
  Open fault, and secret sin.

3 Soon from us the light of day
Shall forever pass away;
Then, from sin and sorrow free,
Take us, Lord, to dwell with thee.

George W. Doane.

SONGS OF WORSHIP.

EVENING HYMN. L. M.   THOMAS TALLIS.

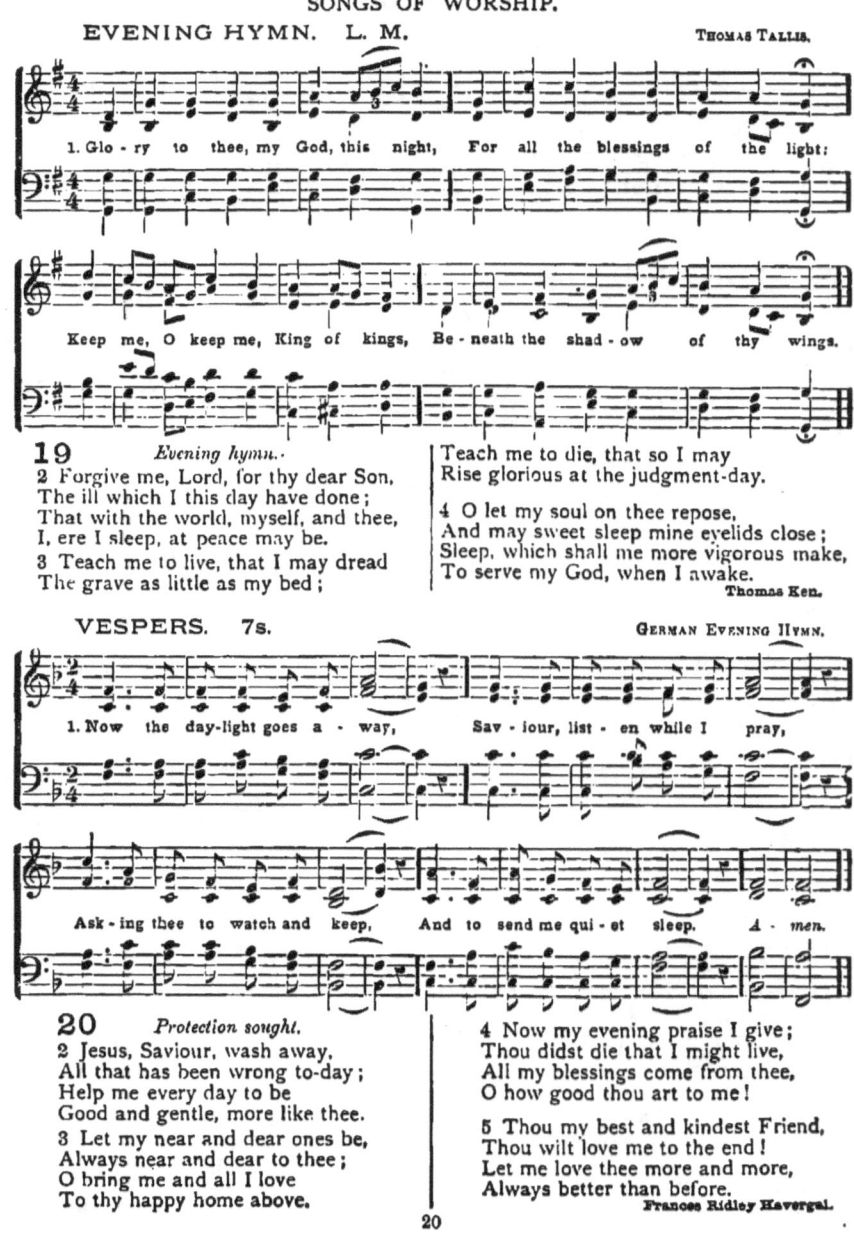

1. Glo-ry to thee, my God, this night, For all the blessings of the light;
Keep me, O keep me, King of kings, Beneath the shadow of thy wings.

19   *Evening hymn.*
2 Forgive me, Lord, for thy dear Son,
The ill which I this day have done;
That with the world, myself, and thee,
I, ere I sleep, at peace may be.

3 Teach me to live, that I may dread
The grave as little as my bed;
Teach me to die, that so I may
Rise glorious at the judgment-day.

4 O let my soul on thee repose,
And may sweet sleep mine eyelids close;
Sleep, which shall me more vigorous make,
To serve my God, when I awake.
                    Thomas Ken.

VESPERS. 7s.   GERMAN EVENING HYMN.

1. Now the day-light goes away, Saviour, listen while I pray,
Asking thee to watch and keep, And to send me quiet sleep. A-men.

20   *Protection sought.*
2 Jesus, Saviour, wash away,
All that has been wrong to-day;
Help me every day to be
Good and gentle, more like thee.

3 Let my near and dear ones be,
Always near and dear to thee;
O bring me and all I love
To thy happy home above.

4 Now my evening praise I give;
Thou didst die that I might live,
All my blessings come from thee,
O how good thou art to me!

5 Thou my best and kindest Friend,
Thou wilt love me to the end!
Let me love thee more and more,
Always better than before.
               Frances Ridley Havergal.

SONGS OF WORSHIP.

EVENTIDE. 10. WILLIAM HENRY MONK.

1. A-bide with me! Fast falls the e-ven-tide, The dark-ness deep-ens— Lord, with me a-bide! When oth-er help-ers fail, and com-forts flee, Help of the help-less, O a-bide with me!

21 *Abide with me.*

2 Swift to its close ebbs out life's little day;
Earth's joys grow dim, its glories pass away;
Change and decay in all around I see;
O thou, who changest not, abide with me!

3 I need thy presence every passing hour;
What but thy grace can foil the tempter's power?
Who, like thyself, my guide and stay can be?
Through cloud and sunshine, Lord, abide with me!

4 I fear no foe, with thee at hand to bless;
Ills have no weight, and tears no bitterness;
Where is death's sting? where, grave, thy victory?
I triumph still, if thou abide with me.

5 Hold thou thy cross before my closing eyes;
Shine through the gloom and point me to the skies;
Heaven's morning breaks, and earth's vain shadows flee;
In life, in death, O Lord, abide with me!
Henry F. Lyte.

STOCKWELL. 8, 7. DARIUS ELIOT JONES.

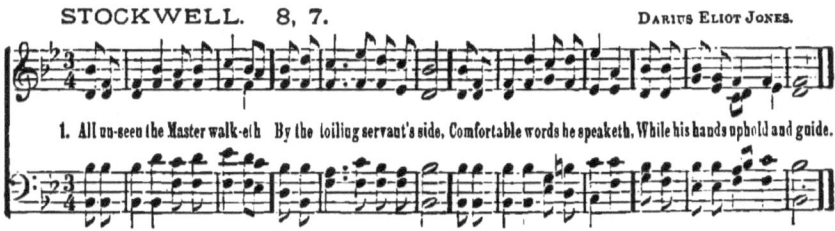

1. All un-seen the Master walk-eth By the toiling servant's side, Comfortable words he speaketh, While his hands uphold and guide.

22 *The Master with us.*

2 Grief, nor pain, nor any sorrow
Rends thy heart, to him unknown,
He to-day, and he to-morrow,
Grace sufficient gives his own.

3 Holy strivings nerve and strengthen,
Long endurance wins the crown,
When the evening shadows lengthen,
Thou shalt lay thy burden down.
Thomas Mackellar.

SONGS OF WORSHIP.

HURSLEY. L. M.   Peter Ritter. Arr. by William Henry Monk.

1. Sun of my soul, thou Saviour dear, It is not night if thou be near:
O may no earth-born cloud arise To hide thee from thy servant's eyes.

23   *Abide with me.*

2 When the soft dews of kindly sleep
My wearied eyelids gently steep,
Be my last thought, how sweet to rest
Forever on my Saviour's breast.

3 Abide with me from morn till eve,
For without thee I cannot live;
Abide with me when night is nigh,
For without thee I dare not die.

4 If some poor wandering child of thine
Have spurned, to-day, the voice divine,
Now, Lord, the gracious work begin;
Let him no more lie down in sin.

5 Come near and bless us when we wake,
Ere through the world our way we take;
Till, in the ocean of thy love,
We lose ourselves in heaven above.
                    John Keble.

24   *Christ present.*

1 ONCE more 'tis eventide, and we,
Oppressed with various ills, draw near;
What if thy form we cannot see?
We know and feel that thou art here.

2 O Saviour, Christ, our woes dispel;
For some are sick, and some are sad,
And some have never loved thee well,
And some have lost the love they had.

3 O Saviour Christ, thou too art man;
Thou hast been troubled, tempted, tried;
Thy kind but searching glance can scan
The very wounds that shame would hide.

4 Thy touch has still its ancient power;
No word from thee can fruitless fall;
Hear in this solemn evening hour,
And in thy mercy heal us all.
                    Rev. Henry Twells.

SETTING SUN. S. M.   Arr. by C. Streatfield.

1. Saviour, abide with us! The day is now far gone: We would obtain a blessing thus By coming to thy throne.

25   *Seeking a blessing.*

2 We have not reached that land,
   That happy land, as yet,
Where holy angels round thee stand,
   Whose sun can never set.

3 Our sun is sinking now;
   Our day is almost o'er;
O Sun of Righteousness, do thou
   Shine on us evermore.
                    John M. Neale.

SONGS OF WORSHIP.

GOD BE WITH YOU.
W. G. TOMER.

26   *The Lord watch between us.*

2 God be with you till we meet again,
'Neath his wings securely hide you;
Daily manna still divide you,
God be with you till we meet again.
   CHO.—Till we meet, etc.

3 God be with you till we meet again,
When life's perils thick confound you;
Put his arms unfailing round you,
God be with you till we meet again.
   CHO.—Till we meet, etc.

4 God be with you till we meet again,
Keep love's banner floating o'er you;
Smite death's threatening wave before you,
God be with you till we meet again.
   CHO.—Till we meet, etc.
                        Rev. J. E. Rankin.

27 *Evening praise.*
2 Lord of life, beneath the dome
Of the universe, thy home,
Gather us who seek thy face
To the fold of thy embrace,
    For thou art nigh.

Holy, holy, holy Lord God of hosts!
Heaven and earth are full of thee!
Heaven and earth are praising thee,
    O Lord most high!

Mary A. Lathbury.

SONGS OF WORSHIP.

EVENING PRAYER.—*Concluded.*

Sin and want we come con-fess-ing, Thou canst save and thou canst heal.

Copyright, 1878, by Geo. C. Stebbins.

28 *Bless us now.*

2 Though destruction walk around us,
  Though the arrows past us fly;
Angel guards from thee surround us,
  We are safe if thou art nigh.

3 Though the night be dark and dreary,
  Darkness cannot hide from thee:

Thou art he who, never weary,
  Watchest where thy people be.

4 Should swift death this night o'ertake us,
  And our couch become our tomb,
May the morn in heaven awake us,
  Clad in bright and deathless bloom.

James Edmeston.

PARTING HYMN. E. J. HOPKINS.

1. Sav-iour, a-gain to thy dear name we raise With one ac-cord our part-ing hymn of praise; We stand to bless thee ere our wor-ship cease, Then, low-ly kneel-ing, wait thy word of peace. A-men.

29 *Close of service.*

2 Grant us thy peace upon our homeward way;
With thee began, with thee shall end the day;
Guard thou the lips from sin, the hearts from shame,
That in this house have called upon thy name.

3 Grant us thy peace, Lord, through the coming night,
Turn thou for us its darkness into light;
From harm and danger keep thy children free,
For dark and light are both alike to thee.

4 Grant us thy peace throughout our earthly life,
Our balm in sorrow and our stay in strife;
Then, when thy voice shall bid our conflict cease,
Call us, O Lord, to thy eternal peace.

John Ellerton.

SONGS OF WORSHIP.

ANGEL VOICES.
Arthur S. Sullivan.

1. An-gel voic-es ev-er sing-ing Round thy throne of light, An-gel harps, for-ev-er ring-ing, Rest not day nor night; Thousands only live to bless thee, And con-fess thee, Lord of might!

30 *Confessing God.*

2 Thou, who art beyond the farthest
   Mental eye can scan,
Can it be that thou regardest
   Songs of sinful man?
Can we feel that thou art near us
   And wilt hear us? Yea, we can.

3 Here, Great God, to-day we offer
   Of thine own to thee;
And for thine acceptance proffer
   All unworthily,
Hearts and minds, and hands and voices,
   In our choicest melody.
Francis Pott.

MY SABBATH SONG.
Wm. B. Bradbury.

1. Strains of mu-sic oft-en greet me, As I join the bu-sy throng, But there's nothing half so pleasant, As the ho-ly Sab-bath song.

CHORUS.
No fear of ill, no fear of wrong, While

Copyright, 1866, by Wm. B. Bradbury.

SONGS OF THE SABBATH.

MY SABBATH SONG. Concluded.

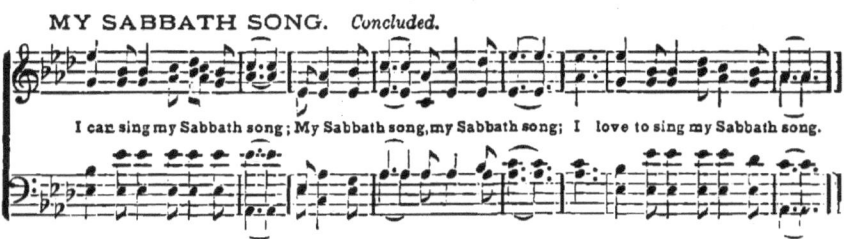

I can sing my Sabbath song; My Sabbath song, my Sabbath song; I love to sing my Sabbath song.

31 *The song of peace.*

2 'Tis a song of love and mercy,
　Speaking peace to all mankind,
Telling sinners poor and needy,
　Where the Saviour they may find.

3 While I live, O, may I ever
　Love the holy Sabbath song,
And when death shall call me homeward,
　Join it with the blood-bought throng.
　　　　　　　　　　Mrs. M. A. Kidder.

SABBATH HOME.   W. H. DOANE.

1. Sweet Sabbath School! more dear to me Than fair-est pal-ace dome, My heart e'er turns with

CHORUS.

joy to thee, My own dear Sabbath Home. Sabbath Home! Blessed Home! Sabbath
　　　　　　　　　　　　　　　　Sweet Home! Sweet Home!

Home! Blessed Home! My heart e'er turns with joy to thee, My own dear Sabbath Home.
Sweet Home! Sweet Home!
　　　　　　　　　　　　　　　Copyright, 1871, by Biglow & Main.

32 *Joy in the Sabbath School.*

2 Here to my willful, wand'ring heart,
　The way of life is shown;
Here may I seek the better part,
　And gain a Sabbath home.—CHO.

3 Here Jesus stands with loving voice,
　Entreating me to come
And make of him my earnest choice,
　In this dear Sabbath Home.—CHO.
　　　　　　　　　　Dr. C. R. Blackall.

SONGS OF THE SABBATH.

MENDEBAS. 7, 6.   *GERMAN MELODY.*

1. O day of rest and gladness, O day of joy and light,
O balm of care and sadness, Most beautiful, most bright;
On thee, the high and lowly, Thro' ages joined in tune,
Sing "Ho-ly, ho-ly, ho-ly," To the great God Tri-une.

33 *Day of rest and gladness.*

2 On thee, at the creation,
  The light first had its birth;
On thee, for our salvation,
  Christ rose from depths of earth;
On thee, our Lord, victorious,
  The Spirit sent from heaven;
And thus on thee, most glorious,
  A triple light was given.

3 New graces ever gaining
  From this our day of rest,
We reach the rest remaining
  To spirits of the blest;
To Holy Ghost be praises,
  To Father, and to Son;
The Church her voice upraises
  To thee, blest Three in One.
              Christopher Wordsworth.

HEBER. C. M.   *GEORGE KINGSLEY.*

1. With joy we hail the sa-cred day, Which God has called his own;
With joy the summons we o-bey, To wor-ship at his throne.

34 *Sabbath and sanctuary joys.*

2 Thy chosen temple, Lord, how fair!
  As here thy servants throng
To breathe the humble, fervent prayer,
  And pour the grateful song.

3 Spirit of grace! O deign to dwell
  Within thy Church below;
Make her in holiness excel,
  With pure devotion glow.

4 Let peace within her walls be found;
  Let all her sons unite;
To spread with holy zeal around
  Her clear and shining light.

5 Great God, we hail the sacred day
  Which thou hast called thine own;
With joy the summons we obey
  To worship at thy throne.
              Harriet Auber.

SONGS OF THE SABBATH.

SABBATH MORN. 7, 6l. — Lowell Mason.

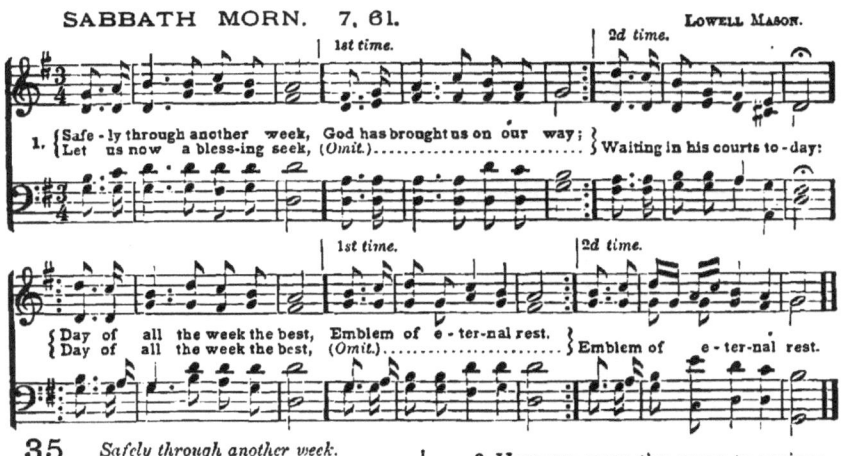

35 *Safely through another week.*

2 While we pray for pardoning grace,
  Through the dear Redeemer's name,
Show thy reconciled face,
  Take away our sin and shame;
From our worldly cares set free,
May we rest this day in thee.

3 Here we come thy name to praise;
  May we feel thy presence near:
May thy glory meet our eyes,
  While we in thy house appear:
Here afford us, Lord, a taste
Of our everlasting feast.
  — John Newton.

SWABIA. S. M. — Arr. by W. H. Havergal.

36 *The Sabbath day.*

2 This is the day of rest;
  Our failing strength renew;
On weary brain and troubled breast
  Shed thou thy freshening dew.

3 This is the day of peace:
  Thy peace our spirits fill;
Bid thou the blasts of discord cease,
  The waves of strife be still.

4 This is the day of prayer:
  Let earth to heaven draw near:
Lift up our hearts to seek thee there;
  Come down to meet us here.
  — John Ellerton.

SONGS OF GOD.

FATHER MOST HOLY.
WM. F. SHERWIN.

1. Fa-ther most ho-ly! To whom all praise be-longs; Thy chil-dren low-ly To thee would bring their songs. Praises nev-er end-ing, All harmonious blend-ing, To thy throne as-cend-ing, Swell from heavenly tongues. Lord, we a-dore thee! And with the Ser-a-phim Bow-ing be-fore thee, Join in their ho-ly hymn.

Copyright, 1885, by Phillips & Hunt.

37 *The Trinity adored.*

2 Jesus, our Saviour,—
  Name more than all most sweet!
Seeking thy favor,
  We worship at thy feet.
All our sins confessing,
Thou our hearts possessing,
May thy gracious blessing
  Here our spirits greet.
Lord, we adore thee! &c.

3 Come, Holy Spirit,
  Kindle devotions fire!
By thine own merit
  Our every thought inspire.
God's own word unsealing,
Precious truth revealing,
Thou canst bring the healing
  Sin-sick souls desire.
Lord, we adore thee! &c.

4 Thus do we bless thee,
O thou great ONE IN THREE!
Gladly confess thee
  Our Lord and King to be.
Hallelujahs swelling,
Shall thy praise be telling,
Till, with Jesus dwelling,
  We thy glory see!
Lord, we adore thee! &c.
                    Wm. F. Sherwin.

SONGS OF GOD.

GIVE PRAISE TO GOD.

Mrs. Joseph F. Knapp.

1. Within God's tem-ple now we meet, To praise his ho-ly name, Give praise to God! Give praise to God!
His wondrous mer-cies we re-peat, His wondrous love pro-claim, Give praise to God! Give praise to God!

CHORUS.
O sing we now our loud ho-san-nas, Till far and wide the ech-oes ring, Give praise, give praise to God, Give praise, give praise to God, Let ev-ery heart, let ev-ery tongue Give praise to God.

Copyright, 1871, by Joseph F. Knapp.

38 *Praise for Redemption.*

2 The gifts he sends us from his hand,
  Our gratitude invite,
Give praise to God! give praise to God!
The peace that now controls the land,
  Bids every heart unite.
Give praise to God! give praise to God!
  O sing we now, etc.

3 But more than any gift beside,
  We prize his holy Son;
Give praise to God! give praise to God!
Who came to earth, was crucified,
  And our redemption won!
Give praise to God! give praise to God!
  O sing we now, etc.
        Josephine Pollard.

SONGS OF GOD.

GOD IS GOOD. 7s.
T. FRANK ALLEN.

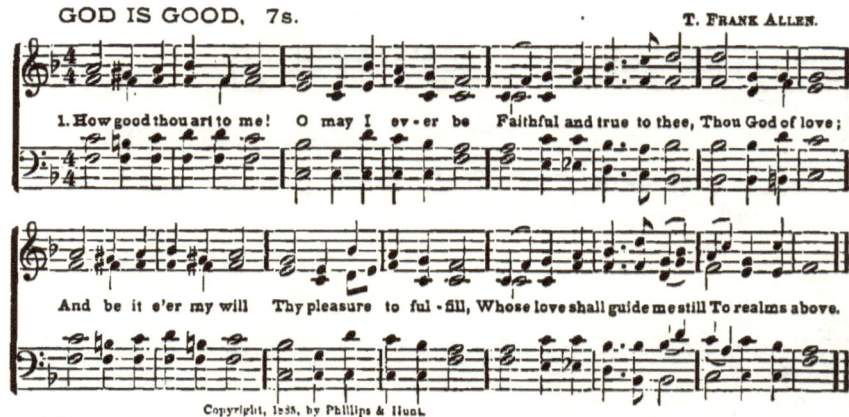

Copyright, 1883, by Phillips & Hunt.

39 *How good is God to me.*

1 How good thou art to me!
Oh may I ever be
Faithful and true to thee,
   Thou God of love;
And be it e'er my will
Thy pleasure to fulfill,
Whose love shall guide me still
   To realms above.

2 Should trials dark and drear
Be my allotment here,
Till all earth's hopes appear
   To fade away;
Let joy my spirit fill
To see therein thy will,
To lead me onward still
   In thy blest way.

3 Faithful and true thou art,
Oh still thy grace impart,
Till my whole life and heart
   From sin be free;
Till I shall live thy praise,
Love thee in all thy ways;
Yea, every moment raise
   Some note to thee.

4 O Christ, receive my prayer!
I would thine image bear,
Would still thy guidance share,
   Till life retires;
Oh make me thine for aye;
Thine while on earth I stay,
And thine where endless day
   Its joy inspires.

R. W. Landis.

GOD IS LOVE.
ENGLISH.

40 *Praise in nature.*

2 Every tree and flower we pass
Every tuft of waving grass,
Every leaf and opening bud,
Seem to tell us "God is good."

3 Little streams that glide along,
Verdant, mossy banks among,
Shadowing forth the clouds above,
Softly murmur, "God is love."

4 He who dwelleth high in heaven,
Unto us hath all things given;
Let us, as through life we move,
Ever feel that "God is love."

SONGS OF GOD.

THE LOVE OF GOD.
Mrs. Joseph F. Knapp.

41   *The love of God.*

1 Let the love of God like the ocean surges roll,
  Sweeping down from the great white throne,
Let it break from the heart, let it burst from the soul,
  Till the world shall be all his own.
    O! the love of God, of its wonders we will sing,
      Of its victories o'er and o'er,
    Till our life-work shall cease and our souls are at peace
      On the beautiful golden shore.

2 'Twas the love of God that beheld and pitied man,
  When his sentence of death was passed,
And a promise it gave, that Messiah should come,
  And the lost should be found at last.
    O! the love of God, etc.

3 'Tis the love of God that shall conquer every foe,
  To its scepter the earth shall bend,
And the cares of to-day soon shall vanish away
  In a morrow that ne'er shall end.
    O! the love of God, etc.

Fanny J. Crosby.

SONGS OF GOD.

MANOAH. C. M.   From F. J. Haydn.

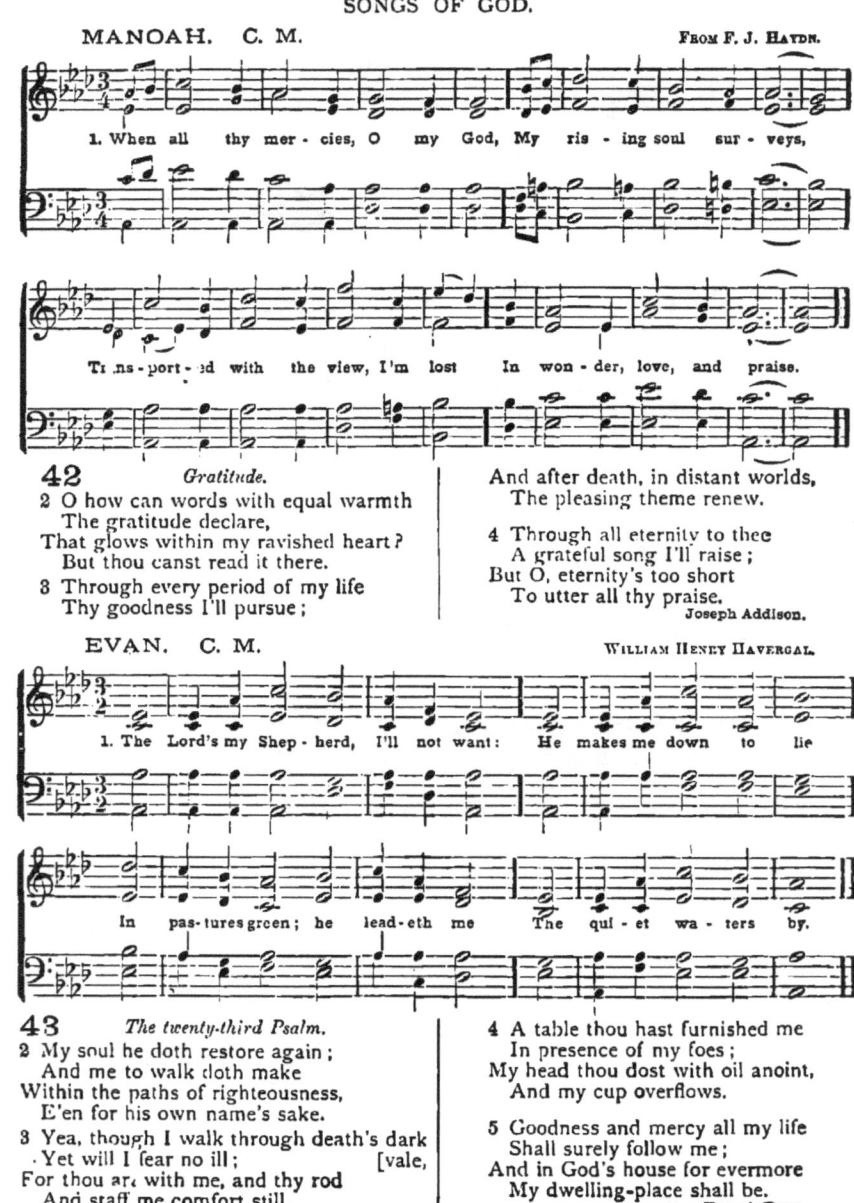

1. When all thy mercies, O my God, My rising soul surveys,
Transported with the view, I'm lost In wonder, love, and praise.

42   *Gratitude.*

2 O how can words with equal warmth
The gratitude declare,
That glows within my ravished heart?
But thou canst read it there.

3 Through every period of my life
Thy goodness I'll pursue;
And after death, in distant worlds,
The pleasing theme renew.

4 Through all eternity to thee
A grateful song I'll raise;
But O, eternity's too short
To utter all thy praise.
               Joseph Addison.

EVAN. C. M.   William Henry Havergal.

1. The Lord's my Shepherd, I'll not want: He makes me down to lie
In pastures green; he leadeth me The quiet waters by.

43   *The twenty-third Psalm.*

2 My soul he doth restore again;
And me to walk doth make
Within the paths of righteousness,
E'en for his own name's sake.

3 Yea, though I walk through death's dark
  Yet will I fear no ill;   [vale,
For thou art with me, and thy rod
  And staff me comfort still.

4 A table thou hast furnished me
In presence of my foes;
My head thou dost with oil anoint,
And my cup overflows.

5 Goodness and mercy all my life
Shall surely follow me;
And in God's house for evermore
My dwelling-place shall be.
               Francis Rous.

SONGS OF GOD.

PRAISE FOR HIS GREATNESS. Mrs. Joseph F. Knapp.

1. Praise, for his excellent greatness, Him who rules the earth and sky;
Praise him with trumpet and cymbal, Glory be to God on high.

CHORUS.
Mighty King, thus we sing, Glory, honor, praise to thee, Praise to thee, praise to thee,
Glory be to God on high; Glory, honor, praise to thee, Glory be to God on high.

Copyright, 1880, by Joseph F. Knapp.

44 *Praises to our King.*

2 Gather the nations before Him,
  Let them know his sovereign power;
He is the hope of his people,
  He their blessed rock and tower.
    Mighty King, etc.

3 Praise to the Lord, our Creator,
  He shall reign for evermore;
Praise to the Lord our Preserver
  He the faithful will restore.
    Mighty King, etc.

4 Under his banner of mercy,
  What have we on earth to fear?
He will defend us from danger,
  He our Shepherd still is near.
    Mighty King, etc.

5 Praise we the Lord our Redeemer,
  Praise his name with heart and voice,
Tell of his wonderful goodness,
  Let the world in him rejoice.
    Mighty King, etc.
        Fanny J. Crosby.

SONGS OF GOD.

LYONS. 10, 11.   FRANCIS JOSEPH HAYDN.

1 Tho' troubles assail, and dangers affright, Tho' friends should all fail, and foes all unite, Yet one thing secures us, whatever betide, The promise assures us, "The Lord will provide."

45   *The Lord will provide.*

2 The birds, without barn or store-house, are fed;
From them let us learn to trust for our bread:
His saints what is fitting shall ne'er be denied,
So long as 'tis written, "The Lord will provide."

3 When Satan appears to stop up our path,
And fills us with fears, we triumph by faith;
He cannot take from us, though oft he has tried,
The heart-cheering promise, "The Lord will provide."

4 He tells us we're weak, our hope is in vain;
The good that we seek we ne'er shall obtain:
But when such suggestions our graces have tried,
This answers all questions, "The Lord will provide."

5 No strength of our own, nor goodness we claim;
Our trust is all thrown on Jesus's name:
In this our strong tower for safety we hide;
The Lord is our power, "The Lord will provide."

6 When life sinks apace, and death is in view,
The word of his grace shall comfort us through:
Not fearing or doubting, with Christ on our side,
We hope to die shouting, "The Lord will provide."
                                             John Newton.

NICÆA. 11, 12, 10.   JOHN BACCHUS DYKES.

1. Holy, holy, holy, Lord God Almighty! Early in the morning our song shall rise to thee;
Holy, holy, holy, merciful and mighty, God in Three Persons, blessed Trinity!

NICÆA. *Concluded.* SONGS OF GOD.

46 *Holy, holy, holy.*

2 Holy, holy, holy! all the saints adore thee,
Casting down their golden crowns around the glassy sea;
Cherubim and seraphim falling down before thee,
Which wert, and art, and evermore shalt be.

3 Holy, holy, holy! though the darkness hide thee,
Though the eye of sinful man thy glory may not see;
Only thou art holy! there is none beside thee,
Perfect in power, in love, and purity.

4 Holy, holy, holy, Lord God Almighty!
All thy works shall praise thy name, in earth, and sky, and sea;
Holy, holy, holy, merciful and mighty,
God in Three Persons, blessed Trinity!
Reginald Heber.

WELLESLEY. 8, 7. LIZZIE S. TOURJEE.

1. There's a wideness in God's mer-cy, Like the wide-ness of the sea:
There's a kindness in his jus-tice, Which is more than lib-er-ty.

47 *The wideness of God's mercy.*

2 There is welcome for the sinner,
And more graces for the good;
There is mercy with the Saviour;
There is healing in his blood.

3 For the love of God is broader
Than the measure of man's mind;
And the heart of the Eternal
Is most wonderfully kind.

4 If our love were but more simple,
We should take him at his word;
And our lives would be all sunshine
In the sweetness of our Lord.
Frederick W. Faber.

HE IS CALLING. (SECOND TUNE.) Arr. by S. J. VAIL.

1. {There's a wideness in God's mercy, Like the wideness of the sea:
   {There's a kindness in his jus-tice Which is more than [*Omit*........} lib-er-ty.

CHORUS.
He is call-ing, "Come to me!" Lord, I'll glad-ly haste to thee.

SONGS OF CHRIST.

SONG OF THE ANGELS.

AMELIA SMITH.

1. Calm on the list'-ning ear of night, Comes heaven's melodious strains; Where wild Ju-de-a stretches far Her sil-ver man-tled plains; Ce-les-tial choirs from courts a-bove Shed sa-cred glo-ries there; And an-gels with their spark-ling lyres, Make mu-sic on the air.

Copyright, 1885, by Phillips & Hunt.

49 *Christmas Anthem.*

2 The answering hills of Palestine
  Send back the glad reply,
And greet from all their holy heights
  The Dayspring from on high:
O'er the blue depths of Galilee
  There comes a holier calm;
And Sharon waves in solemn praise
  Her silent groves of palm.

3 "Glory to God!" the lofty strain
  The realm of ether fills;
How sweeps the song of solemn joy
  O'er Judah's sacred hills!
"Glory to God!" the sounding skies
  Loud with their anthems ring:
"Peace on the earth; good will to men,
  From heaven's eternal King."

4 Light on thy hills, Jerusalem!
  The Saviour now is born!
More bright on Bethlehem's joyous plains
  Breaks the first Christmas morn;
And brighter on Moriah's brow,
  Crowned with her temple spires,
Which first proclaim the new-born light,
  Clothed with its orient fires.

5 This day shall christian tongues be mute,
  And christian hearts be cold?
O catch the anthem that from heaven
  O'er Judah's mountains rolled!
When nightly burst from seraph-harps
  The high and solemn lay,—
"Glory to God; on earth be peace;
  Salvation comes to-day."

Edmund H. Sears.

SONGS OF CHRIST.

ANTIOCH. C. M.  Arr. from Geo. F. Handel.

1. Joy to the world! the Lord is come; Let earth re-ceive her King; Let ev-ery heart pre-pare him room, And heaven and na-ture sing, And heaven, And heaven and na-ture sing, And heaven, And heaven and na-ture sing. sing, And heaven and na-ture sing.

50 *Joy to the world.*

2. Joy to the world! the Saviour reigns;
Let men their songs employ;
While fields and floods, rocks, hills, and plains,
Repeat the sounding joy.

3. No more let sin and sorrow grow,
Nor thorns infest the ground;
He comes to make his blessings flow
Far as the curse is found.

4. He rules the world with truth and grace,
And makes the nations prove
The glories of his righteousness,
And wonders of his love.

Isaac Watts.

CHRISTMAS. C. M. George Frederick Handel.

1. While shepherds watched their flocks by night, All seat-ed on the ground, The an-gel of the Lord came down, And glory shone a-round, And glory shone a-round.
2. "Fear not," said he,—for might-y dread Had seized their troubled mind,— "Glad tidings of great joy I bring, To you and all mankind, To you and all mankind.

SONGS OF CHRIST.

CHRISTMAS. *Concluded.*

51 *Good tidings of great joy.*

3 "To you, in David's town, this day
Is born, of David's line,
The Saviour, who is Christ the Lord;
And this shall be the sign:

4 "The heavenly babe you there shall find
To human view displayed,
All meanly wrapped in swathing-bands,
And in a manger laid."

5 Thus spake the seraph; and forthwith
Appeared a shining throng
Of angels, praising God on high,
Who thus addressed their song:

6 "All glory be to God on high,
And to the earth be peace:
Good-will henceforth from heaven to men,
Begin and never cease."
Tate and Brady.

HERALD ANGELS. 7. D. — Felix Mendelssohn-Bartholdy.

1. Hark! the herald-angels sing, "Glory to the new-born King; Peace on earth, and mercy mild; God and sinners reconciled." Joyful, all ye nations, rise, Join the triumphs of the skies; With angelic hosts proclaim, "Christ is born in Bethlehem," With angelic hosts proclaim, "Christ is born in Bethlehem."

52 *God incarnate.*

2 Christ, by highest heaven adored,
Christ, the everlasting Lord;
Veiled in flesh the Godhead see;
Hail, incarnate Deity!
Hail the heaven-born Prince of peace!

Hail the Sun of righteousness!
Light and life to all he brings,
Risen with healing in his wings.
Light and life to all he brings,
Risen with healing in his wings.
Charles Wesley.

SONGS OF CHRIST.

THIS IS THE WINTER MORN.

Arr. by L. H. Thomas

1. This is the win-ter morn. Our Saviour, Christ, was born, Who left the realms of endless day, To take our sins a-way.

Have ye no Car-ol for the Lord! To spread his love, his love a-broad? Have ye no car-ol for the Lord, To spread, his love, his love a-broad?

Chorus.

Ho-san-na! from all our hearts we raise, Ho-san-na! Ho-san-na! And make our lives his praise.

SONGS OF CHRIST.

THIS IS THE WINTER MORN. — *Concluded.*

53   *A Christmas Carol.*
2 Ring, ring, O happy bells!
A blessed angel tells
The story of his humble birth,
Who came this day to earth.
||: Have ye no praises for the Lord
To spread his love, his love abroad? :||
CHO.—Hosanna! from all our hearts we pour,
  Hosanna! Hosanna!
  And bless him evermore.

3 The shepherds vigils keep
And watch by night their sheep:
Upon the plains of Bethlehem
What glory comes to them!
||: Have ye from heaven no glory felt,
Who all, who all in prayer have knelt? :||
CHO.—Hosanna! in all our hearts is light,
  Hosanna! Hosanna!
  God's worship is delight.

4 All in the lowly place
They find the Royal Grace,
And lo! they fall a worshipping
Before the new-born King.
||: Have ye no worship for the Lord,
To give, to give with one accord? :||
CHO.—Hosanna! in all our hearts we bring,
  Hosanna! Hosanna!
  Our lives our offering.

5 Their grateful hearts are full
Of things most beautiful;
And lo! the wonder of the Lord
They straightway spread abroad.
||: Have ye no beauty of the Christ
Whose love, whose love has long sufficed? :||
CHO.—Hosanna! from all our hearts we raise,
  Hosanna! Hosanna!
  And carry hence his praise.
Osgood E. Fuller.

WAKEN, CHRISTIAN CHILDREN.   ANON.

54   *Welcoming the Saviour.*
2 In a manger lowly
  Sleeps the heavenly Child,
O'er him fondly bendeth
  Mary, mother mild.
Far above that stable,
  Up in heaven so high,
One bright star outshineth,
  Watching silently.

3 Fear not, then, to enter,
  Though we cannot bring
Gold, or myrrh, or incense,
  Fitting for a King.
Gifts he asketh richer,
  Offerings costlier still,
Yet may Christian children
  Bring them if they will.

4 Brighter than all jewels
  Shines the modest eye;
Best of gifts, he loveth
  Infant purity.
Haste we, then, to welcome
  With a joyous lay
Christ, the King of Glory,
  Born for us to-day.
B. C. Hamerton.

SONGS OF CHRIST.

BETHLEHEM. 8, 6. LEWIS H. REDNER.

1. O little town of Bethlehem! How still we see thee lie,
Above thy deep and dreamless sleep, The silent stars go by;
Yet in thy dark streets shineth The everlasting Light;
The hopes and fears of all the years, Are met in thee to-night.

55 *Christmas.*

2 For Christ is born of Mary,
 And gathered all above,
While mortals sleep the angels keep
 Their watch of wondering love.
O morning stars together
 Proclaim the holy birth!
And praises sing to God the King,
 And peace to men on earth.

3 How silently, how silently,
 The wondrous gift is given;
So God imparts to human hearts
 The blessings of his heaven.
No ear may hear his coming,
 But in this world of sin,
Where meek souls will receive him still,
 The dear Christ enters in.

4 O holy child of Bethlehem!
 Descend to us, we pray,
Cast out our sin and enter in,
 Be born in us to-day.
We hear the Christmas angels,
 The great glad tidings tell,
O, come to us, abide with us,
 Our Lord Emmanuel!
  Rev. Phillips Brooks.

SONGS OF CHRIST.

COMMUNION. C. M.
Stephen Jenks

1. Alas! and did my Saviour bleed? And did my Sovereign die?
Would he devote that sacred head For such a worm as I?

56 *Godly sorrow at the cross.*

2 Was it for crimes that I have done,
  He groaned upon the tree?
Amazing pity! grace unknown!
  And love beyond degree!

3 Well might the sun in darkness hide,
  And shut his glories in,
When Christ, the mighty Maker, died,
  For man the creature's sin.

4 Thus might I hide my blushing face
  While his dear cross appears;
Dissolve my heart in thankfulness,
  And melt mine eyes to tears.

5 But drops of grief can ne'er repay
  The debt of love I owe:
Here, Lord, I give myself away,—
  'Tis all that I can do.

Isaac Watts.

REMEMBER ME.
Asa Hull.

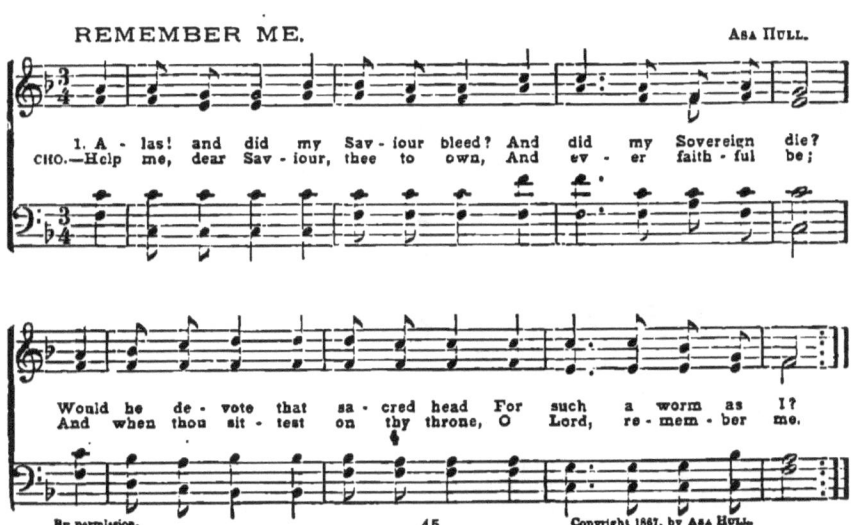

1. Alas! and did my Saviour bleed? And did my Sovereign die?
CHO.—Help me, dear Saviour, thee to own, And ever faithful be;

Would he devote that sacred head For such a worm as I?
And when thou sittest on thy throne, O Lord, remember me.

By permission. Copyright 1867, by Asa Hull.

SONGS OF CHRIST.

EUCHARIST. L. M. — ISAAC BAKER WOODBURY.

1. When I survey the wondrous cross On which the Prince of glory died,
My richest gain I count but loss, And pour contempt on all my pride.

57 *The wondrous cross.*

2 Forbid it, Lord, that I should boast,
Save in the death of Christ, my God;
All the vain things that charm me most,
I sacrifice them to his blood.

3 See, from his head, his hands, his feet,
Sorrow and love flow mingled down:
Did e'er such love and sorrow meet,
Or thorns compose so rich a crown?

4 Were the whole realm of nature mine,
That were a present far too small;
Love so amazing, so divine,
Demands my soul, my life, my all.
Isaac Watts.

RATHBUN. 8, 7. — ITHAMAR CONKEY.

1. In the cross of Christ I glory, Towering o'er the wrecks of time;
All the light of sacred story Gathers round its head sublime.

Copyright, by Permission of O. Ditson & Co.

58 *Glorying in the Cross.*

2 When the woes of life o'ertake me,
Hopes deceive, and fears annoy,
Never shall the cross forsake me;
Lo! it glows with peace and joy.

3 When the sun of bliss is beaming
Light and love upon my way,
From the cross the radiance streaming
Adds more luster to the day.

4 Bane and blessing, pain and pleasure,
By the cross are sanctified;
Peace is there, that knows no measure,
Joys that through all time abide.
Sir John Bowring.

SONGS OF CHRIST.

THE SAVIOUR'S TOMB.
RICHARD REDHEAD.

1. Resting from his work to-day, In the tomb the Saviour lay; Still he slept; from head to feet Shrouded in the winding sheet, Lying in the rock alone, Hidden by the sealed stone.
2. Late at even there was seen Watching long the Magdalene; Early, ere the break of day, Sorrowful she took her way To the holy garden glade Where her buried Lord was laid.

59 *Affections offering.*

3 So with thee, till life shall end,
I would solemn vigil spend:
Let me hew Thee, Lord a shrine
In this rocky heart of mine,
Where in pure embalmèd cell
None but thou may ever dwell.

4 Myrrh and spices will I bring,
True affection's offering;
Close the door from sight and sound
Of the busy world around;
And in patient watch remain
Till my Lord appear again!
Thomas Whytehead.

MORNING RED.
GERMAN AIR.

1. Morning red, Morning red, Now the shadows all are fled; Now the Sabbath's cloudless glory, Tells anew the wondrous story, Christ is risen from the dead.

60 *The risen Saviour.*

2 All around, All around,
Solemn silence reigned profound;
When, with blaze and sudden thunder,
Angels burst the tomb asunder,
And the Saviour was unbound.

3 Forth he came! Forth he came!
Robed in white, celestial flame!
Mary, at his empty prison,
Knew not her Redeemer risen,
Till he called her by her name.

4 Morning red! Morning red!
Christ is risen from the dead!
Still he walketh in the garden,
Speaking words of love and pardon,
Though the crown is on his head.

5 Morning red! Morning red!
Thou dost light his crownèd head!
Brightest jewel of his glory,
Ever shines that wondrous story,
Christ is risen from the dead.
Rossiter W. Raymond.

SONGS OF CHRIST.
NOW ALL THE BELLS ARE RINGING. Anon.

61 *Easter carol.*

2 Alleluia! Alleluia! Alleluia!
  O hasten we to meet him,
    With our companions dear,
  With love and awe to greet him,
    As he is drawing near;
  Of old his friends were bidden
    To haste to Galilee:
  Still in his Church, all glorious,
    Our risen Lord will be.
      Alleluia! Alleluia! Alleluia!

3 Alleluia! Alleluia! Alleluia!
  Still, Jesus! we adore thee
    With faith which may not fail;
  Still, as we kneel before thee,
    We hear thee say "All hail!"
  Thou, who art now descending
    To raise us up to thee,
  An Easter-tide unending
    Grant us in heaven to see.
      Alleluia! Alleluia! Alleluia!
              Anon.

62 *Conqueror over death and the grave.*

2 Victor o'er death and hell!
Cherubic legions swell
　The radiant train.
Praises all heaven inspire;
Each angel sweeps his lyre,
And waves his wings of fire—
　Thou Lamb once slain.—REF.

3 Enter Incarnate God!
No feet but thine have trod
　The serpent down.
Blow the full trumpets, blow!
Wider yon portals throw!
Saviour, triumphant go,
　And take thy crown.—REF.
　　　　　　　Mathew Bridges

SONGS OF CHRIST.
GOD HATH SENT HIS ANGELS.
English.

1. God hath sent his angels to the earth again, Bringing joyful tidings to the sons of men. They who first at Christmas, throng'd the heav'nly way, Now beside the tomb-door, sit on Easter Day. Angels sing his triumph, as you sang his birth, "Christ the Lord is risen," "Peace, good-will on earth."

63   *He giveth his angels charge.*

2 In the dreadful desert, where the Lord was tried,
There the faithful angels gathered at his side.
And when in the garden, grief and pain and care,
Bowed him down with anguish, they were with him there.
    Angels, sing, etc.

3 Yet the Christ they honor, is the same Christ still,
Who, in light and darkness, did his father's will.
And the tomb deserted, shineth like the sky,
Since he passed out from it, into victory.
    Angels, sing, etc.

4 God has still his angels, helping, at his word,
All his faithful children, like their faithful Lord;
Soothing them in sorrow, arming them in strife,
Opening wide the tomb-doors, leading into life.
    Angels, sing, etc.

5 Father, send thine angels unto us, we pray;
Leave us not to wander, all along our way.
Let them guard and guide us, wheresoe'er we be,
Till our resurrection brings us home to thee.
    Angels, sing, etc.

                         Unknown.

SONGS OF CHRIST.

ASCENSION. — ARTHUR SEYMOUR SULLIVAN.

64 *Our ascended Lord.*

2 He who came to save us,
   He who bled and died,
Now is crowned with glory
   At his Father's side;
Never more to suffer;
   Never more to die;

Jesus, King of glory,
   Is gone up on high.
   All his work, &c.
3 Praying for his children
   In that blessed place,
Calling them to glory,

Sending them his grace;
His bright home preparing,
   Little ones for you;
Jesus ever liveth
   Ever loveth too.
      All his work, &c.
   Francis Ridley Havergal.

SONGS OF CHRIST.

CORONATION. C. M. — Oliver Holden.

1. All hail the power of Jesus' name! Let angels prostrate fall; Bring forth the royal diadem, And crown him Lord of all, Bring forth the royal diadem, And crown him Lord of all.

65 *Crown Him Lord of all.*

2 Crown him, ye morning stars of light,
Who fixed this earthly ball;
Now hail the strength of Israel's might,
And crown him Lord of all.

3 Ye chosen seed of Israel's race,
Ye ransomed from the fall,
Hail him who saves you by his grace,
And crown him Lord of all.

4 Sinners, whose love can ne'er forget
The wormwood and the gall;
Go, spread your trophies at his feet,
And crown him Lord of all.

5 Let every kindred, every tribe,
On this terrestrial ball,
To him all majesty ascribe,
And crown him Lord of all.

6 O that with yonder sacred throng
We at his feet may fall!
We'll join the everlasting song,
And crown him Lord of all.
— Edward Perronet, alt.

MILES' LANE. C. M. (SECOND TUNE.) — Wm. Shrubsole.

1. All hail the power of Jesus' name! Let angels prostrate fall; Bring forth the royal diadem, And crown him, crown him, crown him, crown him Lord of all.

SONGS OF CHRIST.

CROWN HIM WITH MANY CROWNS.

Geo. J. Elvey.

1. Crown him with many crowns, The Lamb upon his throne; Hark, how the heavenly anthem drowns All music but its own: Awake, my soul, and sing Of him who died for thee, And hail him as thy matchless King Through all eternity.

66 *Crowning the Saviour.*

2 Crown him the Lord of love:
Behold his hands and side,
Rich wounds yet visible above,
In beauty glorified:
No angel in the sky
Can fully bear that sight,
But downward bends his burning eye
At mysteries so bright.

3 Crown him the Lord of peace:
Whose power a sceptre sways
From pole to pole, that wars may cease,
And all be prayer and praise:

His reign shall know no end,
And round his piercèd feet
Fair flowers of Paradise extend
Their fragrance ever sweet.

4 Crown him the Lord of years,
The Potentate of time,
Creator of the rolling spheres,
Ineffably sublime.
All hail, Redeemer, hail!
For thou hast died for me;
Thy praise shall never, never fail
Throughout eternity.

Matthew Bridges.

SONGS OF CHRIST.

AUTUMN. 8, 7. D. — Spanish Melody, from Marechio.

1. Hail, thou once despised Jesus! Hail, thou Galilean King! Thou didst suffer to release us;
Thou didst free salvation bring. Hail, thou agonizing Saviour, Bearer of our sin and shame!
D. S. By thy merits we find favor; Life is given through thy name.

67 *Our Paschal Lamb.*

2 Paschal Lamb, by God appointed,
  All our sins on thee were laid:
By almighty love anointed,
  Thou hast full atonement made.
All thy people are forgiven,
  Through the virtue of thy blood;
Opened is the gate of heaven;
  Peace is made 'twixt man and God.

3 Jesus, hail! enthroned in glory,
  There forever to abide;
All the heavenly hosts adore thee,
  Seated at thy Father's side:

There for sinners thou art pleading;
  There thou dost our place prepare:
Ever for us interceding,
  Till in glory we appear.

4 Worship, honor, power, and blessing,
  Thou art worthy to receive;
Loudest praises, without ceasing,
  Meet it is for us to give.
Help, ye bright angelic spirits;
  Bring your sweetest, noblest lays;
Help to sing our Saviour's merits;
  Help to chant Immanuel's praise!
                              John Bakewell.

ORTONVILLE. C. M. — Thomas Hastings.

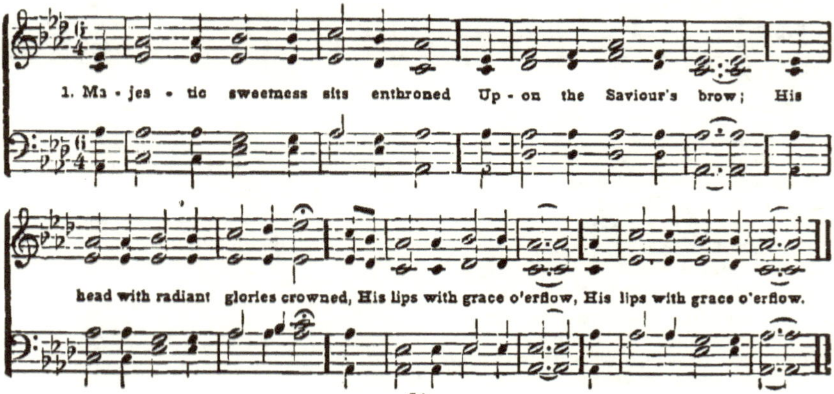

1. Majestic sweetness sits enthroned Upon the Saviour's brow; His head with radiant glories crowned, His lips with grace o'erflow, His lips with grace o'erflow.

SONGS OF CHRIST.

ORTONVILLE. *Concluded.*

68 *Majestic sweetness.*

2 No mortal can with him compare,
Among the sons of men;
Fairer is he than all the fair
That fill the heavenly train.

3 He saw me plunged in deep distress,
He flew to my relief;
For me he bore the shameful cross,
And carried all my grief.

4 To him I owe my life and breath,
And all the joys I have;
He makes me triumph over death,
He saves me from the grave.

5 Since from his bounty I receive
Such proofs of love divine,
Had I a thousand hearts to give,
Lord, they should all be thine.

Samuel Stennett.

TELL ME MORE ABOUT JESUS.   JAMES McGRANAHAN.

By per. of The John Church Co., owners of the Copyright.

69 *That I may know him.*

2 Earth's fairest flowers will droop and die,
Dark clouds o'erspread yon azure sky:
Life's dearest joys flit swiftly by:
  Tell me more about Jesus.
    CHO.—Tell me more, &c.

3 When overwhelmed with unbelief,
When burdened with a blinding grief,
Come kindly then to my relief;
  Tell me more about Jesus.
    CHO.—Tell me more, &c.

4 And when the Glory-land I see,
And take the "place prepared" for me,
Through endless years my song shall be—
  Tell me more about Jesus.
    CHO.—Tell me more, &c.

P. P. Bliss.

SONGS OF CHRIST.

EMMONS. C. M. — FRIEDRICH BURGMÜLLER.

1. Thou dear Redeemer, dy-ing Lamb, I love to hear of thee; No music's like thy charming name, Nor half so sweet can be, Nor half so sweet can be.

70 *Thou dear Redeemer.*

2 O let me even hear thy voice
  In mercy to me speak;
In thee, my Priest, will I rejoice,
  And thy salvation seek.

3 My Jesus shall be still my theme,
  While in this world I stay;
I'll sing my Jesus' lovely name
  When all things else decay.

4 When I appear in yonder cloud,
  With all thy favored throng,
Then will I sing more sweet, more loud,
  And Christ shall be my song.
       John Cennick.

HOLY CROSS. C. M. — MENDELSSOHN.

1. Je-sus, the ver-y thought of thee With sweet-ness fills the breast; But sweet-er far thy face to see, And in thy pres-ence rest.

71 *The sweetest name.*

2 No voice can sing, no heart can frame,
  Nor can the memory find
A sweeter sound than Jesus' name,
  The Saviour of mankind.

3 O Hope of every contrite heart,
  O Joy of all the meek,
To those who ask, how kind thou art!
  How good to those who seek!

4 But what to those who find? Ah, this
  Nor tongue nor pen can show:
The love of Jesus, what it is,
  None but his loved ones know.

5 Jesus, our only joy be thou,
  As thou our prize wilt be;
In thee be all our glory now,
  And through eternity.
    Bernard of Clairvaux. Tr. by E. Caswall.

SONGS OF CHRIST.

I SING OF HIS MERCY.

Rev. Samuel Alman.

72   *"I will sing of his mercy."*

3 I sing of his mercy the mighty to save,
Who came to redeem us from death and the grave;
I sing of a pardon that all may receive,
Who earnestly seek him and truly believe.

4 I sing of his mercy that never can fail,
Tho' storms may o'ertake us and troubles assail;
I sing of his mercy, and still will I sing,
All glory to Jesus my Saviour and King.

Fanny J. Crosby.

73 *Singing of Jesus.*

1 Come, Christian children, come and raise
　Your voice with one accord;
Come, sing in joyful songs of praise
　The glories of your Lord.
Sing of the wonders of his love,
　And loudest praises give,
To him who left his throne above,
　And died that you might live.
Cho.—Come, Christian children, etc.

2 Sing of the wonders of his truth,
　And read in every page
The promise made to earliest youth
　Fulfilled to latest age.
Sing of the wonders of his power,
　Who with his own right arm
Upholds and keeps you hour by hour,
　And shields from every harm.
Cho.—Come, Christian children, etc.

3 Sing of the wonders of his grace,
　Who made and keeps you his,
And guides you to the appointed place
　At his right hand in bliss.
Sing of the wonders of his name,
　And Jesus Christ adore;
Him for your Lord and God proclaim,
　And praise him evermore.
Cho.—Come, Christian children, etc.

Dorothy A. Thrupp.

SONGS OF CHRIST.

THE NAME OF OUR SALVATION.
Jno. Henry Cornell.

1. To the Name of our Sal-va-tion Laud and hon-or let us pay; Which, for many a gen-e-ra-tion Hid in God's foreknowledge lay, But with ho-ly ex-ult-a-tion We may sing a-loud to-day, We may sing a-loud to-day.

From the Hymnary, by per. S. Lasar.

74 *The Lord our salvation.*

2 Jesus is the name we treasure;
Name beyond what words can tell;
Name of gladness, name of pleasure,
Ear and heart delighting well;
Name of sweetness, passing measure,
Saving us from sin and hell.

3 Therefore we, in love revering,
Holy Jesus! thee implore
So to write thy name endearing
In our hearts forevermore,
That at length in heav'n appearing,
We with angels may adore.

Tr. by John Mason Neale.

SING OF JESUS, SING FOREVER.
German Melody.

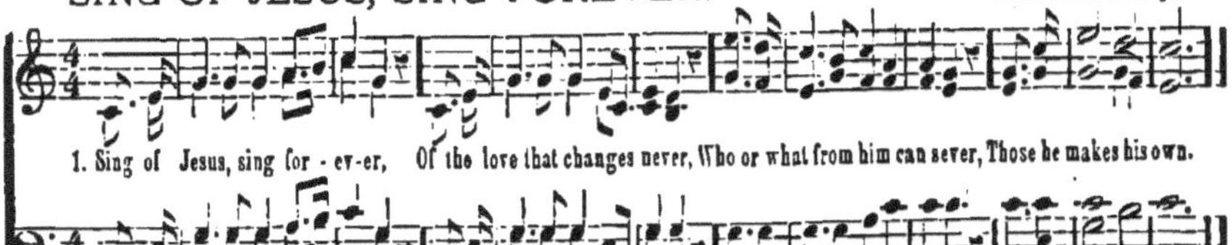

1. Sing of Jesus, sing for-ev-er, Of the love that changes never, Who or what from him can sever, Those he makes his own.

75 *Unchanging Love.*

2 With his blood the Lord has bought them;
When they knew him not, he sought them,
And from all their wanderings brought them;
His the praise alone.

3 Saints in glory, we together
Know the song that ceases never;
Song of Songs thou art, O Saviour,
All that endless day.

Thomas Kelly.

SONGS OF CHRIST.

THE SONG OF THE CHILDREN.

1. Once was heard the song of chil-dren By the Sav-iour when on earth;
Joy-ful in the sa-cred tem-ple Shouts of youth-ful praise have birth;
And ho-san-nas, and ho-san-nas Loud to Da-vid's Son break forth.

76 *Childrens' hosannas.*

2 Palms of victory strewn around him,
  Garments spread beneath his feet,
Prophet of the Lord they crowned him,
  In fair Salem's crowded street,
While hosannas, while hosannas,
  From the lips of children greet.

3 God o'er all, in heaven reigning,
  We this day thy glory sing;
Not with palms thy pathway strewing,
  We would loftier tribute bring,
Glad hosannas, glad hosannas
  To our Prophet, Priest, and King.

4 O, though humble is our off'ring,
  Lord, accept our grateful lays!
These from children once proceeding
  Thou didst deem "perfected praise,"
Now hosannas, now hosannas,
  Saviour, Lord, to thee we raise.

English. Anon 1843.

CRUSADERS' HYMN.
12th Century.

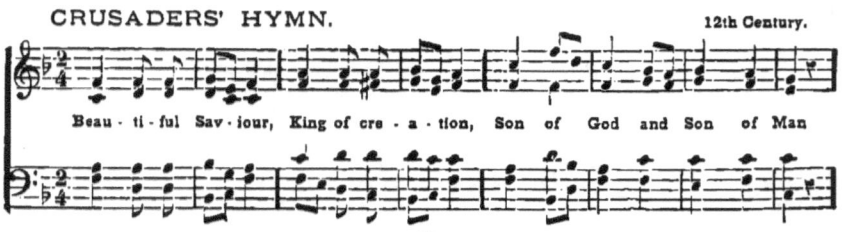

Beau-ti-ful Sav-iour, King of cre-a-tion, Son of God and Son of Man

SONGS OF CHRIST.

CRUSADERS' HYMN.—*Concluded.*

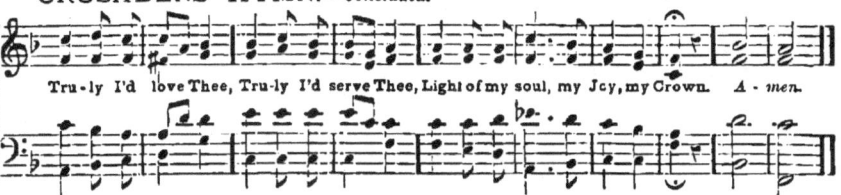

Truly I'd love Thee, Truly I'd serve Thee, Light of my soul, my Joy, my Crown. A-men.

77 *Christ our Captain.*

2 Fair are the meadows,
   Fairer the woodlands,
Robed in flowers of blooming spring;
   Jesus is fairer
   Jesus is purer,
He makes our sorrowing spirits sing.

3 Beautiful Saviour,
   Lord of the nations,
Son of God and Son of man!
   Glory and honor,
   Praise, adoration,
Now and for evermore be Thine.
                              Anon.

WHEN, HIS SALVATION BRINGING.   MOZART.

1. When, His salvation bringing, To Zion, Jesus came, The children all stood singing, "Hosanna to his name!" Nor did their zeal offend him, But as He rode along He let them still attend him, And smiled to hear their song.

78 *Heart and voice for Jesus.*

2 And since the Lord retaineth
   His love for children still—
Though now as King he reigneth
   On Zion's heavenly hill—
We'll flock around his banner
   Who sits upon the throne,
And cry aloud, "Hosanna
   To David's royal Son!"

3 For, should we fail proclaiming
   Our great Redeemer's praise,
The stones, our silence shaming,
   Might well "Hosanna!" raise.
But shall we only render
   The tribute of our words?
No! while our hearts are tender
   They too shall be the Lord's.
                     Rev. John King.

SONGS OF CHRIST.

THE CHILDREN'S FRIEND.

T. R. Matthews.

1. There's a friend for lit-tle chil-dren, A-bove the bright blue sky,
A friend who nev-er chan-ges, Whose love will nev-er die:
Un-like our friends by na-ture, Who change with chang-ing years,
This friend is al-ways wor-thy The pre-cious name he bears.

79 *Suffer them to come unto me.*

2 There's a rest for little children,
　Above the bright blue sky,
Who love the blessed Saviour,
　And to the Father cry,—
A rest from every trouble,
　From sin and danger free;
There every little pilgrim
　Shall rest eternally.

3 There's a home for little children,
　Above the bright blue sky,
Where Jesus reigns in glory,
　A home of peace and joy;
No home on earth is like it,
　Nor can with it compare,
For every one is happy,
　Nor can be happier there.

4 There are crowns for little children,
　Above the bright blue sky,
And all who look to Jesus
　Shall wear them by-and-by;
Yea, crowns of brightest glory
　Which he shall sure bestow,
On all who loved the Saviour,
　And walked with him below.

5 There are songs for little children,
　Above the bright blue sky,
And harps of sweetest music
　For their hymn of victory:
And all above is pleasure,
　And found in Christ alone;
Lord, grant thy little children,
　To know thee as their own.

Albert Midlane.

80 *Sing and rejoice.*

2 His wonderful name makes our victory sure,
We share in his fame, which shall ever endure;
On earth we've his word and the gift of his love;
The joy of the Lord yet awaits us above.—CHO.

3 We bless his dear name through smiles and through tears,
His love all the same hath encompassed our years;
Oh who could be sad when thus held in his care;
Come, let us be glad, and God's goodness declare.—CHO.

Vinnie Vernon.

81

1 Saviour, blessed Saviour
  Listen while we sing,
Hearts and voices raising
  Praises to our King;
All we have to offer,
  All we hope to be,
Body, soul, and spirit,
  All we yield to thee.—REF.

2 Nearer, ever nearer,
  Christ, we draw to thee,
Deep in adoration,
  Bending low the knee;
Thou for our redemption
  Cam'st on earth to die;
Thou, that we might follow,
  Hast gone up on high.—REF.

3 Clearer still and clearer
  Dawns the light from heav'n,
In our sadness bringing
  News of sin forgiv'n;
Life has lost its shadows,
  Pure the light within;
Thou hast shed thy radiance
  On a world of sin.—REF.
            Godfrey Thring, a'a.

SONGS OF CHRIST.

MY SHEPHERD.—*Concluded.*

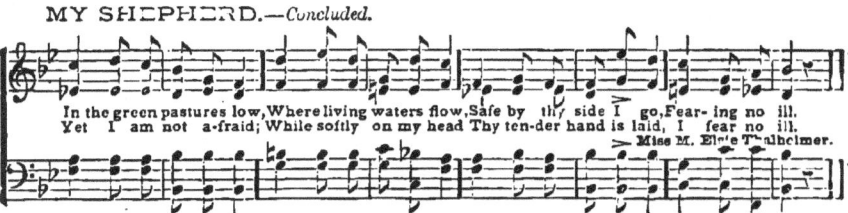

In the green pastures low, Where living waters flow, Safe by thy side I go, Fear-ing no ill.
Yet I am not a-fraid; While softly on my head Thy ten-der hand is laid, I fear no ill.
— Miss M. Elsie Thalheimer.

SECOND HYMN.

83 *Holding to Christ.*
1 Lord do not leave me!
I'm but an erring child,
Weak, poor, and sin defiled,
Afraid, alone;
But thou art strong and wise
No ill can thee surprise;
Beneath thy loving eyes
Danger is none.

2 If thou wilt guide me,
Gladly I'll go with thee;—
No harm can come to me.
Holding thy hand;
And soon my weary feet,
Safe in the golden street,
Where all who love thee meet,
Redeemed shall stand.
— Miss M. Elsie Thalheimer.

NO NAME SO SWEET.   WM. B. BRADBURY, by per.

1. There is no name so sweet on earth, No name so sweet in heaven, The name before his
wondrous birth To Christ the Sav-iour giv-en. We love to sing a-round our King,
And hail him blessed Je-sus; For there's no word ear ev-er heard So dear, so sweet as "Je-sus."

Copyright, 1861, in "Golden Chain," by Wm. B. Bradbury.

84 *The sweetest name.*
2 And when he hung upon the tree,
They wrote this name above him,
That all might see the reason we
Forever more must love him.—REF.

3 So now, upon his Father's throne,
Almighty to release us

From sin and pains, he ever reigns,
The Prince and Saviour, Jesus.—REF.

4 O Jesus! by thy matchless name
Thy grace shall fail us never;
To-day as yesterday the same,
Thou art our God forever.
— Geo. Washington Bethune.

SONGS OF THE HOLY SPIRIT.

ST. MARTIN'S. C. M. — William Tansur.

1. Come, Holy Ghost, our hearts inspire;
Let us thine influence prove;
Source of the old prophetic fire,
Fountain of life and love.

85 *The enlightening Spirit.*

2 Come, Holy Ghost, for moved by thee
The prophets wrote and spoke,
Unlock the truth, thyself the key;
Unseal the sacred book.

3 Expand thy wings, celestial Dove,
Brood o'er our nature's night;
On our disordered spirits move,
And let there now be light.

4 God, through himself, we then shall know,
If thou within us shine;
And sound, with all thy saints below,
The depths of love divine.
— Charles Wesley.

NEW HAVEN. 6, 4. — Thomas Hastings.

1. Come, Holy Ghost, in love, Shed on us from above Thine own bright ray! Divinely good thou art; Thy sacred gifts impart To gladden each sad heart: O come today!

86 *Invocation of the Holy Spirit.*

2 Come, tenderest Friend, and best,
Our most delightful Guest,
With soothing power:
Rest, which the weary know,
Shade, 'mid the noontide glow,
Peace, when deep griefs o'erflow,
Cheer us, this hour!

3 Come, all the faithful bless;
Let all who Christ confess
His praise employ:
Give virtue's rich reward;
Victorious death accord,
And, with our glorious Lord,
Eternal joy!
— Robert II., King of France. Tr. Ray Palmer.

SONGS OF THE HOLY SPIRIT.

HOLY SPIRIT, FAITHFUL GUIDE.
Marcus Morris Wells.

1. Ho-ly Spir-it, faith-ful guide, Ev-er near the Christian's side; Gently lead us by the hand,
Pilgrims in a des-ert land; Wea-ry souls for e'er re-joice, While they hear that sweetest voice
Fol-low me, I'll guide thee home.
D.C.—Whisp'ring softly, wanderer come!

87 *"I will guide thee with mine eye."*

2 Ever present, truest Friend,
Ever near thine aid to lend,
Leave us not to doubt and fear,
Groping on in darkness drear,
When the storms are raging sore,
Hearts grow faint, and hopes give o'er,
Whisper softly, wanderer come !
Follow me, I'll guide thee home.

3 When our days of toil shall cease,
Waiting still for sweet release,
Nothing left but heaven and prayer,
Wond'ring if our names were there ;
Wading deep the dismal flood,
Pleading nought but Jesus' blood,
Whisper softly, wanderer come !
Follow me, I'll guide thee home !
M. M. Wells.

ZEPHYR. L. M.
William B. Bradbury.

1. Al-might-y Spir-it, we con-fess Thee God, and bow with thank-ful-ness;
God with the Fa-ther and the Son; E-ter-nal Three for-ev-er One.

88 *Almighty Spirit.*

2 In thee we live; thy vital breath
First called us from the realm of death,
And each succeeding hour we move
Upheld by thy sustaining love.

3 Thou art our light—the way is dark,
Illume it with thy vital spark ;
Thou art our guide—O lead our feet
To pastures green and waters sweet.

4 Inspire our souls, quicken our sight,
And fill us with thy holy light,
That we may feel thy presence still,
And know and do thy gracious will.
T. C. Reade.

SONGS OF THE SCRIPTURES.

ARMENIA. C. M.   Sylvanus Billings Pond.

1. How precious is the book divine, By inspiration given! Bright as a lamp its doctrines shine, To guide our souls to heaven.

89   *The Bible precious.*

2 It sweetly cheers our drooping hearts,
   In this dark vale of tears;
Life, light, and joy it still imparts,
   And quells our rising fears.

3 This lamp, through all the tedious night
   Of life, shall guide our way;
Till we behold the clearer light
   Of an eternal day.
John Fawcett.

BREAD OF LIFE. 10.   Wm. F. Sherwin.

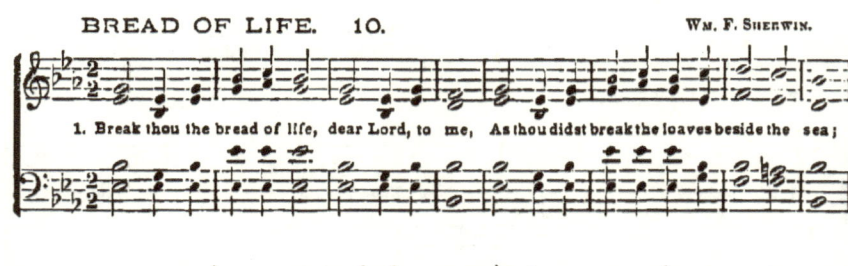

1. Break thou the bread of life, dear Lord, to me, As thou didst break the loaves beside the sea;

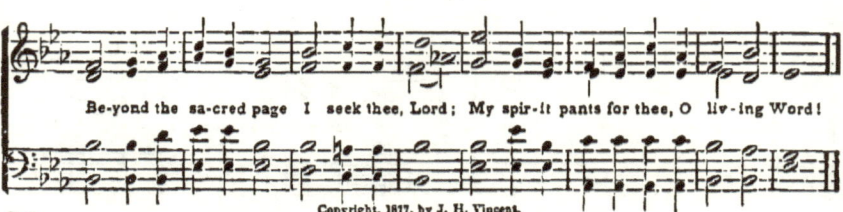

Beyond the sacred page I seek thee, Lord; My spirit pants for thee, O living Word!

Copyright, 1877, by J. H. Vincent.

90   *The Bread of Life.*

1 Break thou the bread of life, dear Lord,
   to me,
  As thou didst break the loaves beside the
   sea;
Beyond the sacred page I seek thee, Lord;
  My spirit pants for thee, O living Word!

2 Bless thou the precious truth, dear Lord,
   to me,
  As thou didst bless the bread by Galilee;
Then shall all bondage cease, all fetters
   fall,
  And I shall find my peace, my all in all!
Mary A. Lathbury.

SONGS OF THE SCRIPTURES.

UXBRIDGE. L. M.   LOWELL MASON.

1. Now let my soul, e-ter-nal King, To thee its grate-ful trib-ute bring; My knee with hum-ble hom-age bow; My tongue perform its sol-emn vow.

91 *The Saviour seen in the Scriptures.*

2 All nature sings thy boundless love,
  In worlds below and worlds above;
  But in thy blessed word I trace
  Diviner wonders of thy grace.

3 There, what delightful truths I read!
  There, I behold the Saviour bleed:
  His name salutes my listening ear,
  Revives my heart and checks my fear.

4 There Jesus bids my sorrows cease;
  And gives my laboring conscience peace;
  He lifts my grateful thoughts on high,
  And points to mansions in the sky.

5 For love like this, O let my song,
  Through endless years, thy praise prolong
  Let distant climes thy name adore,
  Till time and nature are no more.
                  Ottiwell Heginbotham.

DOVER. S. M.   AARON WILLIAMS' COLL.

1. Thy word, al-might-y Lord, Where'er it en-ters in, Is sharp-er than a two-edged sword, To slay the man of sin.

92 *God's word, quick and powerful.*

1 THY word, almighty Lord,
    Where'er it enters in,
  Is sharper than a two-edged sword,
    To slay the man of sin.

2 Thy word is power and life;
    It bids confusion cease,

  And changes envy, hatred, strife,
    To love, and joy, and peace.

3 Then let our hearts obey
    The gospel's glorious sound;
  And all its fruits, from day to day,
    Be in us and abound.
                  James Montgomery.

SONGS OF SALVATION.

LOUVAN. L. M. — Virgil Corydon Taylor.

1. Deep are the wounds which sin has made;
Where shall the sinner find a cure?
In vain, alas! is nature's aid;
The work exceeds her utmost power.

93 *The great Physician.*

2 But can no sovereign balm be found,
And is no kind physician nigh,
To ease the pain and heal the wound,
Ere life and hope forever fly?

3 There is a great Physician near;
Look up, O fainting soul, and live;
See, in his heavenly smiles, appear
Such help as nature cannot give.

4 See, in the Saviour's dying blood,
Life, health, and bliss abundant flow;
And in that sacrificial flood
A balm for all thy grief and woe.
— Anne Steele.

DOWNS. C. M. — Lowell Mason.

1. How sweet the name of Jesus sounds
In a believer's ear!
It soothes his sorrows, heals his wounds,
And drives away his fear.

94 *The dearest name.*

2 It makes the wounded spirit whole,
And calms the troubled breast;
'Tis manna to the hungry soul,
And to the weary, rest.

3 Dear name! the rock on which I build,
My shield and hiding-place;
My never-failing treasure, filled
With boundless stores of grace!

4 Jesus, my Shepherd, Saviour, Friend,
My Prophet, Priest, and King,
My Lord, my Life, my Way, my End,
Accept the praise I bring!

5 I would thy boundless love proclaim
With every fleeting breath;
So shall the music of thy name
Refresh my soul in death.
— John Newton.

SONGS OF SALVATION.

95 *The voice of free grace.*

1 THE voice of free grace cries, "Escape to the mountain;
For Adam's lost race Christ hath opened a fountain:
For sin and uncleanness, and every transgression,
His blood flows most freely in streams of salvation."
  Hallelujah to the Lamb, etc.

2 Now glory to God in the highest is given;
Now glory to God is re-echoed in heaven;
Around the whole earth let us tell the glad story,
And sing of his love, his salvation and glory,

3 O Jesus, ride on,—thy kingdom is glorious;
O'er sin, death, and hell, thou wilt make us victorious:
Thy name shall be praised in the great congregation,
And saints shall ascribe unto thee their salvation.

4 When on Zion we stand, having gained the blest shore,
With our harps in our hands, we will praise evermore:
We'll range the blest fields on the banks of the river,
And sing of redemption forever and ever.
                               Richard Burdsall.

SONGS OF SALVATION.

GREENVILLE. 8, 7, 4.   JEAN JACQUES ROUSSEAU.

1. Come, ye sinners, poor and needy, Weak and wounded, sick and sore; Jesus ready stands to save you, Full of pity, love, and (Omit) power:
D. C. He is a-ble, He is a-ble, He is willing: doubt no more.

96   *Invitation hymn.*

1 COME, ye sinners, poor and needy,
    Weak and wounded, sick and sore;
Jesus ready stands to save you,
    Full of pity, love, and power:
      He is able,
    He is willing: doubt no more.

2 Now, ye needy, come and welcome;
    God's free bounty glorify;
True belief and true repentance,
    Every grace that brings you nigh,
      Without money,
    Come to Jesus Christ and buy.

3 Let not conscience make you linger,
    Nor of fitness fondly dream;
All the fitness he requireth
    Is to feel your need of him:
      This he gives you;
    'Tis the Spirit's glimmering beam.

4 Come, ye weary, heavy-laden,
    Bruised and mangled by the fall;
If you tarry till you're better,
    You will never come at all;
      Not the righteous,—
    Sinners Jesus came to call.

5 Agonizing in the garden,
    Your Redeemer prostrate lies;
On the bloody tree behold him!
    Hear him cry, before he dies,
      "It is finished!"
    Sinners, will not this suffice?

6 Lo! the incarnate God, ascending,
    Pleads the merit of his blood:
Venture on him, venture freely;
    Let no other trust intrude;
      None but Jesus
    Can do helpless sinners good.

7 Saints and angels, joined in concert,
    Sing the praises of the Lamb;
While the blissful seats of heaven
    Sweetly echo with his name:
      Hallelujah!
    Sinners here may do the same.
                                Joseph Hart.

COME, YE SINNERS. 8, 7.   JEREMIAH INGALLS.

1. Come, ye sinners, poor and need-y, Weak and wounded, sick and sore;
Je-sus read-y stands to save you, Full of pit-y, love, and power:
D. C. Glo-ry, hon-or, and sal-va-tion, Christ the Lord is come to reign.

CHORUS.
Turn to the Lord, and seek sal-va-tion, Sound the praise of his dear name;

SONGS OF SALVATION.

WONDERFUL WORDS.

P. P. Bliss.

97 *"They are spirit and they are life."*

1 SING them over again to me,
  Wonderful words of life,
  Let me more of their beauty see,
  Wonderful words of life;
  Words of life and beauty,
  Teach me faith and duty.

CHO.—
  Beautiful words, wonderful words,
  Wonderful words of life;
  Beautiful words, wonderful words,
  Wonderful words of life.

2 Christ, the blessed One gives to all
  Wonderful words of life;
  Sinner, list to the loving call,
  Wonderful words of life;
  All so freely given,
  Wooing us to heaven.—CHO.

3 Sweetly echo the gospel call,
  Wonderful words of life;
  Offer pardon and peace to all,
  Wonderful words of life;
  Jesus, only Saviour,
  Sanctify forever.—CHO.

P. P. Bliss.

SONGS OF SALVATION.

SILVER STREET. S. M.   Isaac Smith.

1. Grace! 'tis a charming sound, Har-mo-nious to the ear; Heaven with the ech-o shall re-sound, And all.... the earth shall hear.

98   *Grace.*

2 Grace first contrived a way
   To save rebellious man;
And all the steps that grace display,
   Which drew the wondrous plan.

3 Grace taught my roving feet
   To tread the heavenly road;
And new supplies each hour I meet,
   While pressing on to God.

4 Grace all the work shall crown
   Through everlasting days;
It lays in heaven the topmost stone,
   And well deserves our praise.
                        Philip Doddridge.

I DO BELIEVE. C. M.

1. Fa-ther, I stretch my hands to thee; No oth-er help I know,
If thou with-draw thy-self from me, Ah! whith-er shall I go?

Cho.—I will be-lieve, I do be-lieve, That Je-sus died for me;
And thro' his blood, his precious blood, I shall from sin be free.

99   *Unwearied earnestness.*

2 What did thine only Son endure,
   Before I drew my breath?
What pain, what labor, to secure
   My soul from endless death!
      I will believe, etc.

3 O Jesus, could I this believe,
   I now should feel thy power;
And all my wants thou wouldst relieve,
   In this accepted hour.
      I will believe, etc.

4 Author of faith! to thee I lift
   My weary, longing eyes:
O, let me now receive that gift,—
   My soul without it dies.
      I will believe, etc.
                      Charles Wesley.

SONGS OF SALVATION.

EVERLASTING LOVE.
Mrs. Joseph F. Knapp.

1. Wondrous words! how rich in bless-ing! Deep-er than th' unfath-omed sea;
Broad-er than its world of wa-ters, Bound-less, in-fi-nite and free:
High-er than the heavens a-bove, Is that Ev-er-last-ing Love;
High-er than the heavens a-bove, Is that Ev-er-last-ing Love.

Copyright by Joseph F. Knapp.

100 *Wondrous words.*

2 Down to lowest depths it reaches—
 The all-loving Father's arm,
Toward his rebel children yearning,
 Drawing them with magic charm;
||: Till the yielding spirits move,
 Touch'd by *Everlasting Love.* :||

3 Weary spirits—sad with toiling,
 'Mid the sorrows of life's way—
Feel their heavy burdens lightened,
 As they journey day by day,
||: How with quickened steps they move,
 Cheered by *Everlasting Love.* :||

4 I have set thee as a signet,
 Graven on my hands thy name;
Lo, I still am with thee always,
 Evermore thy Friend—the same;
||: Never changing—thou wilt prove
 Mine is Everlasting Love. :||

5 In my house of many mansions,
 I've prepared a place for thee,
Where are no dark clouds or tempests,
 Where I am, there thou shalt be—
||: All the untold bliss to prove,
 Of my *Everlasting Love.* :||

Mrs. Mary D. James.

SONGS OF SALVATION.

COWPER. C. M. — Lowell Mason.

1. There is a fountain filled with blood Drawn from Immanuel's veins; And sinners, plunged beneath that flood, Lose all their guilt-y stains, Lose all their guilty stains.

101 *The cleansing fountain.*

2. The dying thief rejoiced to see
That fountain in his day;
And there may I, though vile as he,
Wash all my sins away.

3. Thou dying Lamb! thy precious blood
Shall never lose its power,
Till all the ransomed Church of God
Are saved, to sin no more.

4. E'er since, by faith, I saw the stream
Thy flowing wounds supply,
Redeeming love has been my theme,
And shall be till I die.

5. Then in a nobler, sweeter song,
I'll sing thy power to save,
When this poor lisping, stammering tongue,
Lies silent in the grave.
— William Cowper.

CLEANSING FOUNTAIN. C. M. (SECOND TUNE.) — From Lowell Mason.

1. There is a fountain filled with blood Drawn from Immanuel's veins; And sinners, plunged beneath that flood, Lose all their guilt-y stains, Lose all their guilt-y stains,.... Lose all their guilt-y stains; And sinners, plunged beneath that flood, Lose all their guilty stains.

SONGS OF SALVATION.

CLEANSING WAVE.

MRS. JOSEPH F. KNAPP.

Copyright, 1872, by Joseph F. Knapp.

102 *The fountain of cleansing.*

1 O, NOW I see the crimson wave,
  The fountain deep and wide,
Jesus, my Lord, mighty to save,
  Points to his wounded side.

REFRAIN.

The cleansing stream, I see, I see!
I plunge, and O, it cleanseth me!
O, praise the Lord, it cleanseth me!
It cleanseth me, yes, cleanseth me!

2 I rise to walk in heaven's own light,
  Above the world and sin,
With heart made pure, and garments white,
  And Christ enthroned within.
    The cleansing stream, etc.

3 Amazing grace! 'tis heaven below,
  To feel the blood applied;
And Jesus, only Jesus know,
  My Jesus crucified.
    The cleansing stream, etc.

Phoebe Palmer.

SONGS OF SALVATION.

THE GOSPEL BELL.   T. FRANK ALLEN.

Copyright, 1885, by Phillips & Hunt.

103 *The glad tidings proclaimed.*

2 Inflamed with love, compassion
　To our apostate race,
He by his death and passion
　Revealed his matchless grace;
For us he bore temptations,
　Endured the cross of shame,
He purchased our salvation,
　All glory to his name.
Cho.—The gospel bell is ringing
　　Thro' all the world around,
　　Good news to sinners bringing,
　　How sweet the joyful sound!

3 O come to this good Shepherd,
　That seeks the wand'ring sheep,
He from the wolf and leopard
　Will thee securely keep;
Ye sinners, wildly straying,
　From God no longer roam,
The Shepherds call obeying,
　Ye wanderers, come home.
Cho.—The gospel bell is ringing
　　Thro' all the world around,
　　Good news to sinners bringing,
　　How sweet the joyful sound!
　　　　　　　　　Rev. J. H. Martin.

SONGS OF SALVATION.

OH, COME AT ONCE TO JESUS.   Rev. R. LOWRY.

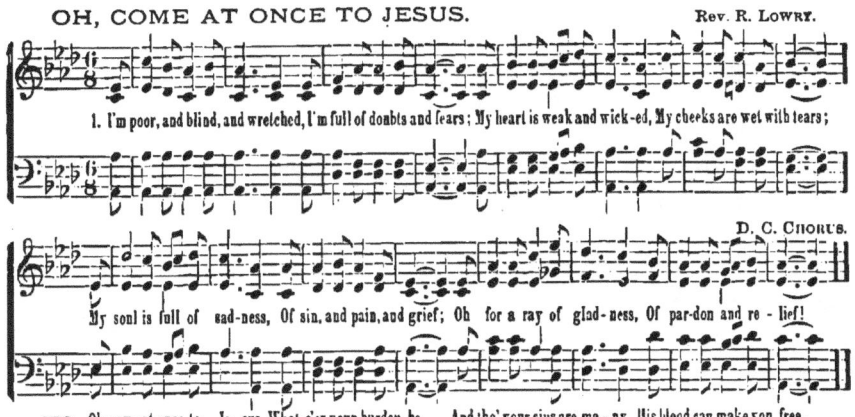

1. I'm poor, and blind, and wretched, I'm full of doubts and fears; My heart is weak and wick-ed, My cheeks are wet with tears;
My soul is full of sad-ness, Of sin, and pain, and grief; Oh for a ray of glad-ness, Of par-don and re-lief!

CHO.—Oh come at once to Je-sus, What-e'er your burden be, And tho' your sins are ma-ny, His blood can make you free.

Copyright, 1873, by Biglow & Main.

104 *Burdened with sin.*
2 And will the blessed Saviour
This guilty soul make pure?
May I be his forever?
May I his love secure?

Oh, then I'll tell the story;
I'll tell the world to come;
For Christ, the king of glory,
Will bid them welcome home.
Archibald Kenyon.

WEARY OF EARTH, AND LADEN.   JAMES LANGRAN.

1. Wea-ry of earth, and lad-en with my sin, I look at heav'n, and long to en-ter in,
But there no e-vil thing may find a home: And yet I hear a voice that bids me "Come."

105 *His life for ours.*
2 It is the voice of Jesus that I hear,
His are the hands stretched out to draw me near,
And his the blood that can for all atone,
And set me faultless there before the throne.

3 Yea, thou wilt answer for me, righteous Lord:
Thine all the merits, mine the great reward;
Thine the sharp thorns, and mine the golden crown,
Mine the life won, and thine the life laid down.
Samuel John Stone.

SONGS OF SALVATION.

HORTON. 7.   XAVIER SCHNYDER.

1. Come, said Jesus' sacred voice, Come, and make my paths your choice; I will guide you to your home; Weary pilgrim, hither come.

106   *The gracious call.*

2 Thou who, houseless, sole, forlorn,
Long hast borne the proud world's scorn,
Long hast roamed the barren waste,
Weary pilgrim, hither haste.

3 Ye who, tossed on beds of pain,
Seek for ease, but seek in vain;
Ye, by fiercer anguish torn,
In remorse for guilt who mourn;

4 Hither come, for here is found
Balm that flows for every wound,
Peace that ever shall endure,
Rest eternal, sacred, sure.
                    Mrs. Anna L. Barbauld.

PLEYEL'S HYMN. 7.   IGNACE PLEYEL.

1. Hasten, sinner, to be wise! Stay not for the morrow's sun: Wisdom if you still despise, Harder is it to be won.

107   *Delay dangerous.*

2 Hasten, mercy to implore!
Stay not for the morrow's sun,
Lest thy season should be o'er
Ere this evening's stage be run.

3 Hasten, sinner, to return!
Stay not for the morrow's sun,
Lest thy lamp should fail to burn
Ere salvation's work is done.

4 Hasten, sinner, to be blest!
Stay not for the morrow's sun,
Lest perdition thee arrest
Ere the morrow is begun.
                    Thomas Scott.

SONGS OF SALVATION.

JESUS IS CALLING.

GEO. C. STEBBINS.

1. Jesus is tenderly calling thee home—Calling to-day, calling to-day;
Why from the sunshine of love wilt thou roam, Farther and farther away?

REFRAIN.
Calling to-day, calling to-day,
Calling, calling to-day, to-day;
Jesus is calling, Is tenderly calling to-day.

Copyright, 1883, by Geo. C. Stebbins.

108 *To-day if ye will hear his voice.*

2 Jesus is calling the weary to rest—
  Calling to-day, calling to-day;
Bring him thy burden and thou shalt be blest;
  He will not turn thee away.—REF.

3 Jesus is waiting, oh, come to him now—
  Waiting to-day, waiting to-day;
Come with thy sins, at his feet lowly bow;
  Come, and no longer delay.—REF.

4 Jesus is pleading, oh, list to his voice—
  Hear him to-day, hear him to-day;
They who believe on his name shall rejoice;
  Quickly arise and away.—REF.

Fanny J. Crosby.

SONGS OF SALVATION.

BLUMENTHAL. 7. D. JACQUES BLUMENTHAL, ARR. BY H. P. M.

1. Depth of mer-cy! can there be Mer-cy still re-served for me? Can my God his wrath for-bear,—Me, the chief of sin-ners, spare? I have long with-stood his grace; Long pro-voked him to his face; Would not hearken to his calls; Grieved him by a thousand falls.

109 *Depth of mercy.*

2 Kindled his relentings are;
Me he now delights to spare;
Cries, "How shall I give thee up?"
Lets the lifted thunder drop.

There for me the Saviour stands,
Shows his wounds and spreads his hands;
God is love! I know, I feel;
Jesus weeps, and loves me still.
  Charles Wesley.

MERCY. 7. (SECOND TUNE.) CHORUS. *Faster. stacc.*

1. { Depth of mer-cy! can there be Mer-cy still re-served for me? }
   { Can my God his wrath for-bear,—Me, the chief of sinners, spare? } God is love! I know, I feel; Jesus weeps, and loves me still; Je-sus weeps, he weeps, and loves me still.

Smoothly. *Repeat pp.*

SONGS OF SALVATION.

FEAST OF BLESSING.
W. H. Doane.

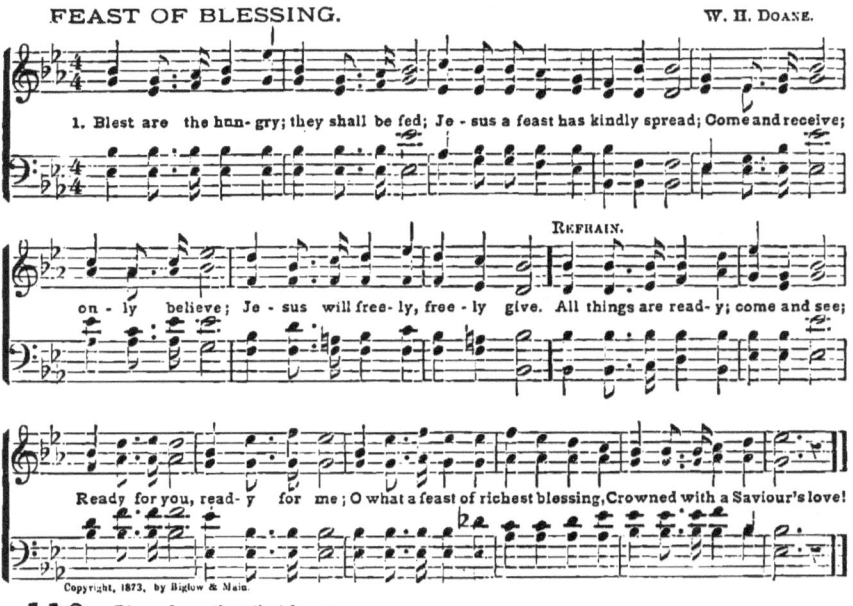

110 *Blessed are they that hunger.*

2 Out in the highway go and proclaim
Welcome to all in Jesus' name;
Bread to the poor, bread evermore,
Jesus will freely, freely give.—REF.

3 Sweet invitation! how can we slight
Him who will make our path so bright?
All we require, all our desire,
Jesus will freely, freely give.—REF.
Fanny J. Crosby.

COME, COME TO JESUS!
Hubert P. Main, 1864, by per.

111 *He waits to welcome.*

2 Come, come to Jesus! He waits to ransom thee,
O slave! so willingly; Come, come to Jesus!

3 Come, come to Jesus! He waits to lighten thee,
O burdened! trustingly Come, come to Jesus!

4 Come, come to Jesus! He waits to shelter thee,
O weary! blessedly Come, come to Jesus!

5 Come, come to Jesus! He waits to carry thee,
O lamb! so lovingly; Come, come to Jesus!
George B. Peck.

SONGS OF SALVATION.

COME TO JESUS.
E. D. Beddall.

1. Come to Jesus and be saved, Come, come to Jesus, Who for you his life he gave, Come, come to Jesus. Come and all your sins confess, Come and he your souls will bless, Come in all thy souls distress, Come, come to Jesus.

CHORUS.
Jesus is waiting, Jesus is waiting, Jesus is waiting in mercy for you.

Copyright, 1885, by Phillips & Hunt.

112 *Jesus is waiting.*

2 Come to Jesus weary one,
　Come, come to Jesus,
He can save you, he alone,
　Come, come to Jesus,
Come, and he will save you now,
Come and at his footstool bow,
Come poor weary sinner thou,
　Come, come to Jesus.
　　Cho.—Jesus is waiting, &c.

3 Come to Jesus don't delay,
　Come, come to Jesus,
Time is flying fast away
　Come, come to Jesus,
Jesus died on Calvary,
Shed his blood for you and me,
Paid the debt to set us free,
　Come, come to Jesus.
　　Cho.—Jesus is waiting, &c.
　　　　　　　　E. D. Beddall.

SONGS OF SALVATION.

INGHAM. L. M. — Lowell Mason.

1. God calling yet! shall I not hear? Earth's pleasures shall I still hold dear?
Shall life's swift passing years all fly, And still my soul in slumber lie?

113 *God calling yet.*

2. God calling yet! shall I not rise?
Can I his loving voice despise,
And basely his kind care repay!
He calls me still; can I delay?

3. God calling yet! and shall he knock,
And I my heart the closer lock?
He still is waiting to receive,
And shall I dare his Spirit grieve?

4. God calling yet! and shall I give
No heed, but still in bondage live?
I wait, but he does not forsake;
He calls me still; my heart, awake!

5. God calling yet! I cannot stay;
My heart I yield without delay:
Vain world, farewell, from thee I part;
The voice of God hath reached my heart.

Gerhard Tersteegen. Tr. by Miss J. Borthwick.

BOYLSTON. S. M. — Lowell Mason.

1. Now is the accepted time, Now is the day of grace;
Now, sinners, come without delay, And seek the Saviour's face.

114 *The day of grace.*

2. Now is the accepted time,
The Saviour calls to-day;
To-morrow it may be too late—
Then why should you delay?

3. Now is the accepted time,
The gospel bids you come;
And every promise in his word
Declares there yet is room.

John Dobell.

SONGS OF SALVATION.

INVITATION ACCEPTED.—*Concluded.*

116 *Implicit faith.*

2 Just as I am, the sin
　That stains my soul,
The load of guilt within
　On thee to roll.
O Jesus hear my cry,
No other hope have I,
Lord save me or I die,
　And make me whole!

3 Just as I am, I bow,
　So glad to know
That e'en to me wilt thou
　Thy mercy show:

For they who seek thy face
Shall not their trust misplace,
On such thy saving grace
　Thou wilt bestow.

4 Just as I am, I give
　Myself to thee;
Thy service while I live
　My joy shall be.
Take thou this heart of mine,
Fill it with love divine,
And seal it wholly thine
　Eternally.
　　　　Rev. Robert M. Offord.

THERE IS A FRIEND.
　　　　　　　　　　Rev. Samuel Alman.

1. There is a friend, A friend you need, A friend with God, To intercede, His precious name is Jesus; A friend thy soul To save from sin, And make thee whole, And pure within, O such a friend is Jesus.

CHORUS.
A friend in need, A friend indeed, O such a friend is Jesus.

Copyright, 1885, by Phillips & Hunt.

117 *"Closer than a brother."*

2 A friend to guide
　Thee day by day,
And by thy side
　To guard the way,
A loving friend is Jesus.
A friend whose power
　Alone can cheer,
In that dark hour—
　When death is near—
No earthly friend like Jesus.

3 O, sinner—stay,
　Why yet offend,
And turn away,
　So great a friend,
As this dear, precious Jesus.
He waiting stands,—
　And pleads to win,—
With outstretched hands—
　Thy heart of sin—
O, what a friend is Jesus.
　　　　Arr. by Rev. Samuel Alman.

SONGS OF SALVATION.

PLEADING WITH THEE.

Rev. ROBERT LOWRY.

1. So near to the kingdom! yet what dost thou lack? So near to the kingdom! what keepeth thee back?
2. So near that thou hearest the songs that resound From those who believing, a pardon have found!

Renounce ev'ry idol, though dear it may be, And come to the Saviour now pleading with thee.
So near, yet unwilling to give up thy sin, When Jesus is waiting to welcome thee in!

REFRAIN.
Pleading with thee, pleading with thee, The Saviour is pleading, is pleading with thee.

Copyright, 1875, by Biglow & Main.

118 *What keepeth thee back?*

3 O come, or thy season of grace will be past,
The door will be closed, and this call be thy last;
O where wouldst thou turn if the light should depart
That comes from the Spirit, and shines on thy heart.—REF.

4 To die with no hope! hast thou counted the cost?
To die out of Christ, and thy soul to be lost!
So near to the kingdom! O come, we implore,
While Jesus is pleading, come, enter the door.—REF.

Fanny J. Crosby.

PASS ME NOT.

W. H. DOANE.

1. Pass me not, O gentle Saviour, Hear my humble cry; While on others Thou art calling, Do not pass me

Copyright, 1870, in "Songs of Devotion," by W. H. Doane.

SONGS OF SALVATION.

PASS ME NOT.—*Concluded.*

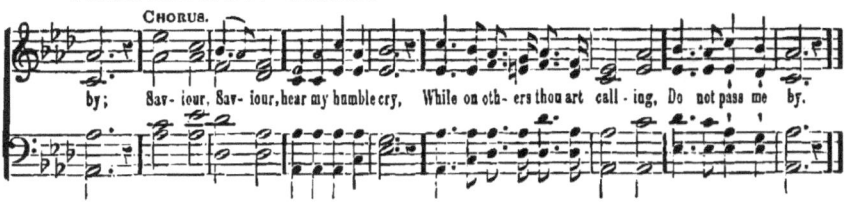

119 *Pleading for mercy.*

2 Let me at a throne of mercy
  Find a sweet relief;
Kneeling there in deep contrition,
  Help my unbelief.—REF.

3 Trusting only in thy merit,
  Would I seek thy face;

Heal my wounded, broken spirit,
  Save me by thy grace.—REF.

4 Thou the spring of all my comfort,
  More than life for me;
Whom have I on earth beside thee?
  Whom in heaven but thee.—REF.

  Fanny J. Crosby.

COME TO THE FOUNTAIN.   GEO. C. STEBBINS.

Copyright, 1883, by Geo. C. Stebbins.

120 *Jesus is waiting to save.*

3 These are the words of the Saviour;
  They who repent and believe,
They who are willing to trust him,
  Life at his hand shall receive.
    CHO.—Haste thee away, &c.

4 Come and be healed at the fountain,
  List to the peace-speaking voice;
Over a sinner returning
  Now let the angels rejoice.
    CHO.—Haste thee away, &c.

    Fanny J. Crosby.

SONGS OF SALVATION.

WHO'LL BE THE NEXT.
Rev. Robert Lowry.

1. Who'll be the next to fol-low Je-sus? Who'll be the next his cross to bear? Some one is read-y, some one is wait-ing; Who'll be the next a crown to wear?

REFRAIN.
Who'll be the next? Who'll be the next? Who'll be the next to fol-low Je-sus? Who'll be the next to fol-low Je-sus now? Fol-low Je-sus now.

Copyright, 1871, by Biglow & Main

121 *Following Jesus.*

2 Who'll be the next to follow Jesus—
Follow his weary, bleeding feet?
Who'll be the next to lay every burden
Down at the Father's mercy seat?—REF.

3 Who'll be the next to follow Jesus?
Who'll be the next to praise his name?

Who'll swell the chorus of free redemption—
Sing, hallelujah! praise the Lamb?—REF.

4 Who'll be the next to follow Jesus,
Down through the Jordan's rolling tide?
Who'll be the next to join with the ransomed,
Singing upon the other side.—REF.

Annie S Hawks.

TO JESUS I WILL GO.
W. H. Doane.

1. There's a gentle voice within calls a-way, 'Tis a warning I have heard o'er and o'er;
But my heart is melt-ed now, I o-bey; From my Saviour I will wan-der no (omit) more.

Copyright, 1869, in Bright Jewels, by Biglow & Main.

SONGS OF SALVATION.

TO JESUS I WILL GO.—Concluded.

122 *The heavenly Monitor.*

2 He has promised all my sins to forgive,
If I ask in simple faith for his love;
In his holy word I learn how to live,
And to labor for his kingdom above.
   CHO.—Yes, I will go, &c.

3 I will try to bear the cross in my youth,
And be faithful to its cause till I die;
If with cheerful step I walk in the truth,
I shall wear a starry crown by and by.
   CHO.—Yes, I will go, &c.

4 Still the gentle voice within calls away,
And its warning I have heard o'er and o'er;
But my heart is melted now, I obey;
From my Saviour I will wander no more.
   CHO.—Yes, I will go, &c.
   Fanny J. Crosby.

NONE BUT JESUS.
Rev. ROBERT LOWRY.

Copyright, 1867, by Robert Lowry.

123 *Salvation through faith.*

2 Working will not save me—
Purest deeds that I can do,
Holiest thoughts and feelings too,
Can not form my soul anew—
   Working will not save me.—REF.

3 Waiting will not save me—
Helpless, guilty, lost I lie;
In my ear is mercy's cry;
If I wait I can but die—
   Waiting will not save me.—REF.

4 Faith in Christ will save me—
Let me trust thy weeping Son,
Trust the work that he has done;
To his arms, Lord, help me run—
   Faith in Christ will save me.—REF.
   Rev. Robert Lowry.

SONGS OF SALVATION.

THE GOSPEL CALL.

Geo. C. Stebbins.

Copyright, 1882, by Geo. C. Stebbins.

124 *Good news to all.*

2 Let every one who hears, say "Come!"
And joyful witness give,
   I heard the sound,
   The stream I found,
I drank and now I live!
   Cho.—The Spirit says, &c.

3 Ye souls who are athirst, forsake
Your broken cisterns first;
   Then come, partake,
   One draught will slake
Your soul's consuming thirst.
   Cho.—The Spirit says, &c.

4 Yea, whosoever will may come,
Your longings Christ can fill;
   The stream is free
   To you and me,
And whosoever will.
   Cho.—The Spirit says, &c.

Arther T. Pierson, D. D.

SONGS OF SALVATION.

TOPLADY. 7, 6 l.
Thomas Hastings.

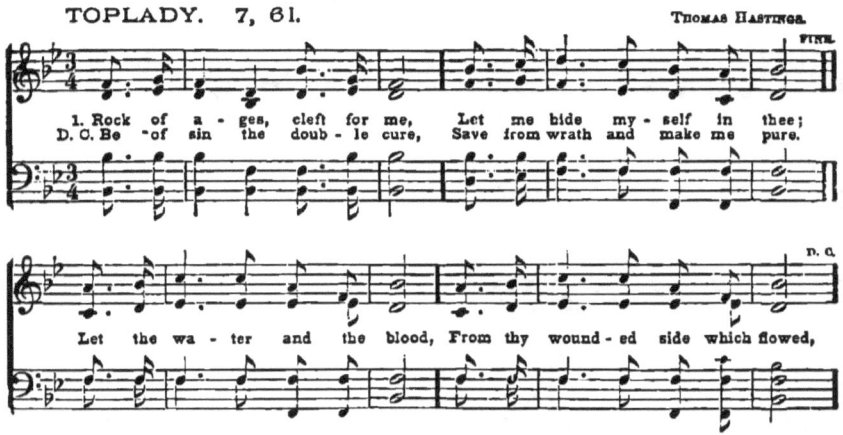

1. Rock of a-ges, cleft for me, Let me hide my-self in thee;
D. C. Be -of sin the doub-le cure, Save from wrath and make me pure.

Let the wa-ter and the blood, From thy wound-ed side which flowed,

125 *Rock of ages.*

2 Could my tears forever flow,
Could my zeal no languor know,
These for sin could not atone:
Thou must save, and thou alone:
In my hand no price I bring;
Simply to thy cross I cling.

3 While I draw this fleeting breath,
When my eyes shall close in death,
When I rise to worlds unknown,
And behold thee on thy throne,
Rock of ages, cleft for me,
Let me hide myself in thee.
Augustus M. Toplady, alt.

EVEN ME. 8, 7, 3.
William B. Bradbury.

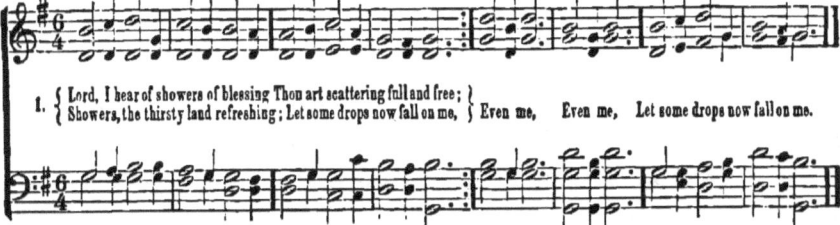

1. { Lord, I hear of showers of blessing Thou art scattering full and free; }
   { Showers, the thirsty land refreshing; Let some drops now fall on me, } Even me, Even me, Let some drops now fall on me.

Copyright, 1862, in "Golden Shower," by Wm. B. Bradbury.

126 *Even me.*

1 LORD, I hear of showers of blessing
    Thou art scattering full and free;
Showers, the thirsty land refreshing;
    Let some drops now fall on me,
        Even me.

2 Pass me not, O God, my Father,
    Sinful though my heart may be;
Thou mightst leave me, but the rather
    Let thy mercy light on me,
        Even me.

3 Pass me not, O gracious Saviour,
    Let me live and cling to thee;
I am longing for thy favor;
    Whilst thou 'rt calling, O call me,
        Even me.

4 Pass me not, O mighty Spirit,
    Thou canst make the blind to see;
Witnesser of Jesus' merit,
    Speak the word of power to me,
        Even me.

5 Love of God, so pure and changeless,
    Blood of Christ, so rich and free,
Grace of God, so strong and boundless,
    Magnify them all in me,
        Even me.
Mrs. Elizabeth Codner.

SONGS OF SALVATION.

WHY DO YOU WAIT?
GEO. F. ROOT.

1. Why do you wait, dear broth-er, Oh, why do you tar-ry so long? Your Saviour is waiting to give you A place in his sanc-ti-fied throng. Why not? why not? Why not come to him now? now?

By per. of The John Church Co., owners of the Copyright.

127 *Arise, he calleth thee.*

2 What do you hope, dear brother,
　To gain by a further delay?
There's no one to save you but Jesus,
There's no other way but his way. CHO.

3 Do you not feel, dear brother,
　His spirit now striving within?
Oh, why not accept his salvation,
　And throw off thy burden of sin. CHO.

4 Why do you wait, dear brother,
　The harvest is passing away.
Your Saviour is longing to bless you,
　There's danger and death in delay. CHO.
　　　　　　　　　　　　G. F. Root.

TAKE ME AS I AM.
GEO. C. STEBBINS.

1. Je-sus my Lord to thee I cry, Un-less thou help me I must die; Oh, bring thy free sal-va-tion nigh, And take me as I am. Take me as I am,

Copyright, 1881, by Geo. C. Stebbins.

SONGS OF SALVATION.

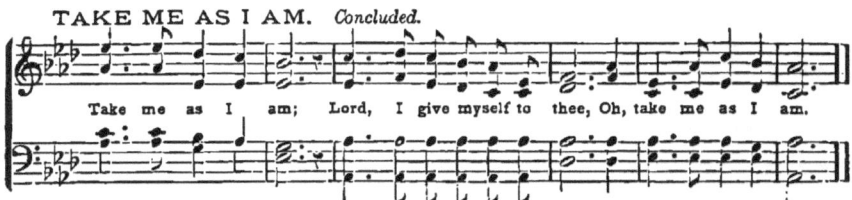

TAKE ME AS I AM. *Concluded.*

Take me as I am; Lord, I give myself to thee, Oh, take me as I am.

128 *Hear my prayer, O Lord.*

2 Helpless I am and full of guilt,
But yet for me thy blood was spilt;
And thou canst make me what thou wilt,
  And take me as I am. CHO.

3 I bow before thy mercy-seat,
Behold me, Saviour, at thy feet;
Thy work begin, thy work complete,
  And take me as I am. CHO.

4 If thou hast work for me to do,
Inspire my will, my heart renew;
And work both in, and by me too,
  And take me as I am. CHO.

5 And when at last the work is done,
The battle fought, the victory won,
Still, still my cry shall be alone.
  Oh take me as I am. CHO.
Eliza H. Hamilton.

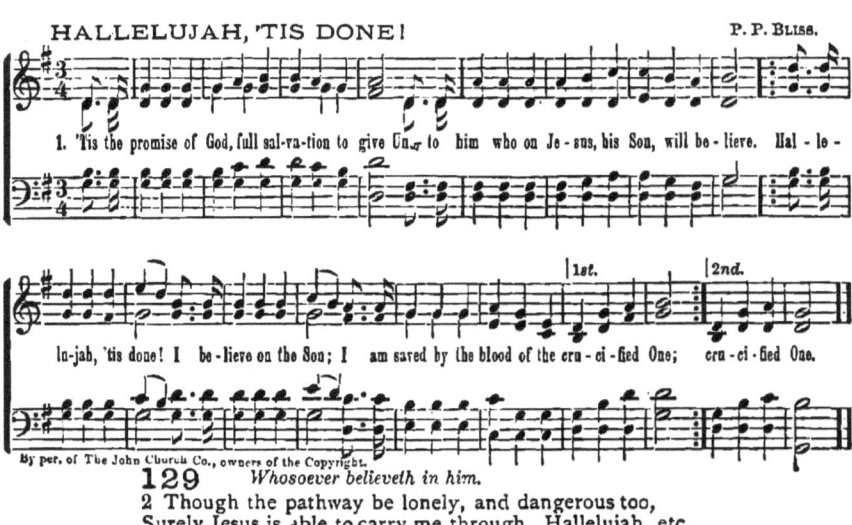

HALLELUJAH, 'TIS DONE! P. P. BLISS.

1. 'Tis the promise of God, full sal-va-tion to give Un-to him who on Je-sus, his Son, will be-lieve. Hal-le-lu-jah, 'tis done! I be-lieve on the Son; I am saved by the blood of the cru-ci-fied One; cru-ci-fied One.

By per. of The John Church Co., owners of the Copyright.

129 *Whosoever believeth in him.*

2 Though the pathway be lonely, and dangerous too,
Surely Jesus is able to carry me through. Hallelujah, etc.

3 Many loved ones have I in yon heavenly throng,
They are safe now in glory and this is their song: Hallelujah, etc.

4 Little children I see standing close by their king,
And he smiles as their song of salvation they sing. Hallelujah, etc.

5 There are prophets and kings in that throng I behold,
And they sing as they march thro' the streets of pure gold: Hallelujah, etc.

6 There's a part in that chorus for you and for me,
And the theme of our praises forever will be: Hallelujah, etc.
P. P. Bliss.

SONGS OF SALVATION.

WOODWORTH. L. M.   WILLIAM B. BRADBURY.

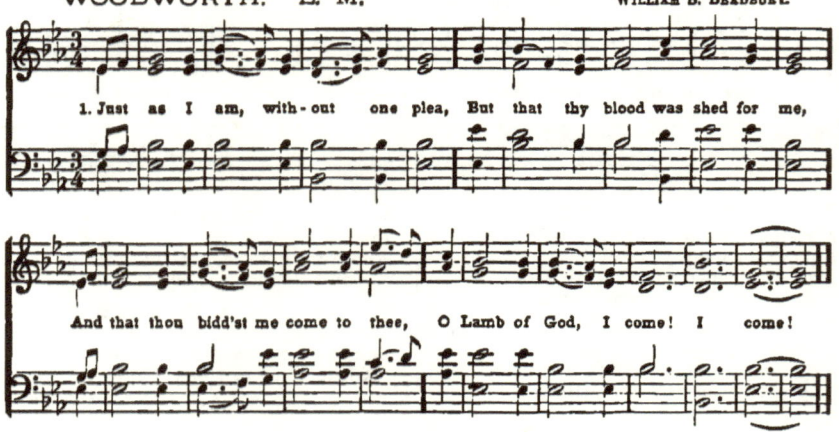

1. Just as I am, with-out one plea, But that thy blood was shed for me,
And that thou bidd'st me come to thee, O Lamb of God, I come! I come!

130   *Just as I am.*

2 Just as I am, and waiting not
To rid my soul of one dark blot,
To thee whose blood can cleanse each spot,
O Lamb of God, I come! I come!

3 Just as I am, though tossed about
With many a conflict, many a doubt,
Fightings within, and fears without,
O Lamb of God, I come! I come!

4 Just as I am—poor, wretched, blind;
Sight, riches, healing of the mind,
Yea, all I need, in thee to find,
O Lamb of God, I come! I come!

5 Just as I am—thou wilt receive,
Wilt welcome, pardon, cleanse, relieve;
Because thy promise I believe,
O Lamb of God, I come! I come!

6 Just as I am—thy love unknown
Hath broken every barrier down;
Now, to be thine, yea, thine alone,
O Lamb of God, I come! I come!
                           Charlotte Elliott.

I AM TRUSTING, LORD, IN THEE.   WM. G. FISCHER.

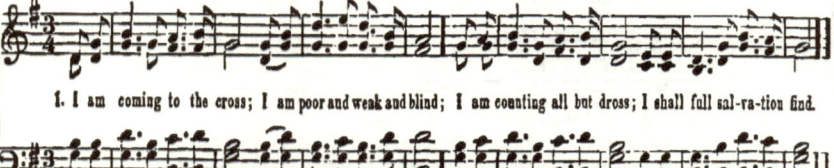

1. I am coming to the cross; I am poor and weak and blind; I am counting all but dross; I shall full sal-va-tion find.

CHO.—I am trusting, Lord, in thee, Dear Lamb of Cal-va-ry; Humbly at thy cross I bow, Save me, Je-sus, save me now.
                          Copyright, 1869, by W. G. Fischer.

131   *Trusting the promises.*

2 Long my heart has sighed for thee
  Long has evil reigned within;
Jesus sweetly speaks to me,
  I will cleanse you from all sin.
      I am trusting, Lord, etc.

3 In thy promises I trust;
  Now I feel the blood applied;
I am prostrate in the dust;
  I with Christ am crucified.
      I am trusting, Lord, etc.
              William McDonald.

SONGS OF SALVATION.

FREELY FOR ME. T. C. O'KANE, by per.

1. Je-sus my Sav-iour, thou Lamb of God, On thee my sins were laid, a mighty load, Now with a joy-ful heart by faith I see Thy precious blood was shed free-ly for me.

REFRAIN.
Free-ly for me, free-ly for me, Thy precious blood was shed freely for me;
Free-ly for me, free-ly for me, Thy precious blood was shed freely for me.

Copyright, 1883, by T C. O Kane

132 *Freely for me.*

2 Jesus my Saviour, thy blood alone
Can for the sinner's guilt fully atone;
This my redemption price, gladly I see
Thy precious blood was shed freely for me.
REF.—Freely for me, freely for me,
  Thy precious blood was shed freely for me:
    Freely for me, freely for me,
  Thy precious blood was shed freely for me.

3 Jesus my Saviour, thy grace to me
Fills all my soul with peace, boundless and free,
This is my steadfast hope, clearly I see
Thy precious blood was shed freely for me.

REF.—Freely for me, freely for me,
  Thy precious blood was shed freely for me,
    Freely for me, freely for me,
  Thy precious blood was shed freely for me.

4 Jesus my Saviour, bought with thy blood,
Living, my life is thine, hidden with God;
Dying, to thee I'll fly, ever to see
Thy precious blood was shed freely for me.
REF.—Freely for me, freely for me,
  Thy precious blood was shed freely for me,
    Freely for me, freely for me,
  Thy precious blood was shed freely for me.
                              J. P. H.

133 *The firm foundation.*

1 How firm a foundation, ye saints of the Lord,
Is laid for your faith in his excellent word!
What more can he say, than to you he hath said,
To you, who for refuge to Jesus have fled?

2 "Fear not, I am with thee, O be not dismayed,
For I am thy God, I will still give thee aid;
I'll strengthen thee, help thee, and cause thee to stand,
Upheld by my gracious, omnipotent hand.

3 "When through the deep waters I call thee to go,
The rivers of sorrow shall not overflow;
For I will be with thee thy trials to bless,
And sanctify to thee thy deepest distress.

4 "When through fiery trials thy pathway shall lie,
My grace, all-sufficient, shall be thy supply,
The flame shall not hurt thee; I only design
Thy dross to consume, and thy gold to refine.

5 "E'en down to old age all my people shall prove
My sovereign, eternal, unchangeable love;
And when hoary hairs shall their temples adorn,
Like lambs they shall still in my bosom be borne.

6 "The soul that on Jesus hath leaned for repose,
I will not, I will not desert to his foes;
That soul, though all hell should endeavor to shake,
I'll never, no never, no never forsake!"
George Keith.

SONGS OF THE CHRISTIAN LIFE.

LOVE DIVINE. 8, 7. D. JOHN ZUNDEL.

1. Love divine, all love excelling, Joy of heaven, to earth come down!
Fix in us thy humble dwelling; All thy faithful mercies crown.
Jesus, thou art all compassion, Pure unbounded love thou art;
Visit us with thy salvation; Enter every trembling heart.

134 *The new creation.*

2 Breathe, O breathe thy loving Spirit
Into every troubled breast!
Let us all in thee inherit,
Let us find that second rest.
Take away our bent to sinning;
Alpha and Omega be;
End of faith, as its beginning,
Set our hearts at liberty.

3 Come, almighty to deliver,
Let us all thy life receive;
Suddenly return, and never,
Never more thy temples leave:

Thee we would be always blessing,
Serve thee as thy hosts above,
Pray, and praise thee without ceasing,
Glory in thy perfect love.

4 Finish then thy new creation;
Pure and spotless let us be;
Let us see thy great salvation,
Perfectly restored in thee:
Changed from glory into glory,
Till in heaven we take our place,
Till we cast our crowns before thee,
Lost in wonder, love, and praise.

Charles Wesley.

SONGS OF THE CHRISTIAN LIFE.

BALERMA. C. M. — R. Simpson.

1. O for a heart to praise my God, A heart from sin set free!
A heart that al-ways feels thy blood, So free-ly spilt for me!

135 *A perfect heart.*

2 A heart resigned, submissive, meek,
My great Redeemer's throne;
Where only Christ is heard to speak,
Where Jesus reigns alone.

3 O for a lowly, contrite heart,
Believing, true, and clean,
Which neither life nor death can part
From him that dwells within!

4 A heart in every thought renewed,
And full of love divine;
Perfect, and right, and pure, and good,
A copy, Lord, of thine.

5 Thy nature, gracious Lord, impart;
Come quickly from above;
Write thy new name upon my heart,
Thy new, best name of Love.
  — Charles Wesley.

AVON. C. M. — Hugh Wilson.

1. For-ev-er here my rest shall be, Close to thy bleed-ing side;
This all my hope, and all my plea, "For me the Sav-iour died."

136 *Entire purification.*

2 My dying Saviour, and my God,
Fountain for guilt and sin,
Sprinkle me ever with thy blood,
And cleanse and keep me clean.

3 Wash me, and make me thus thine own;
Wash me, and mine thou art;

Wash me, but not my feet alone,
My hands, my head, my heart.

4 The atonement of thy blood apply,
Till faith to sight improve;
Till hope in full fruition die,
And all my soul be love.
  — Charles Wesley.

SONGS OF THE CHRISTIAN LIFE.

LOOK UP. Rev. SAMUEL ALMAN.

1. Is this thy time of trou-ble, Look up, look up on high; To him who would re-lieve thee, Who now would draw thee nigh. He sees thy soul is cling-ing, To something here be-low, And wants to make thy rov-ing heart, His great-er love to know. Look up, look up to Je-sus, A present help is he; He has been such to oth-ers, He will be such to thee.

137 *Looking unto Jesus.*

2 Is this thy time of doubting?
  Do fearful thoughts arise?
Lift up thy heart to Jesus,
  He will not thee despise.
Think of his great compassion,
  Think of Gethsemane;
Think why he shed his precious blood,
  And soon thy doubts must flee.
    CHO.—Look up, look up, &c.

3 In every time of trouble,
  Of doubting, or of pain,
Lift up thy heart to Jesus,
  Pray yet and yet again.
He shares in all thy sorrows,
  He feels for all thy griefs,
And though he sends affliction now,
  He soon will send relief.
    CHO.—Look up, look up, &c.
        Anon.

SONGS OF THE CHRISTIAN LIFE.

ST. HILDA. 7, 6.   J. H. KNECHT, and REV. EDWARD HUSBAND.

1. I lay my sins on Jesus, The spotless Lamb of God; He bears them all, and frees us From the accursed load; I bring my guilt to Jesus, To wash my crimson stains White in his blood most precious, Till not a stain remains.

138 *I lay my sins on Jesus.*

2 I lay my wants on Jesus,
   All fullness dwells in him;
He healeth my diseases,
   He doth my soul redeem:
I lay my griefs on Jesus,
   My burdens and my cares;
He from them all releases,
   He all my sorrows shares.

3 I long to be like Jesus,
   Meek, loving, lowly, mild;
I long to be like Jesus,
   The Father's holy child:
I long to be with Jesus
   Amid the heavenly throng,
To sing with saints his praises,
   And learn the angels' song.
                  Horatius Bon

FEAR NOT!   GEO. C. STEBBINS.

1. Fear not! God is thy shield, And be thy great reward; His might has won the field — Thy strength is in the Lord.

Copyright, 1883, by Geo. C. Stebbins.

SONGS OF THE CHRISTIAN LIFE.

FEAR NOT.—*Concluded.*

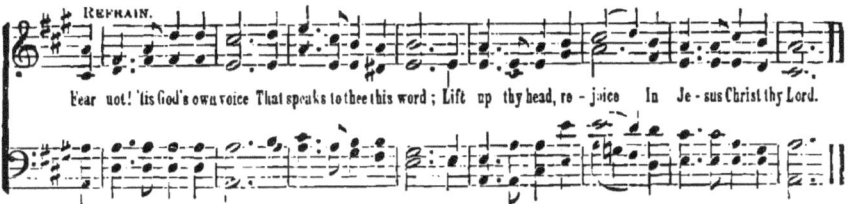

Fear not! 'tis God's own voice That speaks to thee this word; Lift up thy head, re-joice In Je-sus Christ thy Lord.

139 *Fear not little flock.*

2 Fear not! for God has heard
    The cry of thy distress;
The water of his Word
    Thy fainting soul shall bless. REF.

3 Fear not! be not dismayed,
    He, evermore, will be
With thee, to give his aid,
    And he will strengthen thee. REF.

4 Fear not! ye little flock,
    Your Saviour soon will come,
The Glory to unlock,
    And bring you to his home. REF.
                                Rev. Edward G. Taylor.

HIDE THOU ME.
                                                    Rev. Robert Lowry.

1. In thy cleft, O Rock of A-ges, Hide thou me; When the fit-ful tem-pest ra-ges, Hide thou me; Where no mor-tal arm can sev-er From my heart thy love for-ev-er, Hide me, O thou Rock of A-ges, Safe in thee.

Copyright, 1880, by Biglow & Main.

140 *Thou art my hiding place.*

2 From the snare of sinful pleasure
    Hide thou me;
Thou, my soul's eternal treasure,
    Hide thou me;
When the world its power is wielding,
And my heart is almost yielding,
  Hide me, O thou Rock of Ages,
    Safe in thee.

3 In the lonely night of sorrow,
    Hide thou me;
Till in glory dawns the morrow,
    Hide thou me;
In the sight of Jordan's billow,
Let thy bosom be my pillow;
  Hide me, O thou Rock of Ages,
    Safe in thee.
                    Fanny J. Crosby.

SONGS OF THE CHRISTIAN LIFE.

LEAD THOU ME.
JAMES A. SMITH.

1. Sav-iour, let me still a-bide In the shad-ow of thy wings, Let me all my sor-row hide, In the joy thy mer-cy brings; Draw me, keep me day by day, Near-er, near-er, Lord, to thee; All a-long my pil-grim way, O my Sav-iour, lead thou me.

141 *Seeking guidance.*

2 To the cross my soul was brought,
　To the cross, with all its grief;
There a healing balm I sought,
　There I found a sweet relief;
Yet for deeper love I pray,
　Love that clings alone to thee,
All along my pilgrim way,
　O my Saviour, lead thou me.

3 Let me trust thee more and more,
　Let my will and thine be one,
Till my warfare here is o'er,
　Till the vict'ry I have won;
In the light whose blessed ray
　Shining down, by faith I see,
All along my pilgrim way,
　O my Saviour, lead thou me.
　　　　　　Fanny J. Crosby.

TELL IT TO JESUS.
J. B O. CLEMM.

1. Bro-ken in spir-it And la-den with care, Sweet is thy ref-uge, Find it in prayer,

SONGS OF THE CHRISTIAN LIFE.

TELL IT TO JESUS. *Concluded.*

142 *Go and tell Jesus.*

2 Art thou afflicted,
And sighing to know
Why the dear Father
Should chasten thee so? REF.

3 Art thou recalling
The years that have fled,
Weeping in sorrow,
Mourning the dead? REF.

4 Bear thy affliction,
Whatever it be,
Jesus thy Saviour
Bore it for thee. REF.
Arr. Wm. Johnson.

JESUS, MY PORTION. W. J. KIRKPATRICK.

1. I've found a joy in sor-row, A se-cret balm for pain, A beau-ti-ful to-mor-row Of sunshine af-ter rain. 'Tis Je-sus, my portion for-ev-er, 'Tis Je-sus, the First and the Last; A help ver-y present in trou-ble, A shel-ter from ev'-ry blast.

Copyright, 1875, by W. J. Kirkpatrick.

143 *Jesus all in all.*

2 I've found a branch for healing,
Near every bitter spring,
A whispered promise stealing
O'er ev'ry broken string. CHO.

3 I've found a glad hosanna
For ev'ry woe and wail,
A handful of sweet manna,
When grapes of Eschol fail. CHO.

4 An Elim with its coolness,
Its fountains and its shade:
A blessing in its fulness,
When buds of promise fade. CHO.

5 O'er tears of soft contrition
I've seen a rainbow light;
A glory and fruition,
So near!—yet out of sight. CHO.
Mrs. Jane Fox Crewdson.

SONGS OF THE CHRISTIAN LIFE.

THE CHRISTIAN'S HIDING PLACE.
Miss. A. E. GULICK.

Copyright, 1885, by Phillips & Hunt.

144 *Hide me, oh my Father.*

2 Thy pavilion, its foundations
 Are unknown to all save thee,
Who among the nations knoweth
 What the home of God may be?
Only he who spread the heavens,
 God alone who treads the deep,
In mysterious grandeur hiding
 Can his saints in safety keep.

3 We will haste to share thy glory,
 Cling the closer to thy side,
Wrap thy majesty about us,
 In its foldings let us hide!
Then if clouds, or thicker darkness,
 Gather strength from hour to hour,
Still our faith need never falter,
 God will shield us by his power.
 Mrs. J. B. Coats.

SONGS OF THE CHRISTIAN LIFE.

SAVIOUR, LIKE A SHEPHERD. 8, 7, 4.
WILLIAM B. BRADBURY.

1. Saviour, like a shepherd lead us, Much we need thy tenderest care;
In thy pleasant pastures feed us, For our use thy folds prepare: Blessed Jesus, Blessed Jesus,
Thou hast bought us, thine we are, Blessed Jesus, Blessed Jesus, Thou hast bought us, thine we are.

Copyright, 1859, in "Oriola," by Wm. B. Bradbury.

145 *For the Shepherd's care.*

2 We are thine, do thou befriend us,
Be the guardian of our way;
Keep thy flock, from sin defend us,
Seek us when we go astray:
Blessed Jesus,
Hear, O hear us, when we pray.

3 Thou hast promised to receive us,
Poor and sinful though we be;
Thou hast mercy to relieve us,

Grace to cleanse, and power to free:
Blessed Jesus,
We will early turn to thee.

4 Early let us seek thy favor,
Early let us do thy will;
Blessed Lord and only Saviour,
With thy love our bosoms fill:
Blessed Jesus,
Thou hast loved us, love us still.
Dorothy A. Thrupp.

FAITHFUL SHEPHERD. 6, 5.
L. J. HUTTON.

1. Faith-ful Shep-herd, feed me In the pas tures green; Faith-ful Shepherd lead me Where thy steps are seen.
2. Hold me fast, and guide me In the nar-row way; So with thee beside me, I shall nev-er stray.

146 *Within the fold.*

3 Hallow every pleasure,
Every gift and pain;
Be thyself my treasure,
Though none else I gain.

4 Day by day prepare me
As thou seest best,
Then let angels bear me
To thy promised rest.
Rev. T. B. Pollock, abr.

SONGS OF THE CHRISTIAN LIFE.

BETHANY. 6, 4, 6.   Lowell Mason.

*Nearer, my God, to thee! Nearer to thee,
E'en though it be a cross (Omit.......) That raiseth me; Still all my song shall be, Nearer, my God, to thee,
D.C. Nearer, my God, to thee, (Omit.......) Near-er to thee!*

Copyright, used by permission of Oliver Ditson & Co.

147 *Nearer, my God, to thee.*

2 Though like a wanderer,
  The sun gone down,
Darkness be over me,
  My rest a stone,
Yet in my dreams I'd be
Nearer, my God, to thee,
  Nearer to thee!

3 There let the way appear,
  Steps unto heaven;
All that thou sendest me,
  In mercy given;
Angels to beckon me
Nearer, my God, to thee,
  Nearer to thee!

4 Then, with my waking thoughts
  Bright with thy praise,
Out of my stony griefs
  Bethel I'll raise;
So by my woes to be
Nearer, my God, to thee,
  Nearer to thee!

5 Or if, on joyful wing
  Cleaving the sky,
Sun, moon, and stars forgot,
  Upward I fly,
Still all my song shall be,
Nearer, my God, to thee,
  Nearer to thee!

                  Mrs. Sarah F. Adams.

MORE LOVE TO THEE. 6, 4, 6.   William Howard Doane.

*1. More love to thee, O Christ, More love to thee! Hear thou the prayer I make, On bended knee;
This is my earnest plea, More love, O Christ, to thee, More love to thee! More love to thee!*

Copyright 1870, in Songs of Devotion, by W. H. Doane.

148 *More love to Thee.*

2 Once earthly joy I craved,
  Sought peace and rest;
Now thee alone I seek,
  Give what is best;
This all my prayer shall be,
More love, O Christ, to thee,
  More love to thee!

3 Then shall my latest breath
  Whisper thy praise;
This be the parting cry
  My heart shall raise,
This still its prayer shall be,
More love, O Christ, to thee,
  More love to thee!

                  Mrs. Elizabeth P. Prentiss.

SONGS OF THE CHRISTIAN LIFE.

THE YOUNG CHRISTIAN.

Mrs. Joseph F. Knapp.

1. "Just as I am," thine own to be, Friend of the young, who lovest me; To consecrate myself to thee, O Jesus Christ, I come. O Jesus Christ, I come, O Jesus Christ, I come.

REFRAIN.
To consecrate myself to thee, O Jesus Christ, I come.

Copyright, 1886, by Joseph F. Knapp.

149 *Youthful consecration.*

2 In the glad morning of my day,
My life to give, my vows to pay,
With no reserve, and no delay,
   With all my heart I come,
   [:With all my heart I come.:] Ref.

3 I would live ever in the light,
I would work ever for the right,
I would serve thee with all my might,
   Therefore to Thee I come,
   [:Therefore to Thee I come.:] Ref.

4 "Just as I am," young, strong, and free,
To be the best that I can be
For truth, and righteousness, and thee,
   Lord of my life, I come,
   [:Lord of my life, I come.:] Ref.

5 With many dreams of fame and gold,
Success and joy to make me bold;
But dearer still my faith to hold,
   For my whole life I come,
   [:For my whole life I come.:] Ref.

6 And for thy sake to win renown,
And then to take my victor's crown,
And at thy feet to cast it down,
   O Master, Lord, I come,
   [:O Master, Lord, I come.:] Ref.

Marianne Farningham.

SONGS OF THE CHRISTIAN LIFE.

HAPPY DAY. L. M.

1. { O hap-py day, that fixed my choice On thee, my Saviour and my God!
     Well may this glowing heart rejoice, And tell its raptures all abroad. } D.S.—Happy day, happy day,

Happy day, happy day,

When Jesus washed my sins away; He taught me how to watch and pray, And live rejoicing every day;
When Jesus washed my sins away.

150 *O happy day.*

2 O happy bond, that seals my vows
  To him who merits all my love!
  Let cheerful anthems fill his house,
  While to that sacred shrine I move.

3 'Tis done, the great transaction's done;
  I am my Lord's, and he is mine;
  He drew me, and I followed on,
  Charmed to confess the voice divine.

4 Now rest, my long-divided heart;
  Fixed on this blissful center, rest;
  Nor ever from thy Lord depart,
  With him of every good possessed.
                        Philip Doddridge.

ROCKINGHAM. L. M.   LOWELL MASON.

1. I thirst, thou wounded Lamb of God, To wash me in thy cleansing blood;
   To dwell within thy wounds; then pain Is sweet, and life or death is gain.

151 *Thirsting for perfect love.*

2 Take my poor heart, and let it be
  Forever closed to all but thee:
  Seal thou my breast, and let me wear
  That pledge of love forever there.

3 How blest are they who still abide
  Close sheltered in thy bleeding side!
  Who thence their life and strength derive,
  And by thee move, and in thee live.

4 How can it be, thou heavenly King,
  That thou shouldst us to glory bring?
  Make slaves the partners of thy throne,
  Decked with a never-fading crown?

5 Hence our hearts melt, our eyes o'erflow,
  Our words are lost, nor will we know,
  Nor will we think of aught beside,
  "My Lord, my Love is crucified."
       Nicolaus L. Zinzendorf. Tr. by J. Wesley.

SONGS OF THE CHRISTIAN LIFE.

ALL FOR THEE.

WILLIAM G. FISCHER.

1. Take my life, and let it be Con-se-crat-ed, Lord, to Thee; Take my hands, and let them move At the im-pulse of thy love.

CHORUS. Wash me in the Saviour's precious blood, Cleanse me in its pu-ri-fy-ing flood; Lord, I give to thee my life and all to be Thine henceforth, e-ter-nal-ly.

Copyright by Wm. G. Fischer.

152 *Complete surrender.*

2 Take my feet, and let them be
  Swift and beautiful for thee;
Take my voice, and let me sing
  Always, only, for my King.
    Wash me, etc.

3 Take my silver and my gold,
  Not a mite would I withhold;
Take my moments and my days,
  Let them flow in ceaseless praise.
    Wash me, etc.

4 Take my will and make it thine,
  It shall be no longer mine;
Take my heart, it is thine own,
  It shall be thy royal throne.
    Wash me, etc.

5 Take my love; my Lord, I pour
  At thy feet its treasure-store;
Take myself, and I will be
  Ever, only, all for thee.
    Wash me, etc.

Frances Ridley Havergal.

SONGS OF THE CHRISTIAN LIFE.

PRECIOUS PROMISE.
P. P. Bliss.

1. Precious promise God hath given To the weary pass-er by, On the way from earth to hea-ven, "I will guide thee with Mine eye."

REFRAIN.
I will guide thee, I will guide thee, I will guide thee with Mine eye; On the way from earth to hea-ven, I will guide thee with Mine eye.

By per. of The John Church Co., owners of the copyright.

153 *Exceeding great promises.*

2 When temptations almost win thee,
And thy trusted watchers fly,
Let this promise ring within thee,
"I will guide thee with Mine eye."—Ref.

3 When thy secret hopes have perished,
In the grave of years gone by,
Let this promise still be cherished,
"I will guide thee with Mine eye."—Ref.

4 When the shades of life are falling,
And the hour has come to die,
Hear thy trusty Pilot calling,
"I will guide thee with Mine eye."—Ref
  Nathaniel Niles.

ALONE WITH JESUS.
Hubert P. Main.

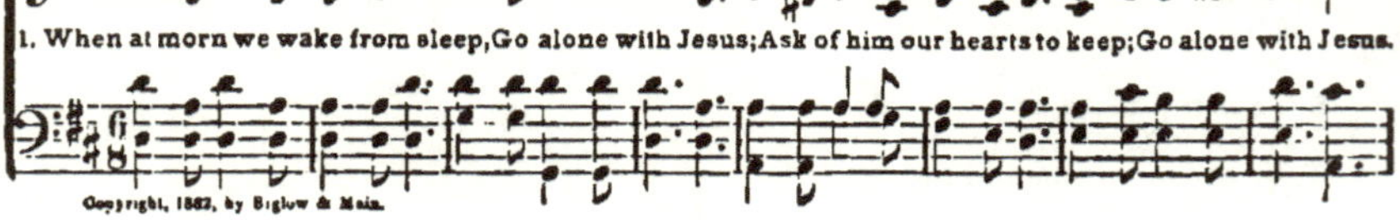

1. When at morn we wake from sleep, Go alone with Jesus; Ask of him our hearts to keep; Go alone with Jesus.

Copyright, 1882, by Biglow & Main.

SONGS OF THE CHRISTIAN LIFE.

ALONE WITH JESUS.—*Concluded.*

Go to him without delay, Only he can guide our way; Don't forget to watch and pray, Go alone with Jesus.

154 *"They went and told Jesus."*

2 When we feel our souls are weak,
　Go alone with Jesus;
He will give the strength we seek,
　Go alone with Jesus.—REF.

3 In the little griefs we bear,
　Go alone with Jesus;
He will lighten every care,
　Go alone with Jesus.—REF.

4 Go to him whate'er we need,
　Go alone with Jesus;
Trust in him, his promise plead,
　Go alone with Jesus.—REF.

Grace J. Frances.

IT IS WELL WITH MY SOUL.　　　P. P. BLISS.

1. When peace, like a riv-er, at-tend-eth my way, When sorrows, like sea-bil-lows, roll; What-
2. Though Sa-tan should buf-fet, tho' tri-als should come, Let this blest as-sur-ance control, That

ev-er my lot, thou hast taught me to say, It is well, it is well with my soul.
Christ hath re-gard-ed my help-less es-tate, And hath shed his own blood for my soul.

CHORUS.
It is well............with my soul..........

It is well with my soul, It is well, it is well with my soul.

By per. of The John Church Co., owners of the Copyright.

155 *"He hath delivered my soul in peace."*

3 My sin—oh, the bliss of this glorious thought—
　My sin—not in part but the whole,
Is nailed to his cross and I bear it no more,
　Praise the Lord, praise the Lord, oh, my soul!—CHO.

4 And Lord, haste the day when the faith shall be sight,
　The clouds be rolled back as a scroll,
The trump shall resound, and the Lord shall descend,
　"Even so"—it is well with my soul.—CHO.

H. G. Spafford.

SONGS OF THE CHRISTIAN LIFE.

ZION. 8, 7, 4. THOMAS HASTINGS.

1 { Guide me, O thou great Jehovah, Pilgrim through this barren land;
    I am weak, but thou art mighty; Hold me with thy powerful hand: } Bread of heaven, Feed me till I want no more. Bread of heaven, Feed me till I want no more.

156 *The pilgrim's Guide.*

2 Open now the crystal fountain,
 Whence the healing waters flow;
Let the fiery, cloudy pillar,
 Lead me all my journey through:
  Strong Deliverer,
Be thou still my strength and shield.

3 When I tread the verge of Jordan,
 Bid my anxious fears subside;
Bear me through the swelling current;
 Land me safe on Canaan's side:
  Songs of praises
 I will ever give to thee.
   William Williams.

FLEMMING. 8, 6. F. F. FLEMMING

1. O holy Saviour! friend unseen, Since on thine arm thou bidd'st me lean, Help me, throughout life's changing scene, By faith to cling to thee.

157 *Clinging to Jesus.*

2 What though the world deceitful prove,
And earthly friends and hopes remove;
With patient, uncomplaining love,
 Still would I cling to thee.

3 Though oft I seem to tread alone
Life's dreary waste, with thorns o'ergrown,

Thy voice of love, in gentlest tone,
 Still whispers, "Cling to me!"

4 Though faith and hope are often tried,
I ask not, need not, aught beside;
So safe, so calm, so satisfied,
 The soul that clings to Thee.
  Charlotte Elliott.

SONGS OF THE CHRISTIAN LIFE.

A WONDERFUL JOY.   JOHN B. SUMNER.

1. A wonderful joy and salvation Has come to my soul;
The Lord in his mercy has spoken And I am made whole,

REFRAIN.
My soul with his glory is flooded 'Tis heav'nly bliss;
No joy like the joy of his presence No rapture like this.

Copyright, 1885, by Phillips & Hunt.

158   *Joy in the Lord.*

2 'Twas down at the fountain of cleansing,
    That I was made pure;
The blood and the spirit attesting
    My covenant sure.

3 From death and from hell he redeemed me,
    And made me his own.
An heir to his kingdom and glory,
    Co-heir to his throne.

4 For infinite love without measure,
    Thanksgiving I bring,
All glory to Jesus forever
    My Saviour and King.
                         Annie Wittenmyer.

SONGS OF THE CHRISTIAN LIFE.

HENLEY. 11, 10.   Lowell Mason.

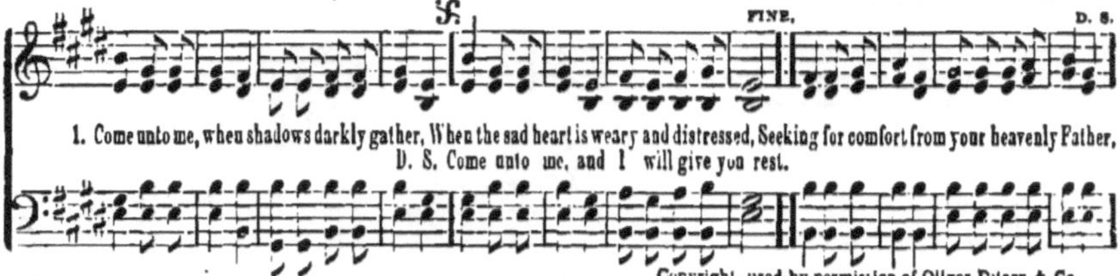

1. Come unto me, when shadows darkly gather, When the sad heart is weary and distressed, Seeking for comfort from your heavenly Father,
D. S. Come unto me, and I will give you rest.

Copyright, used by permission of Oliver Ditson & Co.

159   *Rest for the weary.*

2 Large are the mansions in thy Father's
    dwelling,
Glad are the homes that sorrows never dim;
Sweet are the harps in holy music swelling,
Soft are the tones which raise the heav-
    enly hymn.

3 There, like an Eden blossoming in glad-
    ness,
Bloom the fair flowers the earth too rude-
    ly pressed;
Come unto me, all ye who droop in sadness,
Come unto me, and I will give you rest.
              Mrs. Catherine H. Esling.

PRECIOUS NAME. 8, 7.   William Howard Doane.

1. Take the name of Je-sus with you, Child of sorrow and of woe; It will joy and comfort give you; Take it, then, where'er you go. Precious name, O how sweet! Hope of earth and joy of heaven, Precious name, O how sweet! Hope of earth and joy of heaven.

Precious name, O how sweet, how sweet!

Copyright, 1871, by Biglow & Main

160   *The precious name.*

2 Take the name of Jesus ever,
    As a shield from every snare;
If temptations round you gather,
    Breathe that holy name in prayer.

3 O the precious name of Jesus!
    How it thrills our souls with joy,
When his loving arms receive us,
    And his songs our tongues employ!

4 At the name of Jesus bowing,
    Falling prostrate at his feet,
King of kings in heaven we'll crown him,
    When our journey is complete.
              Mrs. Lydia Baxter.

SONGS OF THE CHRISTIAN LIFE.

IN THE SECRET OF HIS PRESENCE.

Mrs. JOSEPH F. KNAPP.

Psalm 31. 20.

1. In the secret of his presence I am kept from strife of tongues, His pavil-ion is around me, And with-
2. In the secret of his presence All the darkness disappears, For a sun that knows no set-ting Throws a
3. In the secret of his presence Never more can foe alarm, In the shadow of the high-est I can

in are ceaseless songs. Stormy winds, his word fulfilling Beat without, but cannot harm, For the Master's voice is
rainbow on my tears, So the day grows ever lighter, Broad'ning to the perfect noon, So the day grows ev-er
meet them with a psalm, For the strong pavilion hides me, Turns their fiery darts aside, And I know whate'er be-

still-ing, Storm and tempest to a calm, For the Master's voice is stilling Storm and tempest to a calm.
bright-er, Heav'n is coming near and soon, So the day grows ever brighter, Heav'n is coming near and soon.
tide me I shall live because he died, And I know whate'er betide me I shall live because he died.

REFRAIN.

In the secret of his presence Je - sus keeps, I know not how, In the shadow of the

high - est I am resting, hid - ing now.

Copyright, 1885, by Joseph F. Knapp.

161 *Safely Sheltered.*
4 In the secret of his presence
  Is a sweet unbroken rest,
  Pleasures rise to glorious fullness
  Making earth like Eden, blest.
So my peace grows deep and deeper,
  Widening as it nears the sea,
‖:For my Saviour is my keeper,
  Keeping mine, and keeping me.:‖
REF.
                   Henry Burton.

SONGS OF THE CHRISTIAN LIFE.

CHRIST IS NEAR THEE.
HUBERT P. MAIN.

Copyright, 1885, by Bigelow & Main.

162 *Christ all, and in all.*

1 Art thou saddened? Christ will cheer thee,
  He will lift thy heavy load;
Art thou lonely? He is near thee,
  All along the earthly road. REF.

2 Art thou hungry? he will feed thee,
  Hour by hour, and day by day;
Art thou thirsty? he will lead thee
  Where the living waters stray. REF.

3 Art thou weary? he will fold thee,
  In the quiet of his peace;
Art thou sinful? he has told thee,
  He will grant a full release. REF.

4 Art thou fearful? he will hide thee,
  In the cover of his love;
Art thou fainting? he will guide thee
  To the Fatherland above. REF.

Jessie H. Brown.

SONGS OF THE CHRISTIAN LIFE.

JEWETT. 6.   Carl Maria von Weber.

1. My Jesus, as thou wilt: O may thy will be mine; Into thy hand of love I would my all resign. Through sorrow or through joy, Conduct me as thine own, And help me still to say, "My Lord, thy will be done."

163   *Jesus, as thou wilt.*

2 My Jesus, as thou wilt:
  Though seen through many a tear,
Let not my star of hope
  Grow dim or disappear.
Since thou on earth hast wept
  And sorrowed oft alone,
If I must weep with thee,
  My Lord, thy will be done.

3 My Jesus, as thou wilt:
  All shall be well for me;
Each changing future scene
  I gladly trust with thee.
Straight to my home above,
  I travel calmly on,
And sing in life or death,
  "My Lord, thy will be done."
    Benjamin Schmolke. Tr. by Miss J. Borthwick.

SEYMOUR. 7.   Carl Maria von Weber.

1. Come, my soul, thy suit prepare, Jesus loves to answer prayer; He himself invites thee near, Bids thee ask him, waits to hear.

164   *Encouragements to pray.*

2 Lord, I come to thee for rest;
Take possession of my breast;
There thy blood-bought right maintain,
And without a rival reign.

3 While I am a pilgrim here,
Let thy love my spirit cheer;
As my guide, my guard, my friend,
Lead me to my journey's end.

4 Show me what I have to do;
Every hour my strength renew;
Let me live a life of faith,
Let me die thy people's death.
    John Newton.

SONGS OF THE CHRISTIAN LIFE.

WHAT A FRIEND WE HAVE IN JESUS. 8, 7. D.
C. C. Converse

1. What a friend we have in Jesus, All our sins and griefs to bear! What a priv-i-lege to carry Ev-ery thing to God in prayer! O what peace we often for-feit, O what needless pain we bear, All be-cause we do not car-ry Ev-ery thing to God in prayer!

165 *What a Friend we have in Jesus.*

2 Have we trials and temptations?
  Is there trouble anywhere?
We should never be discouraged,
  Take it to the Lord in prayer.
Can we find a friend so faithful
  Who will all our sorrows share?
Jesus knows our every weakness,
  Take it to the Lord in prayer.

3 Are we weak and heavy laden,
  Cumbered with a load of care?—
Precious Saviour, still our refuge,—
  Take it to the Lord in prayer.
Do thy friends despise, forsake thee?
  Take it to the Lord in prayer;
In his arms he'll take and shield thee,
  Thou wilt find a solace there.
                              Unknown.

NETTLETON. 8, 7. D.
John Wyeth, 1823.

1. Come, thou Fount of ev-ery bless-ing, Tune my heart to sing thy grace;
   Streams of mer-cy, nev-er ceas-ing, Call for songs of loud-est praise.
Teach me some me-lo-dious son-net, Sung by flam-ing tongues a-bove;

SONGS OF THE CHRISTIAN LIFE.

NETTLETON.—*Continued.*

Praise the mount—I'm fixed up-on it— Mount of thy re-deem-ing love!

166 *Hitherto hath the Lord helped us.*

2 Here I'll raise mine Ebenezer;
Hither by thy help I'm come;
And I hope, by thy good pleasure,
Safely to arrive at home.
Jesus sought me when a stranger,
Wandering from the fold of God;
He, to rescue me from danger,
Interposed his precious blood.

3 O to grace how great a debtor
Daily I'm constrained to be!
Let thy goodness, like a fetter,
Bind my wandering heart to thee:
Prone to wander, Lord, I feel it,
Prone to leave the God I love;
Here's my heart, O take and seal it;
Seal it for thy courts above.
Robert Robinson.

ARIEL. C. P. M.   ARR. BY LOWELL MASON.

1. O could I speak the match-less worth, O could I sound the glo-ries forth,
Which in my Saviour shine, I'd soar and touch the heavenly strings, And vie with Gabriel
while he sings In notes al-most di-vine, In notes al-most di-vine.

167 *Make His praise glorious.*

2 I'd sing the precious blood he spilt,
My ransom from the dreadful guilt
Of sin, and wrath divine;
I'd sing his glorious righteousness,
In which all-perfect, heavenly dress
My soul shall ever shine.

3 Well, the delightful day will come
When my dear Lord will bring me home
And I shall see his face;
Then with my Saviour, Brother, Friend,
A blest eternity I'll spend,
Triumphant in his grace.
Samuel Medley.

SONGS OF THE CHRISTIAN LIFE.

INVITATION. C. M. D. — Louis Spohr.

1. I heard the voice of Je-sus say, "Come un-to me and rest;
Lay down, thou wea-ry one, lay down Thy head up-on my breast!"
I came to Je-sus as I was, Wea-ry, and worn, and sad;
I found in him a rest-ing-place, And he hath made me glad.

168 *The voice of Jesus.*

2 I heard the voice of Jesus say,
   "Behold, I freely give
The living water; thirsty one,
   Stoop down, and drink, and live!"
I came to Jesus, and I drank
   Of that life-giving stream;
My thirst was quenched, my soul revived,
   And now I live in him.

3 I heard the voice of Jesus say,
   "I am this dark world's Light;
Look unto me, thy morn shall rise
   And all thy day be bright!"
I looked to Jesus, and I found
   In him my Star, my Sun;
And in that light of life I'll walk,
   Till all my journey's done.
                              Horatius Bonar.

LENOX. H. M. — Lewis Edson.

1. Arise, my soul, arise; Shake off thy guilty fears; The bleeding Sacri-fice In my behalf appears:
Before the throne my Surety stands, Before the throne my Surety stands, My name is written on his hands.

SONGS OF THE CHRISTIAN LIFE.

LENOX.—*Continued.*

169 *Abba, father.*—Rom. 8: 15.

2 He ever lives above,
  For me to intercede;
His all-redeeming love,
  His precious blood, to plead;
His blood atoned for all our race,
And sprinkles now the throne of grace.

3 Five bleeding wounds he bears,
  Received on Calvary;
They pour effectual prayers,
  They strongly plead for me:
" Forgive him, O forgive," they cry,
" Nor let that ransomed sinner die."

4 The Father hears him pray,
  His dear anointed One:
He cannot turn away
  The presence of his Son:
His Spirit answers to the blood,
And tells me I am born of God.

5 My God is reconciled;
  His pardoning voice I hear:
He owns me for his child;
  I can no longer fear:
With confidence I now draw nigh,
And, " Father, Abba, Father," cry.
Charles Wesley.

LEBANON. S. M. D. JOHN ZUNDEL.

1. I was a wandering sheep, I did not love the fold; I did not love my Shepherd's voice, I would not be con-troll'd; I was a way-ward child, I did not love my home, I did not love my Father's voice,—I loved a-far to roam.

170 *No more a wandering sheep.*

2 The Shepherd sought his sheep,
  The Father sought his child;
He followed me o'er vale and hill,
  O'er deserts waste and wild:
He found me nigh to death,
  Famished, and faint, and lone;
He bound me with the bands of love,
  He saved the wandering one.

3 No more a wandering sheep,
  I love to be controlled,
I love my tender Shepherd's voice,
  I love the peaceful fold:
No more a wayward child,
  I seek no more to roam;
I love my heavenly Father's voice,
  I love, I love his home.
Horatius Bonar.

SONGS OF THE CHRISTIAN LIFE.

BROWNE. 6, 8, 4.   Miss Mari Anne Browne.

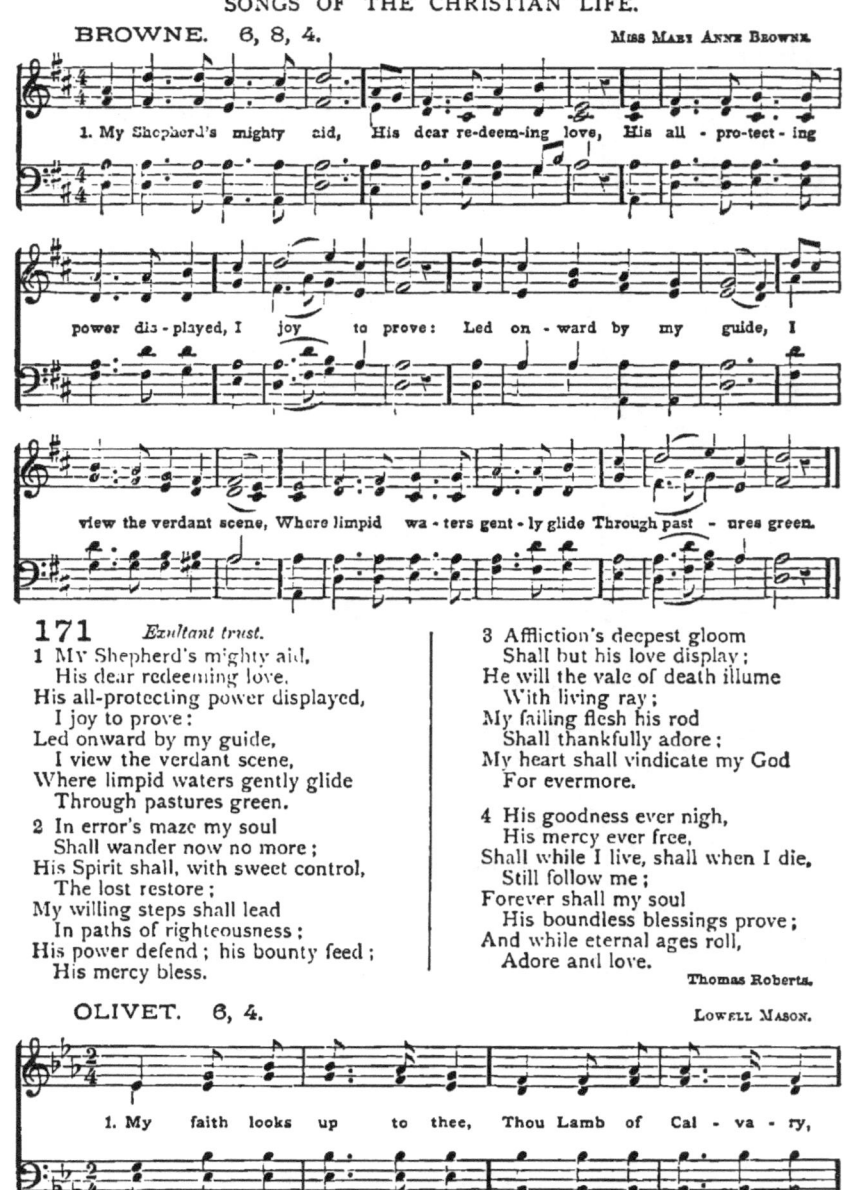

171   *Exultant trust.*

1 My Shepherd's mighty aid,
   His dear redeeming love,
His all-protecting power displayed,
   I joy to prove:
Led onward by my guide,
   I view the verdant scene,
Where limpid waters gently glide
   Through pastures green.

2 In error's maze my soul
   Shall wander now no more;
His Spirit shall, with sweet control,
   The lost restore;
My willing steps shall lead
   In paths of righteousness;
His power defend; his bounty feed;
   His mercy bless.

3 Affliction's deepest gloom
   Shall but his love display;
He will the vale of death illume
   With living ray;
My failing flesh his rod
   Shall thankfully adore;
My heart shall vindicate my God
   For evermore.

4 His goodness ever nigh,
   His mercy ever free,
Shall while I live, shall when I die,
   Still follow me;
Forever shall my soul
   His boundless blessings prove;
And while eternal ages roll,
   Adore and love.

                                        Thomas Roberts.

OLIVET. 6, 4.   Lowell Mason.

SONGS OF THE CHRISTIAN LIFE.

OLIVET. 6, 4.—*Continued.*

Sav-iour di-vine: Now hear me while I pray, Take all my guilt a-way, O let me from this day Be whol-ly thine.

172 *Before the cross.*

2 May thy rich grace impart
Strength to my fainting heart,
  My zeal inspire;
As thou hast died for me,
O may my love to thee
Pure, warm, and changeless be,—
  A living fire.

3 While life's dark maze I tread,
And griefs around me spread,
  Be thou my guide;
Bid darkness turn to day,
Wipe sorrow's tears away,
Nor let me ever stray
  From thee aside.

4 When ends life's transient dream,
When death's cold, sullen stream
  Shall o'er me roll;
Blest Saviour, then, in love,
Fear and distrust remove;
O bear me safe above,—
  A ransomed soul.

                      Ray Palmer.

I NEED THEE EVERY HOUR. 6, 4, 7.   Rev. Robert Lowry.

1. I need thee every hour, Most gracious Lord; No tender voice like thine Can peace afford.
2. I need thee every hour; Stay thou near by; Temptations lose their power When thou art nigh.
3. I need thee every hour, In joy or pain; Come quickly and a-bide, Or life is vain.

Refrain.

I need thee, O I need thee; Every hour I need thee; O bless me now, my Saviour, I come to thee!

Copyright 1872, by Robert Lowry.

173 *I need Thee every hour.*

4 I need thee every hour;
  Teach me thy will;
And thy rich promises
  In me fulfill.

5 I need thee every hour,
  Most Holy One;
O make me thine indeed,
  Thou blessed Son!
            Mrs. Annie S. Hawks.

SONGS OF THE CHRISTIAN LIFE.

DUANE STREET. L. M. D. — Rev. George Coles.

1. Jesus, my all, to heaven is gone, He whom I fix my hopes upon; His track I see, and I'll pursue The narrow way, till him I view. The way the holy prophets went, The road that leads from banishment, The King's highway of holiness, I'll go, for all his paths are peace.

174 *The highway of holiness.*

2 This is the way I long have sought,
And mourned because I found it not ;
My grief a burden long has been,
Because I was not saved from sin.
The more I strove against its power,
I felt its weight and guilt the more ;
Till late I heard my Saviour say,
"Come hither, soul, I am the way."

3 Lo! glad I come; and thou, blest Lamb,
Shalt take me to thee, as I am ;
Nothing but sin have I to give ;
Nothing but love shall I receive.
Then will I tell to sinners round,
What a dear Saviour I have found ;
I'll point to thy redeeming blood,
And say, "Behold the way to God."
— John Cennick.

ALETTA. 7. — William B. Bradbury.

1. Prince of peace, control my will; Bid this struggling heart be still; Bid my fears and doubtings cease, Hush my spirit into peace.

Copyright, 1857, in "The Jubilee," by Wm. B. Bradbury.

175 *Perfect peace.*

2 Thou hast bought me with thy blood,
Opened wide the gate to God :
Peace I ask—but peace must be,
Lord, in being one with thee.

3 May thy will, not mine, be done;
May thy will and mine be one :

Chase these doubtings from my heart ;
Now thy perfect peace impart.

4 Saviour, at thy feet I fall ;
Thou my Life, my God, my All !
Let thy happy servant be
One for evermore with thee !
— Mary A. S. Barber.

SONGS OF THE CHRISTIAN LIFE.

ALL THE WAY. Rev. Robert Lowry.

Copyright, 1875, by Biglow & Main.

176   *Our faithful Guide.*

1 ALL the way my Saviour leads me;
   What have I to ask beside?
   Can I doubt his tender mercy,
   Who through life has been my guide?
   Heavenly peace, divinest comfort,
   Here by faith in him to dwell!
   For I know, whate'er befall me,
   Jesus doeth all things well;
   For I know, whate'er befall me,
   Jesus doeth all things well.

2 All the way my Saviour leads me;
   Cheers each winding path I tread;
   Gives me grace for every trial,
   Feeds me with the living bread;
   &c.

Though my weary steps may falter,
   And my soul athirst may be,
Gushing from the Rock before me,
   Lo! a spring of joy I see;
   Gushing from the Rock, &c.

3 All the way my Saviour leads me;
   Oh, the fullness of his love!
   Perfect rest to me is promised
   In my Father's house above;
   When my spirit, clothed immortal,
   Wings it flight to realms of day,
   This my song through endless ages—
   Jesus led me all the way;
   This my song, &c.
                         Fanny J. Crosby.

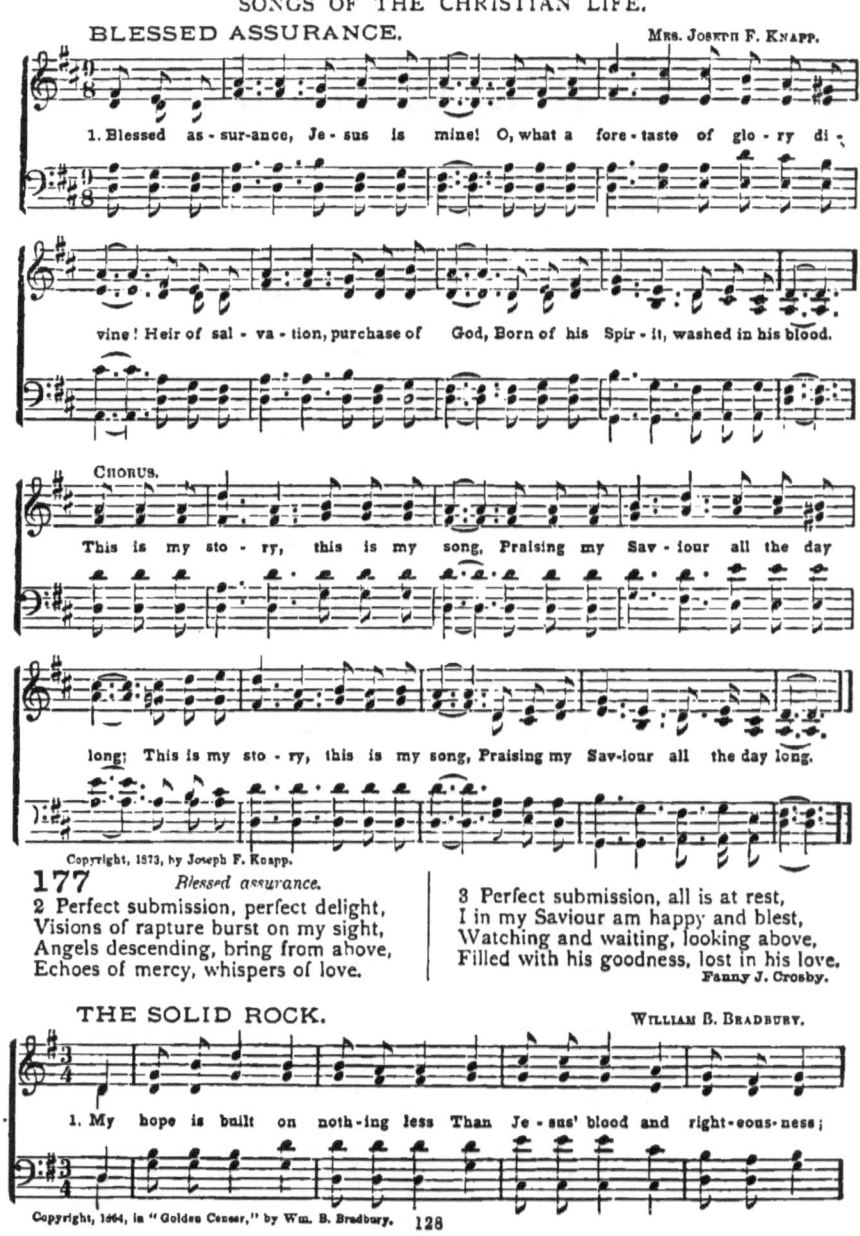

SONGS OF THE CHRISTIAN LIFE.

BLESSED ASSURANCE.
Mrs. Joseph F. Knapp.

1. Blessed as-sur-ance, Je-sus is mine! O, what a fore-taste of glo-ry di-vine! Heir of sal-va-tion, purchase of God, Born of his Spir-it, washed in his blood.

Chorus.
This is my sto-ry, this is my song, Praising my Sav-iour all the day long; This is my sto-ry, this is my song, Praising my Sav-iour all the day long.

Copyright, 1873, by Joseph F. Knapp.

177 *Blessed assurance.*

2 Perfect submission, perfect delight,
Visions of rapture burst on my sight,
Angels descending, bring from above,
Echoes of mercy, whispers of love.

3 Perfect submission, all is at rest,
I in my Saviour am happy and blest,
Watching and waiting, looking above,
Filled with his goodness, lost in his love.
— Fanny J. Crosby.

THE SOLID ROCK.
William B. Bradbury.

1. My hope is built on noth-ing less Than Je-sus' blood and right-eous-ness;

Copyright, 1864, in "Golden Censer," by Wm. B. Bradbury.

SONGS OF THE CHRISTIAN LIFE.

THE SOLID ROCK. *Concluded.*

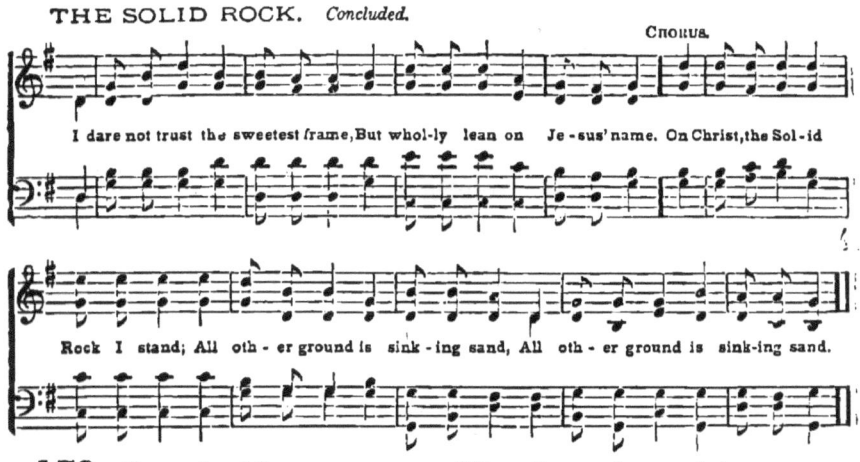

I dare not trust the sweetest frame, But wholly lean on Jesus' name. On Christ, the Solid Rock I stand; All other ground is sinking sand, All other ground is sinking sand.

178 *The sure foundation.*

2 When darkness veils his lovely face
I rest on his unchanging grace;
In every high and stormy gale,
My anchor holds within the vail.

3 His oath, his covenant, his blood,
Support me in the whelming flood;
When all around my soul gives way,
He then is all my hope and stay.

4 When he shall come with trumpet sound,
O, may I then in him be found;
Drest in his righteousness alone,
Faultless to stand before the throne !
Edward Mote.

GREENWOOD. S. M. Jos. E. Sweetser.

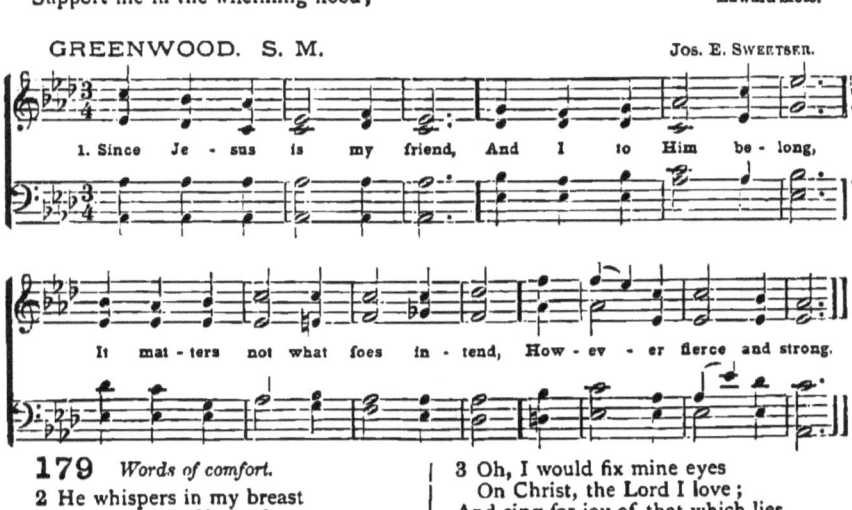

1. Since Jesus is my friend, And I to Him belong,
It matters not what foes intend, However fierce and strong.

179 *Words of comfort.*

2 He whispers in my breast
  Sweet words of holy cheer,
How they who seek in God their rest,
  Shall ever find him near.

3 Oh, I would fix mine eyes
  On Christ, the Lord I love;
And sing for joy of that which lies
  Stored up for me above.
P. Gerhardt.

SONGS OF THE CHRISTIAN LIFE.

HE LEADETH ME. L. M.   William B. Bradbury.

1. He leadeth me! O blessed thought! O words with heavenly comfort fraught! Whate'er I do, wher-e'er I be, Still 'tis God's hand that leadeth me.

CHORUS.

He leadeth me, he leadeth me, By his own hand he leadeth me: His faithful follower I would be, For by his hand he leadeth me.

Copyright, 1864, in "Golden Censer," by Wm. B. Bradbury.

180   *He leadeth me.*

2 Sometimes 'mid scenes of deepest gloom,
Sometimes where Eden's bowers bloom,
By waters still, o'er troubled sea,—
Still 'tis his hand that leadeth me!

3 Lord, I would clasp thy hand in mine,
Nor ever murmur nor repine,
Content, whatever lot I see,
Since 'tis my God that leadeth me!

4 And when my task on earth is done,
When, by thy grace, the victory's won,
E'en death's cold wave I will not flee,
Since God through Jordan leadeth me.
               J. H. Gilmore.

NAOMI. C. M.   Hans Georg Nägeli.

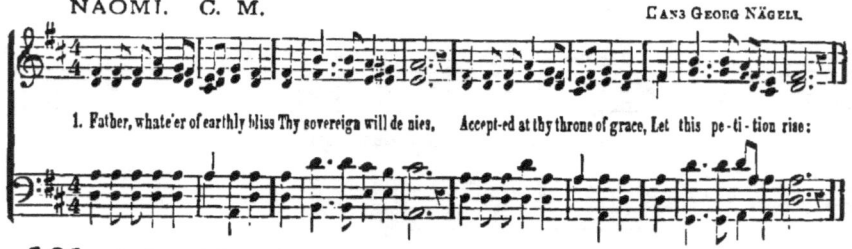

1. Father, whate'er of earthly bliss Thy sovereign will denies, Accept-ed at thy throne of grace, Let this pe-ti-tion rise:

181   *A calm and thankful heart.*

2 Give me a calm, a thankful heart,
From every murmur free;
The blessings of thy grace impart,
And make me live to thee.

3 Let the sweet hope that thou art mine
My life and death attend;
Thy presence through my journey shine,
And crown my journey's end.
               Anne Steele.

SONGS OF THE CHRISTIAN LIFE.

NEVER ALONE.
FERD. SILCHER.

1. Far out on the desolate bil-low, The sai-lor sails the sea. A-lone with the night and the temp-est, Where count-less dan-gers be. Yet, nev-er a-lone is the Christian, Who lives by faith and prayer; For God is a friend un-fail-ing, And God is ev-ery-where.

182 *Always with us.*

2 Far down in the earth's dark bosom,
   The miner mines the ore;
   Death lurks in the dark behind him,
   And hides in the rock before. CHO.

3 Forth into the dreadful battle
   The steadfast soldier goes,
   No friend, when he lies a dying
   His eyes to tenderly close. CHO.

4 Lord, grant as we sail life's ocean,
   Or delve in its mines of woe;
   Or fight in its terrible conflict,
   This comfort all to know. That never, &c.
   Rossiter W. Raymond.

A BROTHER'S CARE.
Mrs. CHARLES BARNARD.

1. Yes! for me, for me he careth, With a brother's tender care, Yes! with me, with me he shareth, Every bur-den, every care.

183 *His guardian care.*

2 Yes! o'er me, o'er me he watcheth,
   Ceaseless watcheth night and day;
   Yes! e'en me, e'en me he snatcheth
   From the perils of the way.

3 Yes! for me he standeth pleading
   At the mercy-seat above;
   Ever for me interceding,
   Constant in untiring love.

4 Yes! in me, in me he dwelleth,
   I in him, and he in me;
   And my empty soul he filleth,
   Here, and through eternity.

5 Thus I wait for his returning,
   Singing all the way to heaven;
   Such the joyful song of morning,
   Such the joyful song of even.
   Horatius Bonar.

SONGS OF THE CHRISTIAN LIFE.

SAFE IN THE ARMS OF JESUS.
W. H. DOANE.

1. Safe in the arms of Jesus, Safe on his gentle breast, There by his love o'er-shaded, Sweetly my soul shall rest. Hark! 'tis the voice of angels, Borne in a song to me, Over the fields of glory, Over the jasper sea.

2. Safe in the arms of Jesus, Safe from corroding care, Safe from the world's temptations, Sin cannot harm me there. Free from the blight of sorrow, Free from my doubts and fears; Only a few more trials, Only a few more tears!

CHO.—Safe in the arms of Jesus, Safe on his gentle breast, There by his love o'ershaded, Sweetly my soul shall rest.

184 *Sweetly resting.*

3 Jesus, my heart's dear refuge,
Jesus has died for me;
Firm on the Rock of Ages,
Ever my trust shall be.

Here let me wait with patience,
Wait till the night is o'er;
Wait till I see the morning
Break on the golden shore. CHO.
Fanny J. Crosby.

SAVIOUR, TEACH ME.
ANON.

1. Saviour, teach me, day by day, Love's sweet lesson to obey; Sweeter lesson cannot be—Loving him who first loved me.

185 *Love's sweet lesson.*

2 With a childlike heart of love,
At thy bidding may I move;
Prompt to serve and follow thee,
Loving him who first loved me.

3 Teach me all thy steps to trace,
Strong to follow in thy grace,

Learning how to love from thee,
Loving him who first loved me.

4 Thus may I rejoice to show
That I feel the love I owe;
Singing, till Thy face I see,
Of his love who first loved me.
Jane E. Leeson.

SONGS OF THE CHRISTIAN LIFE.

THE LORD WILL PROVIDE.
C. S. Harrington, by per. E. Tourjee.

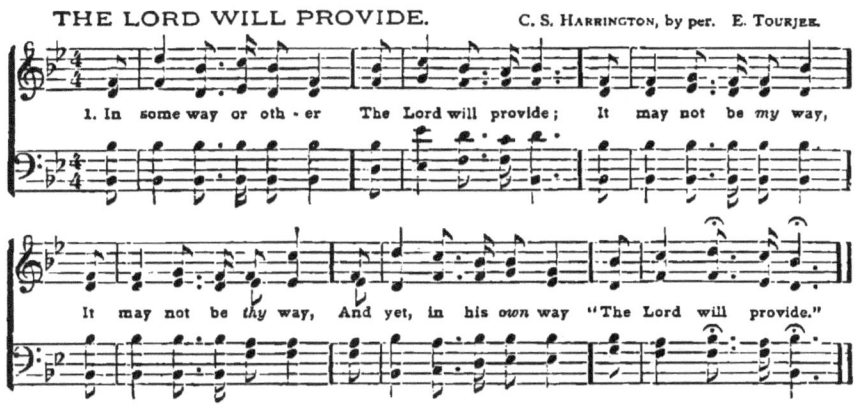

1. In some way or other The Lord will provide; It may not be *my* way, It may not be *thy* way, And yet, in his *own* way "The Lord will provide."

186 *Thy way not mine.*

2 At some time or other
  The Lord will provide;
It may not be *my* time,
It may not be *thy* time,
And yet, in his *own* time,
"The Lord will provide."

3 Despond then no longer:
  The Lord will provide;
And this be the token—

No word he hath spoken
Was ever yet broken,—
"The Lord will provide."

4 March on, then, right boldly;
  The sea shall divide;
The pathway made glorious,
With shoutings victorious,
We'll join in the chorus,
"The Lord will provide."
　　　　Mrs. M. A. W. Cooke.

FATHER, LEAD ME.
German.

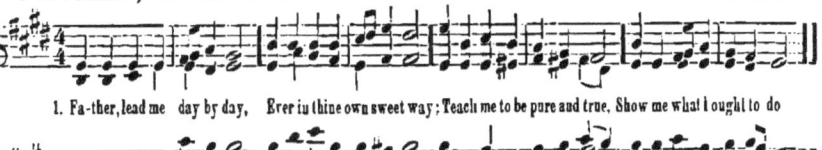

1. Father, lead me day by day, Ever in thine own sweet way; Teach me to be pure and true, Show me what I ought to do

137 *Patient continuance.*

2 When in danger, make me brave;
Make me know that thou canst save;
Keep me safe by thy dear side;
Let me in thy love abide.

3 When I'm tempted to do wrong,
Make me steadfast, wise, and strong;
And when all alone I stand,
Shield me with thy mighty hand.

4 When my heart is full of glee,
Help me to remember thee,—

Happy most of all to know
That my Father loves me so.

5 When my work seems hard and dry,
May I press on cheerily;
Help me patiently to bear
Pain and hardship, toil and care.

6 May I do the good I know,
Be thy loving child below,
Then at last go home to thee.
Evermore thy child to be.
　　　　Anon.

SONGS OF THE CHRISTIAN LIFE.

LUX BENIGNA. 10, 4, 10.   John Bacchus Dykes.

1. Lead, kindly Light a-mid the encircling gloom, Lead thou me on! The night is dark, and I am far from home; Lead thou me on! Keep thou my feet; I do not ask to see The dis-tant scene; one step e-nough for me.

188   *Lead, kindly Light.*

2 I was not ever thus, nor prayed that thou
    Shouldst lead me on;
I loved to choose and see my path; but now
    Lead thou me on!
I loved the garish day, and, spite of fears,
Pride ruled my will. Remember not past
    years!

3 So long thy power hath blest me, sure it
    Will lead me on   [still
O'er moor and fen, o'er crag and torrent, till
    The night is gone,
And with the morn those angel faces smile
Which I have loved long since, and lost
    awhile!
                          John H. Newman.

THINE FOR EVER.   Charles Thirtle.

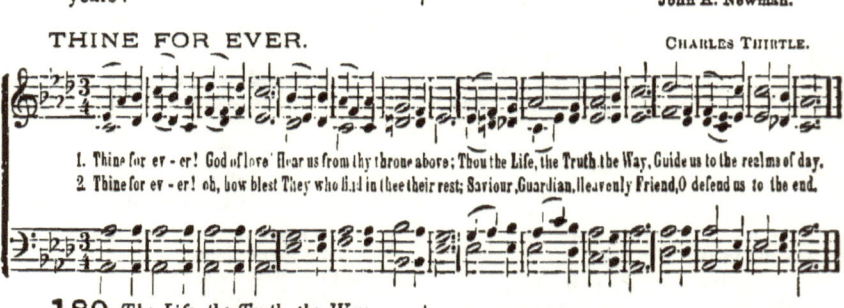

1. Thine for ev-er! God of love! Hear us from thy throne above; Thou the Life, the Truth, the Way, Guide us to the realms of day.
2. Thine for ev-er! oh, how blest They who find in thee their rest; Saviour, Guardian, Heavenly Friend, O defend us to the end.

189   *The Life, the Truth, the Way.*

3 Thine for ever! Saviour keep
Us, thy frail and trembling sheep;
Safe alone beneath thy care,
Let us all thy goodness share.

4 Thine for ever! thou our guide,
All our wants by thee supplied;
All our sins by thee forgiven,
Lead us, Lord, from earth to heaven.
                          Mary Fawler Maude.

SONGS OF THE CHRISTIAN LIFE.

TRUSTING IN HIS WORD.
GEO. C. STEBBINS.

1. All my doubts I give to Jesus, I've his gracious promise heard; I shall never be confounded, I am trusting in his word.

CHORUS.
I am trusting, fully trusting, Sweetly trusting in his word, I am trusting, ful-ly trusting, Sweetly trusting in his word.

Copyright, 1876, by Ira D. Sankey.

190 *Casting all on Jesus.*

2 All my sin I lay on Jesus,
  He doth wash me in his blood;
  He will keep me pure and holy,
  He will bring me home to God. REF.

3 All my fears I give to Jesus,
  Rests my weary soul on him;
  Though my way be hid in darkness,
  Never can my light grow dim. REF.

4 All in all I have in Jesus,
  Poor, yet rich as cherubim;
  Ignorant and full of weakness,
  Heaven's own store I find in him. REF.
  J. C. Morgan, M. D.

MILWAUKEE. 8. 7.
JOHN ZUNDEL.

1. Sav-iour, who thy flock art feed-ing With the Shep-herd's kind-est care,
All the fee-ble, gent-ly lead-ing, While the lambs thy bo-som share.

191 *The shepherd's care.*

2 Now, these little ones receiving,
  Fold them in thy gracious arm,
  There, we know, thy word believing,
  Only there, secure from harm.

3 Never, from thy pasture roving,
  Let them be the lion's prey;
  Let thy tenderness, so loving,
  Keep them thro' life's dangerous way.

4 Then within thy fold eternal,
  Let them find a resting-place,
  Feed in pastures ever vernal,
  Drink the rivers of thy grace.
  Wm. A. Muhlenberg.

SONGS OF THE CHRISTIAN LIFE.

GOD'S ANVIL. QUISQUAM.

1. Pain's fur-nace heat with-in me quiv-ers, God's breath up-on the flame doth blow, And all my heart in anguish shivers, And trembles at the fie-ry glow: And yet I whisper, 'As God will,' And in his hottest fire hold still. I will not murmur at the sor-row That on-ly longer-liv'd would be, The end may come, and that to-morrow, When God hath wrought his will in me; And so I whisper, 'As God will,' And trusting to the end hold still.

192 *God's will be done.*

2 He comes and lays my heart all heated,
On his hard anvil, minded so;
Yet in his own fair form to beat it,
With his great hammer, blow by blow:
And yet, &c.

3 He takes my soften'd heart and beats it;
The sparks fly off at every blow:
He turns it o'er and o'er, and heats it,
And let's it cool, and makes it glow.
And yet, &c.

4 He kindles for my profit, purely,
Affliction's glowing, fiery brand;
For all his heaviest blows are surely
Inflicted by a Master hand:
And yet, &c.

Julius Sturm. Tr. by Rev. Charles T. Brooks.

SONGS OF THE CHRISTIAN LIFE.

THE WILL OF GOD.

JNO. E. SEARLES, JR.

1. I love thy will, O God, Thy bless-ed, per-fect will, In which this once re-bel-lious heart Lies sat-is-fied and still.

Copyright, 1885, by Phillips & Hunt.

193 *God's will accepted.*

2 I love thy will, O God!
  It is my joy, my rest;
  It glorifies my common task,
  It makes each trial blest.

3 I love thy will, O God!
  The sunshine or the rain;
  Some days are bright with praise, and some
  Sweet with accepted pain.

4 I love thy will, O God!
  O hear my earnest plea,
  That as thy will is done in heaven,
  It may be done in me!

Bessie P. MacLaughlin.

COME, YE DISCONSOLATE. 11, 10.

SAMUEL WEBBE.

1. Come, ye dis-con-so-late, where'er ye languish; Come to the mercy-seat, fer-vent-ly kneel; Here bring your wounded hearts, here tell your anguish; Earth has no sorrow that Heaven cannot heal

194 *Come, ye disconsolate.*

2 Joy of the desolate, light of the straying,
  Hope of the penitent, fadeless and pure,
  Here speaks the Comforter, tenderly saying,
  "Earth has no sorrow that Heaven cannot cure."

3 Here see the bread of life; see waters flowing
  Forth from the throne of God, pure from above;
  Come to the feast of love; come, ever knowing
  Earth has no sorrow but Heaven can remove.

Thomas Moore, alt.
and Thos. Hastings.

SONGS OF THE CHRISTIAN LIFE.

I WILL SING FOR JESUS.
PHILIP PHILLIPS.

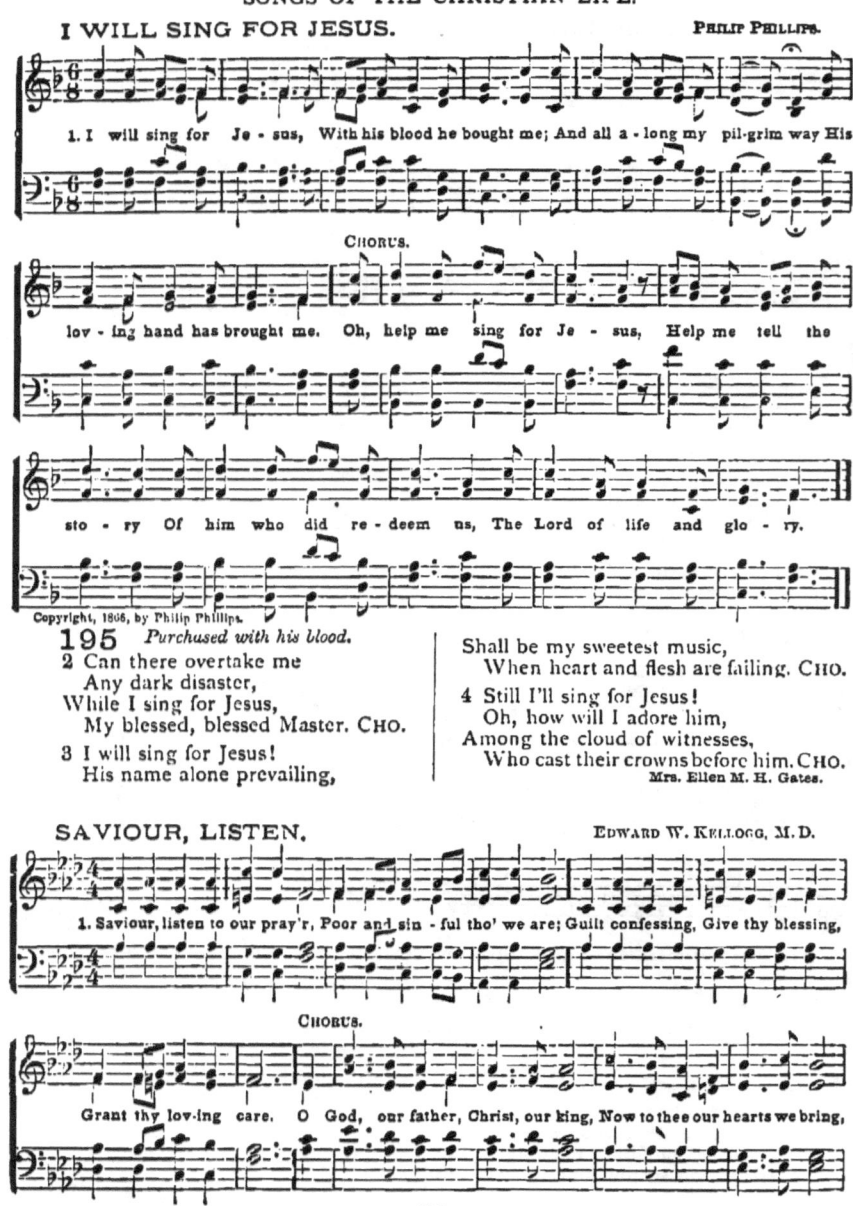

1. I will sing for Je-sus, With his blood he bought me; And all a-long my pil-grim way His lov-ing hand has brought me. Oh, help me sing for Je-sus, Help me tell the sto-ry Of him who did re-deem us, The Lord of life and glo-ry.

Copyright, 1866, by Philip Phillips.

195 *Purchased with his blood.*

2 Can there overtake me
  Any dark disaster,
While I sing for Jesus,
  My blessed, blessed Master. CHO.

3 I will sing for Jesus!
  His name alone prevailing,

Shall be my sweetest music,
  When heart and flesh are failing. CHO.

4 Still I'll sing for Jesus!
  Oh, how will I adore him,
Among the cloud of witnesses,
  Who cast their crowns before him. CHO.

Mrs. Ellen M. H. Gates.

SAVIOUR, LISTEN.
EDWARD W. KELLOGG, M.D.

1. Saviour, listen to our pray'r, Poor and sin-ful tho' we are; Guilt confessing, Give thy blessing, Grant thy lov-ing care. O God, our father, Christ, our king, Now to thee our hearts we bring,

SONGS OF THE CHRISTIAN LIFE.

SAVIOUR, LISTEN.—Concluded.

Keep them ev-er, Bless-ed Sav-iour, Till in heav'n thy love we sing.

196 *Seeking strength.*
2 Strength is thine; we often stray
From the pure and holy way;
  Wilt thou guide us,
  Walk beside us
Nearer every day! CHO.

3 Then may we, when life is o'er,
Stand with thee on yonder shore;
  Freed from sinning,
  Heaven winning,
Praising evermore! CHO.
           Anon.

O MY SAVIOUR, HEAR ME.
HUBERT P. MAIN.

1. "O my Saviour hear me, Draw me close to thee;" Thou hast paid my ransom, Thou hast died for me; Now by simple faith I claim Pardon thro' thy gracious name; Thou, my ark of safety, Let me fly to thee.

Copyright, 1875, by Biglow & Main.

197 *Seeking pardon.*
2 O my Saviour, bless me,
  Bless me while I pray;
Grant thy grace to help me,
  Take my fear away;
I believe thy promise, Lord;
I will trust thy holy word;
Thou, my soul's Redeemer,
  Bless me while I pray.

3 O my Saviour, love me,
  Make me all thine own;
Leave me not to wander
  In this world alone;

Bless my way with light divine,
Let thy glory round me shine;
Thou my rock, my refuge,
  Make me all thine own.

4 O my Saviour, guard me,
  Keep me evermore;
Bless me, love and guide me,
  Till my work is o'er,
May I then, with glad surprise,
Chant thy praise beyond the skies;
There with thee, my Saviour,
  Dwell for ever more.
           Fanny J. Crosby.

SONGS OF THE CHRISTIAN LIFE.

RETREAT. L. M. — Thomas Hastings.

1. From every stormy wind that blows, From every swelling tide of woes, There is a calm, a sure retreat: 'Tis found beneath the mercy-seat.

198 *The mercy-seat.*

2 There is a place where Jesus sheds
The oil of gladness on our heads;
A place than all besides more sweet:
It is the blood-bought mercy-seat.

3 There is a scene where spirits blend,
Where friend holds fellowship with friend:
Though sundered far, by faith they meet
Around one common mercy-seat.

4 There, there on eagle wings we soar,
And sin and sense molest no more;
And heaven comes down our souls to greet,
While glory crowns the mercy-seat.
Hugh Stowell.

SWEET HOUR OF PRAYER. L. M. D. — William B. Bradbury.

1. Sweet hour of prayer, sweet hour of prayer, That calls me from a world of care, And bids me, at my Father's throne, Make all my wants and (Omit) wishes known!
D. C. And oft escaped the tempter's snare, By thy return, sweet (Omit) hour of prayer.

In seasons of distress and grief, My soul has often found relief,

Copyright, 1859, by Wm. B. Bradbury.

199 *Sweet hour of prayer.*

2 Sweet hour of prayer, sweet hour of prayer,
Thy wings shall my petition bear
To Him, whose truth and faithfulness
Engage the waiting soul to bless:
And since he bids me seek his face,
Believe his word, and trust his grace,
I'll cast on him my every care,
And wait for thee, sweet hour of prayer.

3 Sweet hour of prayer, sweet hour of prayer,
May I thy consolation share.
Till, from Mount Pisgah's lofty height,
I view my home, and take my flight:
This robe of flesh I'll drop, and rise,
To seize the everlasting prize;
And shout, while passing through the air,
Farewell, farewell, sweet hour of prayer!
William W. Walford.

SONGS OF THE CHRISTIAN LIFE.

JESUS, MY ALL.
Scotch Air.

1. Lord, at Thy mercy-seat, Humbly I fall; Pleading Thy promise sweet, Lord, hear my call; Now let thy work begin, Oh, make me pure within, Cleanse me from every sin, Je-sus, my all.

200 *Pleading the promises.*

2 Tears of repentant grief
  Silently fall;
Help thou my unbelief,
  Hear thou my call,
Oh, how I pine for thee!
'Tis all my hope, and plea:
Jesus has died for me,
  Jesus, my all.

3 Still at thy mercy-seat
  Humbly I fall;
Pleading Thy promise sweet,
  Heard is my call.
Faith wings my soul to thee;
This all my hope shall be,
Jesus has died for me,
  Jesus, my all.
  — *Fanny J. Crosby.*

SELVIN. S. M.
GERMAN, ARR. BY LOWELL MASON.

1. If, on a quiet sea, Toward heaven we calmly sail, With grateful hearts, O God, to thee, We'll own the favoring gale, With grateful hearts, O God, to thee, We'll own the favoring gale.

201 *Walking by faith.*

2 But should the surges rise,
  And rest delay to come,
Blest be the tempest, kind the storm,
  Which drives us nearer home.

3 Soon shall our doubts and fears
  All yield to thy control;
Thy tender mercies shall illume
  The midnight of the soul.

4 Teach us, in every state,
  To make thy will our own;
And when the joys of sense depart,
  To live by faith alone.
  — *Augustus M. Toplady.*

SONGS OF THE CHRISTIAN LIFE.

REFUGE. 7. D.   Joseph P. Holbrook.

202   *The only refuge.*

1 JESUS, Lover of my soul,
    Let me to thy bosom fly,
While the nearer waters roll,
    While the tempest still is high!
Hide me, O my Saviour, hide,
    Till the storm of life is past;
Safe into the haven guide,
    O receive my soul at last!

2 Other refuge have I none;
    Hangs my helpless soul on thee:
Leave, O leave me not alone,
    Still support and comfort me:
All my trust on thee is stayed,
    All my help from thee I bring;
Cover my defenseless head
    With the shadow of thy wing!

3 Thou, O Christ, art all I want;
    More than all in thee I find;
Raise the fallen, cheer the faint,
    Heal the sick, and lead the blind.
Just and holy is thy name,
    I am all unrighteousness:
False and full of sin I am,
    Thou art full of truth and grace.

4 Plenteous grace with thee is found,
    Grace to cover all my sin:
Let the healing streams abound:
    Make and keep me pure within.
Thou of life the fountain art,
    Freely let me take of thee:
Spring thou up within my heart,
    Rise to all eternity.

                                            Charles Wesley.

MARTYN. 7. D.   Simeon Butler Marsh.

SONGS OF THE CHRISTIAN LIFE.

KEEP THOU MY WAY.
Hubert P. Main.

1. Keep thou my way, O Lord; Myself I can-not guide; Nor dare I trust my err-ing steps One moment from thy side: I can-not think a-right, Un-less in-spired by thee; My heart would fail with-out thy aid; Choose thou my thoughts for me.

Copyright, 1869, in Bright Jewels by Biglow & Main.

203 *Self distrusted.*

2 For every act of faith,
And every pure design,—
For all of good my soul can know,
The glory, Lord, be thine;
Free grace my pardon seals,
Through thy atoning blood;
Free grace the full assurance brings,
Of peace with thee, my God.

3 O speak, and I will hear;
Command, and I obey,
My willing feet with joy shall haste
To run the heav'nly way;
Keep thou my wand'ring heart,
And bid it cease to roam;
O bear me safe o'er death's cold wave
To heaven, my blissful home.
Fanny J. Crosby.

MY TIMES ARE IN THY HAND.
Alexander Ernst Fesca.

1. "My times are in thy hand;" My God! I wish them there: My life, my soul, my all, I leave En-tire-ly to thy care.

From "The Hymnary" by per. S. Lasar.

204 *God's way the best.*

2 "My times are in thy hand:"
Whatever they may be;
Pleasing or painful, dark or bright,
As best may seem to thee.

3 "My times are in thy hand,"
Why should I doubt or fear?
My Father's hand will never cause
His child a needless tear.

4 "My times are in thy hand;"
I always trust in thee;
Till I possess the promised land,
And all thy glory see.
Wm. Freeman Lloyd.

SONGS OF THE CHRISTIAN LIFE.

YIELD NOT TO TEMPTATION.
H. R. Palmer, by per.

1. Yield not to temp-ta-tion, For yield-ing is sin, Each vic-t'ry will help you
Some oth-er to win; Fight man-ful-ly on-ward, Dark pas-sions sub-due,
Look ev-er to Je-sus, He'll car-ry you through. Ask the Saviour to help you,
Comfort, strengthen, and keep you: He is will-ing to aid you, He will car-ry you through.

Copyright 1868, by H. R. Palmer.

205 *Resisting evil.*

2 Shun evil companions,
　Bad language disdain,
God's name hold in reverence,
　Nor take it in vain;
Be thoughtful and earnest,
　Kindhearted and true,
Look ever to Jesus,
　He'll carry you through.
Cho.—Ask the Saviour to help you,
　Comfort, strengthen, and keep you,
　He is willing to aid you,
　He will carry you through.

3 To him that o'ercometh
　God giveth a crown,
Through faith we shall conquer,
　Though often cast down;
He who is our Saviour,
　Our strength will renew,
Look ever to Jesus,
　He'll carry you through.
Cho.—Ask the Saviour to help you,
　Comfort, strengthen, and keep you;
　He is willing to aid you,
　He will carry you through.

H. R. Palmer.

SONGS OF THE CHRISTIAN LIFE.

WHITER THAN SNOW.

WM. G. FISCHER, 1872.

1. Lord Jesus, I long to be perfectly whole; I want thee forever, to live in my soul; Break down every idol, cast out every foe; Now wash me, and I shall be whiter than snow. Whiter than snow, yes, whiter than snow; Now wash me, and I shall be whiter than snow.

Copyright, 1871, by Wm. G. Fischer.

206 *Wash me, and I shall be whiter than snow.*

2 Lord Jesus, look down from thy throne in the skies,
And help me to make a complete sacrifice;
I give up myself, and whatever I know—
Now wash me, and I shall be whiter than snow. CHO.

3 Lord Jesus, for this I most humbly entreat;
I wait, blessed Lord, at thy crucified feet,
By faith, for my cleansing, I see thy blood flow—
Now wash me, and I shall be whiter than snow. CHO.

4 Lord Jesus, thou seest I patiently wait;
Come now, and within me a new heart create;
To those who have sought thee, thou never said'st No—
Now wash me, and I shall be whiter than snow. CHO.

James Nicholson.

SONGS OF THE CHRISTIAN LIFE.

SING ALWAYS.
W. F. Sherwin.

1. Sing with a tuneful spirit, Sing with a cheerful lay, Praise to thy great Creator, While on the pilgrim way, Sing when the birds are waking, Sing with the morning light; Sing in the noontide's golden beam, Sing in the hush of night.
2. Sing when the heart is troubled, Sing when the hours are long, Sing when the storm-cloud gathers; Sweet is the voice of song. Sing when the sky is darkest, Sing when the thunders roll; Sing of a land where rest remains, Rest for the weary soul.

207 *The song of trust.*

3 Sing in the vale of shadows,
Sing in the hour of death,
And when the eyes are closing,
Sing with the latest breath.
Sing till the heart's deep longings
Cease on the other shore;
Then with the countless numbers [there,
Sing on, forever more.

Fanny J. Crosby.

DARE TO DO RIGHT.
Wm. B. Bradbury.

1. Dare to do right! Dare to be true! You have a work that no other can do; Do it so bravely, so kindly, so well, Angels will hasten the story to tell.

Copyrighted, 1864, in Golden Censer, by Wm. B. Bradbury.

SONGS OF THE CHRISTIAN LIFE.

DARE TO DO RIGHT. *Concluded.*

Dare, Dare, Dare to do right, Dare, Dare, Dare to be true! Dare, Dare to do right, Dare to be true!

208 *True to God and man.*

2 Dare to do right! Dare to be true!
Other men's failures can never save you;
Stand by your conscience, your honor your faith;
Stand like a hero, and battle to death.

3 Dare to do right! Dare to be true!
God, who created you, cares for you too,
Treasures the tears that his striving ones shed,
Counts and protects every hair of your head.

4 Dare to do right! Dare to be true!
Jesus, your Saviour, will carry you thro';
City and mansion and throne all in sight,
Can you not dare to be true, and do right?

Rev. Geo. L. Taylor.

WILL JESUS FIND US WATCHING?

W. H. Doane, by per.

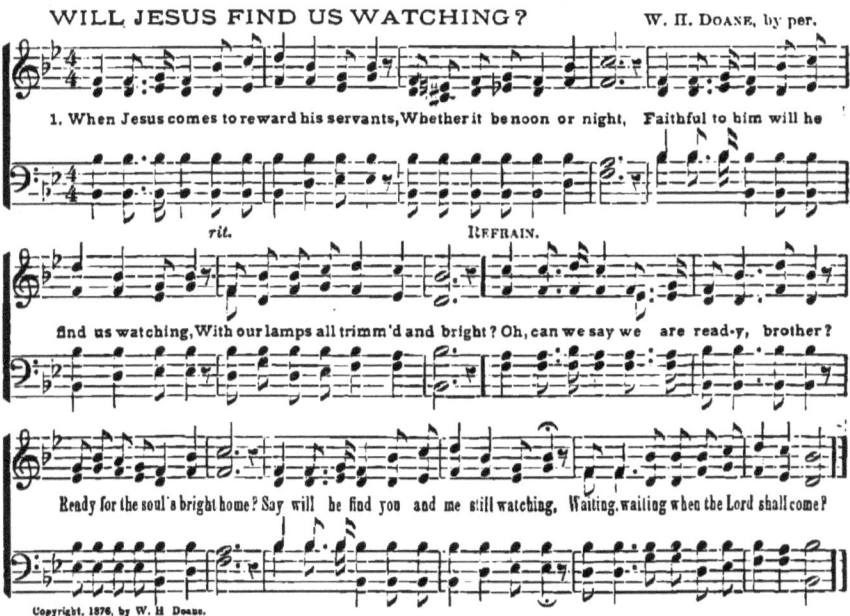

1. When Jesus comes to reward his servants, Whether it be noon or night, Faithful to him will he find us watching, With our lamps all trimm'd and bright? Oh, can we say we are read-y, brother? Ready for the soul's bright home? Say will he find you and me still watching, Waiting, waiting when the Lord shall come?

Copyright, 1876, by W. H. Doane.

209 *"Watch therefore."*

2 If at the dawn of the early morning,
  He shall call us one by one,
When to the Lord we restore our talents,
  Will he answer thee—"Well done?" REF.

3 Have we been true to the trust he left us?
  Do we seek to do our best?
If in our hearts there is naught condemns us,
  We shall have a glorious rest. REF.

4 Blessed are those whom the Lord finds watching,
  In his glory they shall share;
If he shall come at the dawn or midnight,
  Will he find us watching there? REF.

Fanny J. Crosby.

SONGS OF THE CHRISTIAN LIFE.

IS MY NAME WRITTEN THERE?

FRANK M. DAVIS, by per.

1. Lord, I care not for rich-es, Nei-ther sil-ver nor gold; I would make sure of heav-en, I would en-ter the fold. In the book of thy king-dom, With its pa-ges so fair, Tell me, Je-sus, my Sav-iour, Is my name writ-ten there? Is my name written there, On the page white and fair? In the book of thy kingdom, Is my name written there?

210 *"Your names are written in heaven."*

2 Lord, my sins they are many,
  Like the sands of the sea,
But thy blood, oh, my Saviour!
  Is sufficient for me;
For thy promise is written,
  In bright letters that glow,
"Though your sins be as scarlet,
  I will make them like snow."
CHO.—Yes, my name's written there,
  On the page white and fair;
In the book of thy kingdom,
  Yes, my name's written there.

3 Oh! that beautiful city,
  With its mansions of light,
With its glorified beings,
  In pure garments of white;
Where no evil thing cometh,
  To despoil what is fair;
Where the angels are watching,
  Yes, my name's written there.
CHO.—Yes, my name's written there,
  On the page white and fair;
In the book of thy kingdom,
  Yes, my name's written there.

Mrs. Mary A. Kidder.

SONGS OF THE CHRISTIAN LIFE.

CHILD OF A KING.

Rev. JOHN B. SUMNER, arr.

1. My Father is rich in houses and lands, He holdeth the wealth of the world in his hands; Of rubies and diamonds of silver and gold, His coffers are full, He has riches untold.

CHORUS.
I'm the child of a King, The child of a King; With Jesus my Saviour, I'm the child of a King.

Copyright, 1877, by Bigelow & Main.

211 *Joint heirs with Christ.*

2 My Father's own Son, who saves us from sin,
Once wandered on earth as the poorest of men;
But now he is reigning forever on high,
And will give me a home with himself by-and-by.—CHO.

3 I once was an outcast stranger on earth,
A sinner by choice, and an "alien" by birth;
But I've been "adopted," my name's written down,
An heir to a mansion, a robe and a crown.—CHO.

4 A tent or a cottage, why should I care?
They're building a palace for me over there;
Though exiled from home, yet my heart still may sing.
All glory to God, I'm the child of a King.—CHO.

Hattie E. Buell, arr.

SONGS OF THE CHRISTIAN LIFE.

MARCHING TO ZION. Rev. Robert Lowry.

1. Come ye that love the Lord, And let your joys be known, Join in a song with sweet accord, Join in a song with sweet accord, And thus sur-round the throne, And thus surround the throne.

thus surround the throne, And thus surround the throne.

CHORUS.
We're march--ing to Zi-on, Beau-ti-ful, beau-ti-ful Zi-on; We're
We're march-ing on to Zi-on,

marching up-ward to Zi- - -on, The beau-ti-ful cit-y of God.
Zi-on, Zi-on,

Copyright, 1867, by Rev. Robert Lowry.

212 *The heavenly road.*

1 COME, ye that love the Lord,
  And let your joys be known,
  Join in a song with sweet accord,
  Join in a song with sweet accord,
    And thus surround the throne,
    And thus surround the throne. CHO.

2 Let those refuse to sing,
  Who never knew our God;
  But children of the heavenly king,
  But children of the heavenly king,
    May speak their joys abroad,
    May speak their joys abroad. CHO.

3 The hill of Zion yields
  A thousand sacred sweets,
  Before we reach the heavenly fields,
  Before we reach the heavenly fields,
    Or walk the golden streets,
    Or walk the golden streets. CHO.

4 Then let our songs abound,
  And every tear be dry;
  We're marching thro' Immanuel's ground,
  We're marching thro' Immanuel's ground,
    To fairer worlds on high,
    To fairer worlds on high. CHO.
      Isaac Watts.

213 *I love to tell the story.*

2 I love to tell the story;
More wonderful it seems
Than all the golden fancies
Of all our golden dreams.
I love to tell the story,
It did so much for me;
And that is just the reason
I tell it now to thee.

3 I love to tell the story;
'Tis pleasant to repeat
What seems, each time I tell it,
More wonderfully sweet.
I love to tell the story;
For some have never heard
The message of salvation
From God's own holy word.

4 I love to tell the story;
For those who know it best
Seem hungering and thirsting
To hear it like the rest.
And when, in scenes of glory,
I sing the new, new song,
'Twill be the old, old story
That I have loved so long.
                        Catharine Hankey.

SONGS OF THE CHRISTIAN LIFE.

ARLINGTON. C. M.   Thomas Augustine Arne.

1. Am I a soldier of the cross, A follower of the Lamb, And shall I fear to own his cause, Or blush to speak his name?

214 *Faith sees the final triumph.*

2 Are there no foes for me to face?
   Must I not stem the flood?
  Is this vile world a friend to grace,
   To help me on to God?

3 Sure I must fight, if I would reign;
   Increase my courage, Lord;
  I'll bear the toil, endure the pain,
   Supported by thy word.

4 Thy saints in all this glorious war
   Shall conquer, though they die:
  They see the triumph from afar,
   By faith they bring it nigh.

5 When that illustrious day shall rise,
   And all thy armies shine
  In robes of victory through the skies,
   The glory shall be thine.
                     Isaac Watts.

MAITLAND. C. M.   George N. Allen.

1. Must Jesus bear the cross alone, And all the world go free? No, there's a cross for every one, And there's a cross for me.

215 *No cross, no crown.*

2 How happy are the saints above,
   Who once went sorrowing here!
  But now they taste unmingled love,
   And joy without a tear.

3 The consecrated cross I'll bear,
   Till death shall set me free;
  And then go home my crown to wear,
   For there's a crown for me.
                     Thomas Shepherd, alt.

SONGS OF THE CHRISTIAN LIFE.

MY YOUTH IS THINE.
ROBERT THALLON.

1. O God, my youth is thine, With all its mirth and glee, The sweet-est gar-lands love can twine I glad-ly bring to thee. My hap-py, hap-py gold-en days To thee, to thee, O Lord, I give, And strive in all my youth-ful ways, For thee, for thee, a-lone to live.

Copyright, 1885, by Phillips & Hunt

216 *Youth's offering.*

2 In thee I seek my joys;
    Without thee all is drear;
'Tis sweet to hear thy gentle voice,
    And feel thy presence near.
Thine, thine, O Lord, my youthful heart,
    Yea, thine its truest, purest love;
And from thee it shall ne'er depart
    Till called to dwell with thee above.

3 My life—its days, its hours—
    All, Saviour, blest, divine,
My energies and all my powers
    Shall be forever thine.
My off'ring, Lord, is poor and small,
    But fully, freely, gladly given,
'Tis all I have—accept my all,
    And guide, O guide, my steps to heaven.
                  Thomas E. Boach.

SONGS OF THE CHRISTIAN LIFE.

CAN YE NOT WATCH ONE LITTLE HOUR? Geo. C. Stebbins

1. One little hour for watching with the Master, Eternal years to walk with him in white; One little hour to bravely meet disaster, Eternal years to reign with him in light.

CHORUS.
Then souls, be brave, and watch until the morrow! Awake! arise! your lamps of purpose trim; Your Saviour speaks across the night of sorrow; Can ye not watch one little hour with him?

Copyright, 1885, by Phillips & Hunt.

217 *Watching with Jesus.*

2 One little hour to suffer scorn and losses,
   Eternal years beyond earth's cruel frowns;
One little hour to carry heavy crosses,
   Eternal years to wear unfading crowns.
Cho.—Then souls, be brave, and watch until the morrow! &c.

3 One little hour for weary toils and trials,
   Eternal years for calm and peaceful rest;
One little hour for patient self-denials,
   Eternal years of life where life is blest.
Cho.—Then souls, be brave, and watch until the morrow! &c.

Jessie H. Brown.

SONGS OF THE CHRISTIAN LIFE.

SOMETHING FOR JESUS.
Rev. R. Lowry.

1. Saviour! thy dy-ing love Thou gavest me, Nor should I aught withhold. Dear Lord, from thee;
2. At the blest mer-cy-seat, Pleading for me, My fee-ble faith looks up, Je-sus, to thee:

In love my soul would bow, My heart fulfill its vow, Some offering bring thee now, Something for thee.
Help me the cross to bear, Thy wondrous love declare, Some song to raise, or prayer, Something for thee.

Copyright, 1871, by Biglow & Main.

218 *"Lord, what wilt thou have me to do?"*

3 Give me a faithful heart—
　Likeness to thee—
That each departing day
　Henceforth may see
Some work of love begun,
Some deed of kindness done,
Some wand'rer sought and won
　Something for thee.

4 All that I am and have—
　Thy gifts so free,
In joy, in grief, through life,
　Dear Lord, for thee!
And when thy face I see,
My ransomed soul shall be,
Through all eternity,
　Something for thee.

S. D. Phelps.

REVIVE US AGAIN.
J. J. Husband.

1. We praise thee, O God! for the Son of thy love, For Je-sus who died, and is now gone a-bove.

Chorus.

{ Hal-le-lu-jah! Thine the glo-ry; Hal-le-lu-jah! A-men! }
{ Hal-le-lu-jah! Thine the glo-ry; [Omit............] } Re-vive us a-gain.

219 *Thine the Glory.*

2 We praise thee, O God! for thy spirit of light,
　Who has shown us our Saviour and scattered our night.
3 All glory and praise to the Lamb that was slain,
　Who has borne all our sins, and has cleansed every stain.
4 All glory and praise to the God of all grace,
　Who has bought us, and sought us, and guided our ways.
5 Revive us again; fill each heart with thy love;
　May each soul be rekindled with fire from above.

Wm. Paton Mackay.

SONGS OF THE CHRISTIAN LIFE.

EARNESTLY FIGHTING FOR JESUS.
THEODORE WOOD.

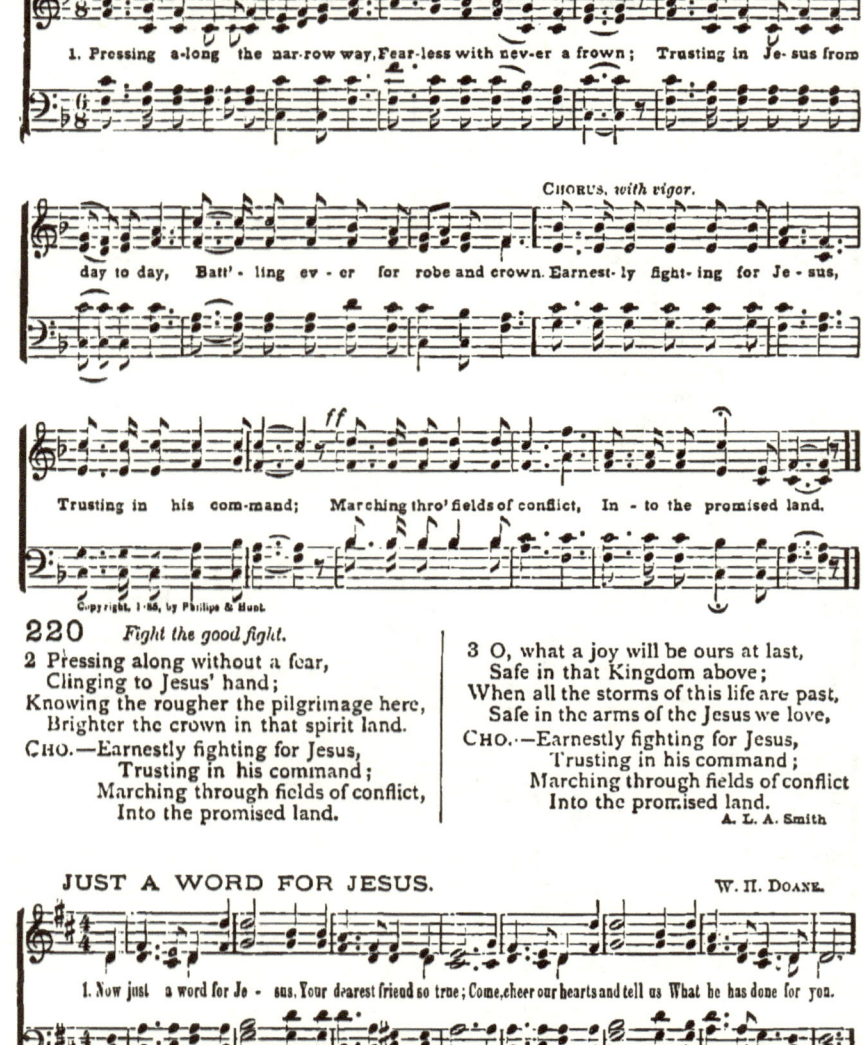

1. Pressing a-long the nar-row way, Fear-less with nev-er a frown; Trusting in Je-sus from day to day, Batt'-ling ev-er for robe and crown. Earnest-ly fight-ing for Je-sus, Trusting in his com-mand; Marching thro' fields of conflict, In-to the promised land.

Copyright, 1-85, by Phillips & Hunt.

220 *Fight the good fight.*

2 Pressing along without a fear,
　Clinging to Jesus' hand;
Knowing the rougher the pilgrimage here,
　Brighter the crown in that spirit land.
CHO.—Earnestly fighting for Jesus,
　　Trusting in his command;
　　Marching through fields of conflict,
　　Into the promised land.

3 O, what a joy will be ours at last,
　Safe in that Kingdom above;
When all the storms of this life are past,
　Safe in the arms of the Jesus we love,
CHO.—Earnestly fighting for Jesus,
　　Trusting in his command;
　　Marching through fields of conflict
　　Into the promised land.
　　　　　　　　　A. L. A. Smith

JUST A WORD FOR JESUS.
W. H. DOANE.

1. Now just a word for Je-sus, Your dearest friend so true; Come, cheer our hearts and tell us What he has done for you.

Copyright, 1878, by Biglow & Main.

SONGS OF THE CHRISTIAN LIFE.

JUST A WORD FOR JESUS.—Concluded.

221 *"Will thou not tell."*

2 Now just a word for Jesus;
 You feel your sins forgiven,
And by his grace are striving
 To reach a home in heaven.—REF.

3 Now just a word for Jesus;
 A cross it cannot be
To say, I love my Saviour
 Who gave his life for me.—REF.

4 Now just a word for Jesus;
 Let not the time be lost;
The heart's neglected duty
 Brings sorrow to its cost.—REF.

5 Now just a word for Jesus;
 And if your faith be dim,
Arise in all your weakness,
 And leave the rest to him.—REF.
                      Fanny J. Crosby.

WHEN THE KING COMES IN.
E. S. LORENZ.

From "Songs of Grace," by per.

222 *The wedding garment.*

2 Crowns on the head where the thorns have been,
 Glorified he who once died for men;
Splendid the vision before us then,
 When the King comes in.—REF.

3 Like lightning's flash will that instant show
Things hidden long from both friend and foe,
Just what we are, every one will know,
 When the King comes in.—REF.

4 Joyful his eyes on each one shall rest
Who is in white wedding garments dressed—
Ah! well for us if we stand the test,
 When the King comes in.—REF.
                      J. E. Landor.

SONGS OF THE CHRISTIAN LIFE.

TAKE UP THE CROSS.
Rev. ROBERT LOWRY.

1. If my dis-ci-ple thou wouldst be, Take up the cross and fol-low me;
Rough tho' the jour-ney, strait the road, This is the way that leads to God;
Free-ly I give my-self for thee; Take up the cross and fol-low me.

REFRAIN.
Take up the cross, Take up the cross, Take up the cross and fol-low me.

Copyright, 1878, by Biglow & Main.

223. *Glorying in the cross.*

2 What if the world reproach thy name?
Take up the cross, despise the shame;
Glory in this, that love divine
Brings thee a ransom, makes thee mine;
Think of the thorns I wore for thee;
Take up the cross and follow me.—REF.

3 Bearing the cross in good or ill,
Trusting the hand that guides thee still,
Soon thou wilt reach the gates of light,
Soon will thy faith be changed to sight;
There is a crown of life for thee;
Take up the cross and follow me.—REF.
Fanny J. Crosby.

BATTLING FOR THE LORD.
T. E. PERKINS, by per.

1. We've list-ed in a ho-ly war, Battling for the Lord! E-ter-nal life, e-

SONGS OF THE CHRISTIAN LIFE.

BATTLING FOR THE LORD.—*Concluded.*

224 *Fight the good fight.*

2 We've girded on our armor bright,
  Battling for the Lord!
Our Captain's word our strength and might,
  Battling for the Lord!—Cho.

3 We'll stand like heroes on the field,
  Battling for the Lord!
And in his strength we'll never yield,
  Battling for the Lord!—Cho.
                    Mrs. M. A. Kidder, alt.

VICTORY. 7.   J. B. CALKIN.

225 *The sure reward.*

2 His no crowns that pass away;
  His no palm that sees decay;
  His the joy that shall not fade;
  His the light that knows no shade.

3 His the home for spirits blest,
  Where he gives them peaceful rest,
  Far above the starry skies,
  In the bliss of Paradise.

4 Here on earth ye can but clasp
  Things that perish in the grasp;
  Lift your hearts then to the skies;
  God himself shall be your prize.

5 Praise we now with saints at rest,
  Father, Son and Spirit blest;
  For his promises are sure,
  His reward shall aye endure.
                    Isaac Williams.

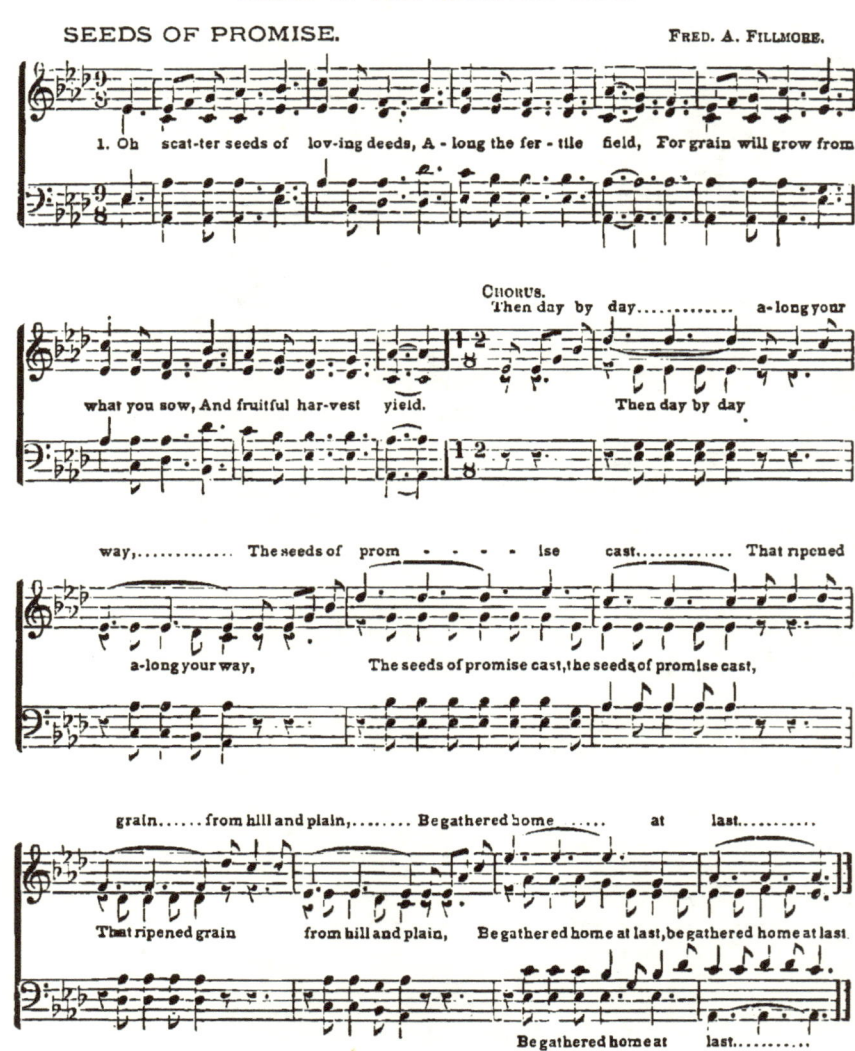

226 *"In the morning sow thy seed."*

2 Tho' sown in tears thro' weary years,
　The seed will surely live;
　Though great the cost it is not lost,
　For God will fruitage give. CHO.

3 The harvest-home of God will come,
　And after toil and care;
　With joy untold your sheaves of gold,
　Will all be garnered there. CHO.

　　　　　　　　　　　　Jessie H. Brown.

SONGS OF THE CHRISTIAN LIFE.

I LOVE TO SING THE STORY.
Rev. S. ALMAN.

1. I love to sing the sto-ry, So precious and so true; It comforts and it gladdens, As noth-ing else can do. In times of deep-est sor-row, When all seems dark and drear; I love to sing the sto-ry It fills my soul with cheer.

CHORUS.
I love to sing the sto-ry, Its joy-ful strains pro-long; I love to sing the sto-ry, The grand old Gos-pel song.

Copyright, 1885, by Phillips & Hunt.

227 *"My tongue shall sing aloud."*

2 I love to sing the story,
  'Tis such a joyful strain;
It tells me of my Saviour,
  All glory to his name.
It helps to keep me faithful,
  To overcome the wrong;
I love to sing the story
  'Tis such a cheerful song.

CHO.—I love to sing the story, &c.

3 I love to sing the story,
  Of Jesus' dying love;
Of pardon and of promise,
  And blessings from above.
When life on earth is ended,
  And here is hushed my song,
In heav'n I'll sing the story
  That here I've sung so long.

CHO.—I love to sing the story, &c.

Samuel Alman.

SONGS OF THE CHRISTIAN LIFE.

WORK SONG. 7, 6, 5.   Lowell Mason.

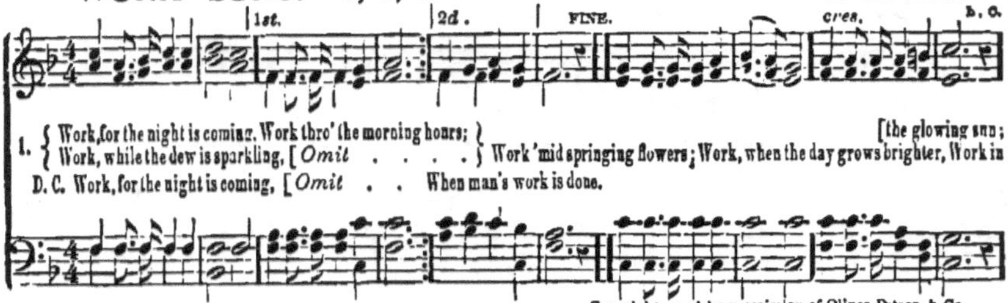

1. Work, for the night is coming, Work thro' the morning hours;
Work, while the dew is sparkling, [*Omit* . . . .] Work 'mid springing flowers; Work, when the day grows brighter, Work in [the glowing sun;
D. C. Work, for the night is coming, [*Omit* . . When man's work is done.

Copyright, used by permission of Oliver Ditson & Co.

228 *Work, while it is day.*

2 Work, for the night is coming,
  Work through the sunny noon;
Fill brightest hours with labor,
  Rest comes sure and soon.
Give every flying minute
  Something to keep in store:
Work, for the night is coming,
  When man works no more.

3 Work, for the night is coming,
  Under the sunset skies;
While their bright tints are glowing,
  Work, for daylight flies.
Work till the last beam fadeth,
  Fadeth to shine no more;
Work while the night is darkening,
  When man's work is o'er.
                  Anna L. Walker.

CALEDONIA. 7, 7, 7, 6.   Scotch.

1. Soldiers of the cross, arise! Lo! your Leader from the skies Waves before you glory's prize, The prize of vic-to-ry.

Seize your armor, gird it on; Now the bat-tle will be won; See, the strife will soon be done; Then struggle manfully.

229 *The spiritual warfare.*

2 Now the fight of faith begin,
Be no more the slaves of sin,
Strive the victor's palm to win,
  Trusting in the Lord:
Gird ye on the armor bright,
Warriors of the King of light,
Never yield, nor lose by flight
  Your divine reward.

3 Jesus conquered when he fell,
Met and vanquished earth and hell;
Now he leads you on to swell
  The triumphs of his cross.

Though all earth and hell appear,
Who will doubt, or who can fear?
God, our strength and shield, is near;
  We cannot lose our cause.

4 Onward, then, ye hosts of God!
Jesus points the victor's rod;
Follow where your Leader trod;
  You soon shall see his face.
Soon, your enemies all slain,
Crowns of glory you shall gain,
Soon you'll join that glorious train
  Who shout their Saviour's praise.
                  Jared B. Waterbury.

SONGS OF THE CHRISTIAN LIFE.

SOME WORK TO DO.   E. C. Phelps.

Copyright 1885, by Phillips & Hunt.

230 *"Lord, what wilt thou have me to do?"*

2 If I may never bear
   Rich sheaves of golden wheat,
I still may glean an humble share,
   To lay at thy dear feet.
And should thy reapers fail,
   Scorched by the noontide heat;
My hands though weak, may then avail
   The harvest to complete.
     Give me some work to do,
     Some work to do.

3 Show me thy will, O Lord,
   What seemeth to thee best,
I'll gladly do, helped by thy word,
   Leaving to thee, the rest,
Thrice happy if at last
   Beneath life's setting sun,
All labor o'er, the harvest past,
   I hear thy sweet " Well done."
     Give me some work to do,
     Some work to do.
             Mrs. Lanta Wilson Smith.

SONGS OF THE CHRISTIAN LIFE.

231 *Fight the good fight.*

1 SOUND the battle-cry!
See! the foe is nigh;
Raise the standard high
　For the Lord;
Gird your armor on,
Stand firm every one;
Rest your cause upon
　His holy word. CHO.

2 Strong to meet the foe,
Marching on we go,
While our cause we know,
　Must prevail;
Shield and banner bright
Gleaming in the light;
Battling for the right
　We ne'er can fail. CHO.

3 Oh! thou God of all,
Hear us when we call,
Help us one and all
　By thy grace;
When the battle's done,
And the vict'ry won,
May we wear the crown
　Before thy face. CHO.
　　　　Wm. F. Sherwin.

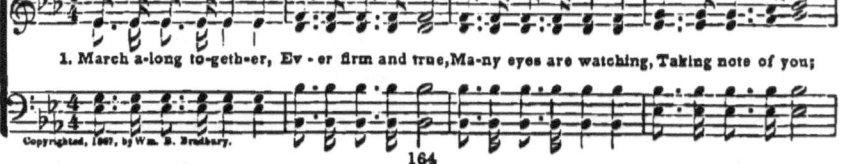

SONGS OF THE CHRISTIAN LIFE.

KEEP TO THE RIGHT.—*Concluded.*

Pleasant winds or foul ones, Cloudy days or bright, Keep to the right, boys, Keep to the right, right.

232 *The conquering army.*

2 Raise on high your banner,
  That its folds may fly
Like the wing of eagle,
  Sweeping to the sky;
If you wish to conquer
  Every foe you fight,
Keep to the right, boys,
  Keep to the right.

3 Of your heavenly Father,
  Strength and courage seek;
Swords are ever worthless,
  If the heart be weak;
Every heart endowing
  With a warrior's might,
Keep to the right, boys,
  Keep to the right.

4 *Love* should be your motto,
  Duty be your aim;
Ever " overcoming,"
  Till a crown you claim;
For a fame undying,
  Strive with all your might,
Keep to the right, boys,
  Keep to the right.
              Josephine Pollard.

STRIKE FOR VICTORY.
W. H. DOANE.

1. Strike! O strike for vic-t'ry Soldiers of the Lord, Hoping in his mer-cy, Trusting in his word;
2. Strike! O strike for vic-t'ry He-roes of the cross, Sac-ri-fic-ing pleasure, Glo-ry-ing in loss;

Lift the gos-pel ban-ner High above the world; Let its folds of beauty Ev-er be un-furl'd.
Ev - er pressing onward, Onward to the light, Till we reach the Jordan, With our home in sight.

CHORUS.
Strike! strike for Vict'ry, Heroes bold; Strike! till the Vict'ry You behold; Strike! strike for Vict'ry, Ne'er give o'er; Rest then in glo-ry Ev - er - more.

Copyright, 1871, by Biglow & Main.

233 *Unfurling the gospel banner.*

3 Hand to hand united,
  Heart to heart as one,
Let us still keep marching
  Till our journey's done,
Till we see the angels
  Come in glory down,
With the shining garments
  And the victor's crown.
              Mrs. Mary A. Kidder.

SONGS OF THE CHRISTIAN LIFE.

WEBB. 7, 6. GEORGE JAMES WEBB.

1. Stand up, stand up for Jesus, Ye soldiers of the cross; Lift high his royal banner, It must not suffer loss: From victory unto victory His army shall he lead, Till every foe is vanquished And Christ is Lord indeed.

234 *Stand up for Jesus.*

2 Stand up, stand up for Jesus,
   Stand in his strength alone;
The arm of flesh will fail you;
   Ye dare not trust your own:
Put on the gospel armor,
   Each piece put on with prayer;
Where duty calls, or danger,
   Be never wanting there.

3 Stand up, stand up for Jesus,
   The strife will not be long;
This day the noise of battle,
   The next the victor's song:
To him that overcometh,
   A crown of life shall be;
He with the King of glory
   Shall reign eternally.
George Duffield, Jr.

COURAGE. 7. HENRY J. GAUNTLETT.

1. Oft in danger, oft in woe, Onward, Christians, onward go: Fight the fight, maintain the strife, Strengthen'd with the bread of life.

235 *Onward march.*

2 Onward, Christians, onward go,
Join the war and face the foe:
Will ye flee in danger's hour?
Know ye not your Captain's power?

3 Let your drooping hearts be glad;
March in heavenly armor clad:

Fight, nor think the battle long,
Victory soon shall tune your song.

4 Onward then in battle move,
More than conquerors ye shall prove:
Though opposed by many a foe,
Christian soldiers, onward go.
Henry Kirke White.

SONGS OF THE CHRISTIAN LIFE.

ONWARD. (Christus Victor.) 6, 5.   Arthur Seymour Sullivan.

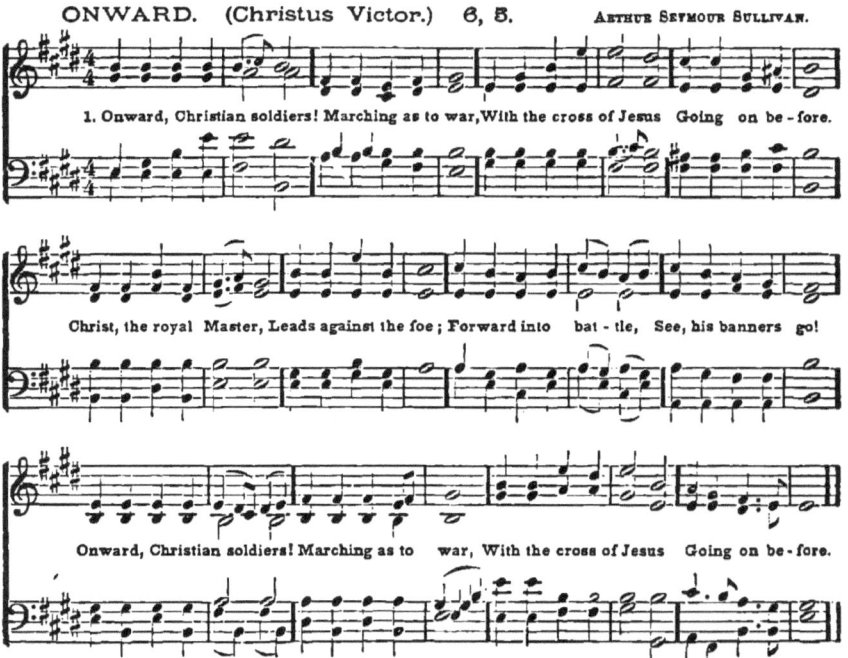

236 *Onward, Christian soldiers.*

1 ONWARD, Christian soldiers!
   Marching as to war,
With the cross of Jesus
   Going on before.
Christ, the royal Master,
   Leads against the foe;
Forward into battle,
   See, his banners go!
      Onward, Christian soldiers!
        Marching as to war,
      With the cross of Jesus
        Going on before.

2 At the sign of triumph
   Satan's host doth flee;
On, then, Christian soldiers,
   On to victory!
Hell's foundations quiver
   At the shout of praise;
Brothers, lift your voices,
   Loud your anthems raise.

3 Like a mighty army
   Moves the Church of God;
Brothers, we are treading
   Where the saints have trod;
We are not divided,
   All one body we,
One in hope and doctrine,
   One in charity.

4 Crowns and thrones may perish,
   Kingdoms rise and wane
But the Church of Jesus
   Constant will remain;
Gates of hell can never
   'Gainst that Church prevail;
We have Christ's own promise,
   And that cannot fail.

5 Onward, then, ye people!
   Join our happy throng,
Blend with ours your voices
   In the triumph-song;
Glory, laud, and honor
   Unto Christ the King,
This through countless ages
   Men and angels sing.
                  Sabine Baring-Gould.

SONGS OF THE CHRISTIAN LIFE.

ELMSWOOD. S. M.   Isaac B. Woodbury.

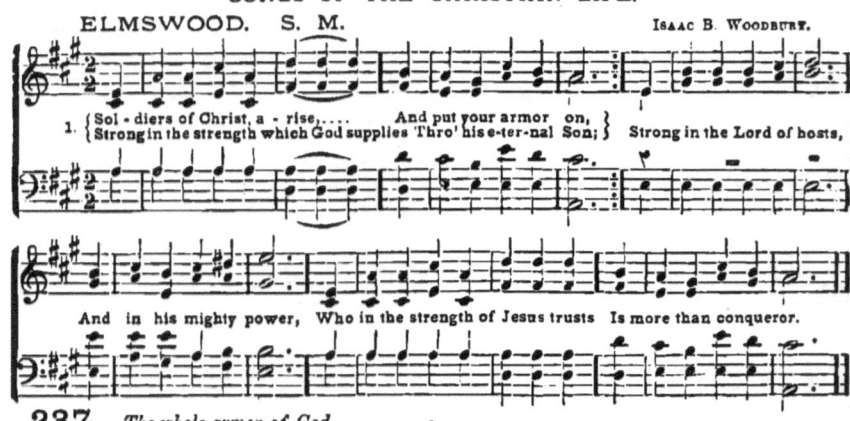

1. Sol-diers of Christ, a-rise,.... And put your armor on,
   Strong in the strength which God supplies Thro' his e-ter-nal Son;
   Strong in the Lord of hosts, And in his mighty power, Who in the strength of Jesus trusts Is more than conqueror.

237   *The whole armor of God.*

2 Stand, then, in his great might,
   With all his strength endued;
But take, to arm you for the fight,
   The panoply of God:
That, having all things done,
   And all your conflicts passed,
Ye may o'ercome through Christ alone,
   And stand entire at last.

3 Leave no unguarded place,
   No weakness of the soul;
Take every virtue, every grace,
   And fortify the whole:
Indissolubly joined,
   To battle all proceed;
But arm yourselves with all the mind
   That was in Christ, your Head.
                      Charles Wesley.

AWAKE, MY SOUL. C. M.   George Frederick Handel.

1. A-wake, my soul, stretch ev-ery nerve, And press with vig-or on; A heavenly race demands thy zeal, And an immortal crown, And an immortal crown.

238   *The race for glory.*

2 A cloud of witnesses around
   Hold thee in full survey;
Forget the steps already trod,
   And onward urge thy way.

3 'Tis God's all-animating voice
   That calls thee from on high;
'Tis his own hand presents the prize
   To thine aspiring eye:—

4 Blest Saviour, introduced by thee,
   Have I my race begun;
And, crowned with victory, at thy feet
   I'll lay my honors down.
                      Philip Doddridge.

SONGS OF THE CHRISTIAN LIFE.

UP FOR JESUS STAND.

Mrs. Joseph F. Knapp.

Copyright, 1851, by Joseph F. Knapp.

239 *Soldiers of the eternal King.*

2 Label it on every door,
  Place it high the pulpit o'er,
Let it stand for evermore!
  Up! for Jesus stand.
Blazon it in mansion halls,
  Pencil it on prison walls;
Do and dare, as duty calls;
  Up! for Jesus stand.

3 Place it on the chiseled stone,
  Where the mourners weep alone;
'Grave it on the monarch's throne!
  Up! for Jesus stand.
Let the press, whose wheels of might
  Roll for reason and for right,
Flash it on the nation's sight;
  Up! for Jesus stand.

J. H.

240 *God in the midst of her.*

2 See, the streams of living waters,
Springing from eternal love,
Still supply thy sons and daughters,
And all fear of want remove:
Who can faint while such a river
Ever flows our thirst to assuage?
Grace, which, like the Lord, the giver,
Never fails from age to age.

3 Round each habitation hovering,
See the cloud and fire appear,
For a glory and a covering,
Showing that the Lord is near!
He who gives us daily manna,
He who listens when we cry,
Let him hear the loud hosanna
Rising to his throne on high.
John Newton.

SONGS OF THE CHURCH.

ST. THOMAS.—Continued.

241 *Love of Zion.*

2 I love thy Church, O God!
  Her walls before thee stand,
Dear as the apple of thine eye,
  And graven on thy hand.

3 For her my tears shall fall,
  For her my prayers ascend;
To her my cares and toils be given,
  Till toils and cares shall end.

4 Beyond my highest joy,
  I prize her heavenly ways,
Her sweet communion, solemn vows,
  Her hymns of love and praise.

5 Sure as thy truth shall last,
  To Zion shall be given
The brightest glories earth can yield,
  And brighter bliss of heaven.
  Timothy Dwight.

GARDEN.   JER. INGALLS.

1. The Lord in-to his garden comes, The spi-ces yield their rich perfumes, The lil-ies grow and thrive; The lil-ies grow and thrive; Re-fresh-ing show'rs of grace di-vine, From Je-sus flow to ev-'ry vine, And make the dead re-vive, And make the dead re-vive.

242 *The Lord's garden.*

2 O that this dry and barren ground,
  In springs of water may abound,—
    A fruitful soil become;
The desert blossoms like the rose,
When Jesus conquers all his foes,
  And makes his people one.

3 Come, brethren, you that love the Lord,
  Who taste the sweetness of his word,
    In Jesus' ways go on;
Our troubles and our trials here,
Will only make us richer there,
  When we arrive at home.
  Anon.

SONGS OF THE CHURCH.

AURELIA. 7, 6, D. SAMUEL SEBASTIAN WESLEY.

1. The Church's one foun-da-tion Is Je-sus Christ her Lord; She is his new cre-a-tion By wa-ter and the word: From heav'n he came and sought her To be his ho-ly bride; With his own blood he bought her, And for her life he died.

243 *The Church his Bride.*

2 Elect from every nation,
  Yet one o'er all the earth,
Her charter of salvation
  One Lord, one faith, one birth;
One Holy Name she blesses,
  Partakes one holy food,
And to one hope she presses,
  With every grace endued.

3 Yet she on earth hath union
  With God the Three in One,
And mystic sweet communion
  With those whose rest is won:
O happy ones and holy!
  Lord, give us grace that we
Like them, the meek and lowly,
  On high may dwell with thee.

Samuel John Stone.

ENDSLEIGH. 7, 6. S. SALVATORI.

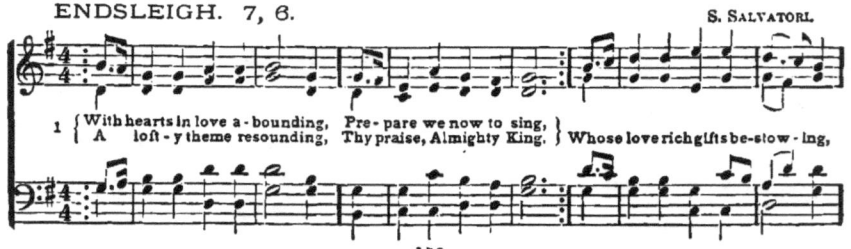

1 { With hearts in love a-bounding, Pre-pare we now to sing, }
  { A-loft-y theme resounding, Thy praise, Almighty King. } Whose love rich gifts be-stow-ing,

SONGS OF THE CHURCH.

ENDSLEIGH.—*Concluded.*

Redeemed the human race; Whose lips with zeal o'er-flow-ing, Breathe words of truth and grace.

244 *The Redeemer's kingdom.*

2 So reign, O God, of Heaven,
  Eternally the same;
And endless praise be given
  To thy Almighty Name.
Clothed in thy dazzling brightness
  Thy Church on earth behold,
In robe of purest whiteness,
  In raiment wrought in gold.

3 And let each Gentile nation
  Come gladly in her train,
To share thy great salvation,
  And join her grateful strain;
Then ne'er shall note of sadness
  Awake the trembling string;
One song of joy and gladness
  The ransomed world shall sing.
  —Harriet Auber.

BLOW THE TRUMPET. WM. J. KIRKPATRICK.

1. Watchman blow the gospel trum-pet, Ev-'ry soul a warning give, Who-so-ev-er hears the message, May repent, and turn and live.

CHORUS. Blow the trumpet, trusty watchman, Blow it loud o'er land and sea;..... God commissions, sound the mes-sage, Ev-'ry cap-tive may be free.

Copyright, 1884, by Wm. J. Kirkpatrick.

245 *The glad tidings.*

Sound it loud o'er ev'ry hill-top,
  Gloomy shade and sunny plain;
Ocean depths repeat the message,
  Full salvation's glad refrain.—CHO.

3 Sound it in the hedge and highway,
  Earth's dark spots where exiles roam,

Let it tell all things are ready,
  Father waits to welcome home.—CHO.

4 Sound it for the heavy-laden,
  Weary, longing to be free;
Sound a Saviour's invitation,
  Sweetly saying, "Come to me."—CHO.
  —H. L. Gilmour.

SONGS OF THE CHURCH.

WEBB. 7, 6.   GEORGE JAMES WEBB.

1. The morning light is breaking; The darkness disappears; The sons of earth are wak-ing To pen-i-tential tears; Each breeze that sweeps the ocean Brings tidings from a-far, Of nations in com-mo-tion, Prepared for Zion's war.

246 *The morning light is breaking.*

2 See heathen nations bending
   Before the God we love,
And thousand hearts ascending
   In gratitude above;
While sinners, now confessing,
   The gospel call obey,
And seek the Saviour's blessing,
   A nation in a day.

3 Blest river of salvation,
   Pursue thine onward way:
Flow thou to every nation,
   Nor in thy richness stay:
Stay not till all the lowly
   Triumphant reach their home:
Stay not till all the holy
   Proclaim, "The Lord is come!"
                        Samuel F. Smith.

MISSIONARY HYMN. 7, 6.   LOWELL MASON.

1. From Greenland's i-cy mountains, From India's cor-al strand; Where Afric's sunny fountains Roll down their gold-en sand; From many an an-cient riv-er, From many a palm-y plain, They call us to de-liv-er Their land from error's chain.

SONGS OF THE CHURCH.

MISSIONARY HYMN.—*Continued.*

247 *Missionary hymn.*

1 FROM Greenland's icy mountains,
 From India's coral strand;
Where Afric's sunny fountains
 Roll down their golden sand;
From many an ancient river,
 From many a palmy plain,
They call us to deliver
 Their land from error's chain.

2 What though the spicy breezes
 Blow soft o'er Ceylon's isle;
Though every prospect pleases,
 And only man is vile?
In vain with lavish kindness
 The gifts of God are strown;
The heathen in his blindness
 Bows down to wood and stone.

3 Shall we, whose souls are lighted
 With wisdom from on high,
Shall we to men benighted
 The lamp of life deny?
Salvation! O salvation!
 The joyful sound proclaim,
Till earth's remotest nation
 Has learned Messiah's name.

4 Waft, waft, ye winds, his story,
 And you, ye waters, roll,
Till, like a sea of glory,
 It spreads from pole to pole:
Till o'er our ransomed nature
 The Lamb for sinners slain,
Redeemer, King, Creator,
 In bliss returns to reign.
  Reginald Heber.

OVER THE OCEAN WAVE.
WILLIAM B. BRADBURY.

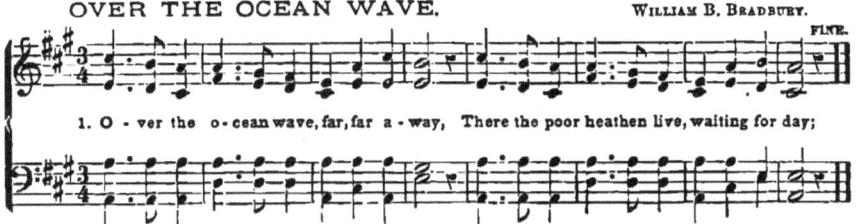

1. O-ver the o-cean wave, far, far a-way, There the poor heathen live, waiting for day;

CHO.—Pit-y them, pit-y them, Christians at home, Haste with the bread of life, hasten and come.

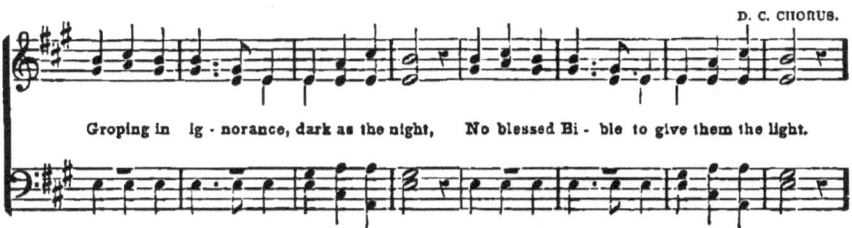

Groping in ig-norance, dark as the night, No blessed Bi-ble to give them the light.

248 *"The heathen for thine inheritance."*

2 Here in this happy land we have the light
 Shining from God's own word, free, pure, and bright;
Shall we not send to them Bibles to read,
 Teachers, and preachers, and all that they need?
  Pity them, pity them, Christians at home,
   Haste with the bread of life, hasten and come.

3 Then, while the mission ships glad tidings bring,
 List! as that heathen band joyfully sing,
"Over the ocean wave, O, see them come,
 Bringing the bread of life, guiding us home."
  Pity them, pity them, Christians at home,
   Haste with the bread of life, hasten and come.
     Anon.

SONGS OF THE CHURCH.

JESUS SHALL REIGN. L. M.
Karl Wilhelm, arr.

1. Jesus shall reign where'er the sun
Does his successive journeys run;
His kingdom spread from shore to shore,
Till moons shall wax and wane no more.

From north to south the princes meet,
To pay their homage at his feet;
While western empires own their Lord,
And savage tribes attend his word.

249 *Christ's all-embracing empire.*

2 To him shall endless prayer be made,
And endless praises crown his head;
His name like sweet perfume shall rise
With every morning sacrifice.

People and realms of every tongue
Dwell on his love with sweetest song,
And infant voices shall proclaim
Their early blessings on his name.
— *Isaac Watts.*

MISSIONARY CHANT. L. M.
Heinrich Christopher Zeuner.

1. Jesus shall reign where'er the sun Does his successive journeys run; His kingdom spread from shore to shore, Till moons shall wax and wane so

[more.

SONGS OF THE CHURCH.

ARISE, GO FORTH TO CONQUER.
HUBERT P. MAIN.

1. A-rise, go forth to con-quer, Young champions for the Lord; Fling out the roy-al standard, Unsheath the mighty sword; The church that sword has wielded In many a dreadful fray, Till Satan's ar-my trembled, And, vanquished, fled a-way. *CHORUS.* A-rise, go forth to con-quer, Young champions for the Lord; Fling out the roy-al stan-dard, Unsheath the might-y sword.

Copyright, 1878, by Biglow & Main.

250 *Young recruits.*

2 Go forth, go forth, young soldiers,
  The grand old cause defend;
Take up the cross and bear it,
  Be faithful to the end;
Go forth to fill their places,
  Whose work is almost done,
Whose course is well-nigh finished,
  Whose crowns are nearly won.
    Arise, go forth, &c.

3 O swell our ranks, young soldiers,
  And, by our Captain led,
From conquering still to conquer,
  March on with fearless tread;
Fight manfully and bravely,
  We'll die with sword in hand,
And leave, for those who follow,
  Our foot-prints in the sand.
    Arise, go forth, &c.

Grace J. Frances.

SONGS OF THE CHURCH.

CHURCH RALLYING SONG.

Jno. R. Sweney

1. A-wake! a-wake! the Master now is calling us, A-rise! a-rise! and trusting in his word, Go forth, go forth! proclaim the year of ju-bi-lee. And take the cross, the bless-ed cross, of Christ our Lord.

CHORUS.

On, on, swell the cho-rus; On, on, the morning-star is shining o'er us; On, on, while before us Our mighty, mighty Saviour leads the way: { Glory, glo-ry, hear the everlasting throng } { Shout hosanna, while we boldly march along; } Faithful soldiers here below, On-ly Je-sus will we know, Shouting "free salvation" o'er the world, we go

On, on, on, swell the chorus, On, on, on, On, on, on, while before, leads the way,

Copyright, 1882, by John J. Hood.

SONGS OF THE CHURCH.

CHURCH RALLYING SONG.—*Concluded.*
251   *Soldiers of the cross.*

2 A cry for light from dying ones in heathen lands:
   It comes, it comes across the ocean's foam;
Then haste, oh, haste to spread the words of truth abroad,
   Forgetting not the starving poor at home, dear home.—CHO.

3 O church of God, extend thy kind maternal arms
   To save the lost on mountains dark and cold,
Reach out thy hand with loving smile to rescue them,
   And bring them to the shelter of the Saviour's fold.—CHO.

4 Look up! look up! the promised day is drawing near,
   When all shall hail, shall hail the Saviour King,
When peace and joy shall fold their wings in every clime,
   And "Glory, hallelujah," o'er the earth shall ring.—CHO.
Fanny J. Crosby.

STAND UP FOR JESUS.   ASA HULL, by per.

1. Stand up for Je-sus, Christian stand! Firm as a rock on o-cean's strand!
Beat back the waves of sin that roll, Like rag-ing floods, a-round thy soul.

CHORUS.
Stand up for Je-sus, no-bly stand! Firm as a rock on o-cean's strand!
Stand up, his righteous cause de-fend; Stand up for Je-sus your best friend.

Copyright 1864, by ASA HULL.

252   *Work and warfare.*

2 Stand up for Jesus, Christian stand!
Sound forth his name o'er sea and land!
Spread ye his glorious word abroad,
Till all the world shall own him Lord!

3 Stand up for Jesus, Christian stand!
Soon with the blest immortal band
We'll dwell for aye, life's journey o'er
In realms of light on heaven's bright shore.
B. Torrey, Jr.

SONGS OF THE CHURCH.

RESCUE THE PERISHING.
W. H. DOANE.

1 Rescue the perishing, Care for the dying, Snatch them in pity from sin and the grave; Weep o'er the erring one, Lift up the fallen, Tell them of Jesus the mighty to save.

CHORUS. Rescue the perishing, Care for the dying; Jesus is merciful, Jesus will save.

Copyright, 1870, by W. H. Doane, in Songs of Devotion.

253 *"Compel them to come in."*

2 Though they are slighting him,
   Still he is waiting,
Waiting the penitent child to receive,
   Plead with them earnestly,
   Plead with them gently:
He will forgive if they only believe.

3 Down in the human heart,
   Crushed by the tempter,
Feelings lie buried that grace can restore:

Touched by a loving heart,
   Wakened by kindness,
Chords that were broken will vibrate once more.

4 Rescue the perishing,
   Duty demands it;
Strength for thy labor the Lord will provide:
   Back to the narrow way
   Patiently win them;
Tell the poor wanderer a Saviour has died.

Fanny J. Crosby.

SONGS OF THE CHURCH.

254 *Work for all.*

2 To the work! to the work! let the hungry be fed;
To the fountain of Life let the weary be led;
In the cross and its banner our glory shall be
While we herald the tidings, "*Salvation is free!*"—Cho.

3 To the work! to the work! there is labor for all,
For the kingdom of darkness and error shall fall;
And the name of Jehovah exalted shall be
In the loud swelling chorus, "*Salvation is free!*"—Cho.

4 To the work! to the work! in the strength of the Lord,
And a robe and a crown shall our labor reward;
When the home of the faithful our dwelling shall be,
And we shout with the ransomed "*Salvation is free!*"—Cho.

Fanny J. Crosby.

SONGS OF THE CHURCH.

THE CALL FOR REAPERS. J. B. O. CLEMM.

1. Far and near the fields are teem-ing, With the waves of rip-ened grain;
Far and near their gold is gleam-ing, O'er the sun-ny slope and plain.

CHORUS.
Lord of Har-vest, send forth reap-ers! Hear us, Lord, to thee we cry;
Send them now the sheaves to gath-er, Ere the har-vest time pass by.

Copyright, 1885, by Phillips & Hunt.

255 *"The harvest is great."*

2 Send them forth with morn's first beaming,
 Send them in the noontide's glare;
 When the sun's last rays are gleaming,
 Bid them gather everywhere.
  CHO.—Lord of Harvest, &c.

3 O thou, whom thy Lord is sending,
 Gather now the sheaves of gold,
 Heavenward then at evening wending
 Thou shalt come with joy untold.
  CHO.—Lord of Harvest, &c. J. O. Thompson.

SONGS OF THE CHURCH.

256 *"Compel them to come in."*

1 GATHER them in for there yet is room,
　At the feast that a King has spread,
O gather them in, let his house be filled,
　And the hungry and poor be fed.
CH. Out in the highway, out in the by way,
　　Out in the dark depths of sin,
　Go forth! go forth with a loving heart,
　　And gather the wand'rers in.

2 Gather them in for there yet is room,
　But our hearts how they throb with pain,
To think of the many who slight the call,
　That may never be heard again.
CH. Out in the highway, out in the by way,
　　Out in the dark depths of sin,
　Go forth! go forth with a loving heart,
　　And gather the wand'rers in.

3 Gather them in for there yet is room,
　'Tis a message from God above,
O gather them in to the fold of grace,
　And the arms of the Saviour's love.
CH. Out in the highway, out in the by way,
　　Out in the dark depths of sin,
　Go forth! go forth with a loving heart,
　　And gather the wand'rers in.

　　　　　　　　　　　Fanny J. Crosby.

SONGS OF THE CHURCH.

257   *The Lord is King.*

3 Tell it out among the people, Jesus reigns above;
   Tell it out! Tell it out!
Tell it out among the nations that his reign is love;
   Tell it out! Tell it out!
Tell it out among the highways and the lanes at home,
Let it ring across the mountains and the ocean's foam,
That the weary, heavy-laden, need no longer roam;
   Tell it out! Tell it out!

Frances R. Havergal.

SONGS OF THE CHURCH.

FINAL VICTORY.
W. F. Sherwin.

1. When that glorious morn shall come, Long foretold by prophets old,
When the church shall be call'd home, Saints shall stand with courage bold;
All who then on Christ believe— Safely gather'd at his side—
Shall the crown of life receive— Ever with their Lord abide.—

Copyright, 1885, by Phillips & Hunt.

258 *The church triumphant.*

2 All their warfare now is o'er,
   All their foes are left behind;
Safe on Canaan's peaceful shore—
   Rest eternal they shall find,
No more wand'rings to and fro,
   In the wilderness of sin;
No more pain or earthly woe,
   When their heavenly joys begin

3 See! the everlasting doors
   Lift their shining portals high;
Light divine, effulgent pours,
   As the banner'd host draws nigh;
Shouts of joyous welcome rise,
   From the arch angelic throng,
Hallelujahs rend the skies,
   While the saints awake the song.—

4 Unto him who hath redeem'd,
   Wash'd us in his precious blood,
Sav'd us from a world of sin
   Made us kings, and priests to God—
Unto him the praise belongs,
   Unto him all glory be,
Unto Christ, our choicest songs
   We will raise eternally.
                 W. Bennett.

SONGS OF THE CHURCH.

DENNIS. S. M. — Hans Georg Nägeli

1. Blest be the tie that binds Our hearts in Christian love; The fellowship of kindred minds Is like to that above.

259 *Sympathy and mutual love.*

2 Before our Father's throne,
  We pour our ardent prayers;
Our fears, our hopes, our aims are one,
  Our comforts and our cares.

3 We share our mutual woes,
  Our mutual burdens bear;
And often for each other flows
  The sympathizing tear.

4 When we asunder part,
  It gives us inward pain;
But we shall still be joined in heart,
  And hope to meet again.
  —John Fawcett.

NUREMBERG. 7. — Johann Rudolf Ahle

1. Glory be to God above, God, from whom all blessings flow; Make we mention of his love, Publish we his praise below:

260 *Sweet counsel.*

2 Called together by his grace,
  We are met in Jesus' name;
See with joy each other's face,
  Foll'wers of the bleeding Lamb.

3 Build we each the other up;
  Pray we for our faith's increase;
Solid comfort, settled hope,
  Constant joy, and lasting peace.

4 More and more let love abound;
  Let us never, never rest,
Till we are in Jesus found,
  Of our paradise possessed.
  —Charles Wesley.

SONGS OF HEAVEN.

HEAVEN IS MY HOME. 6,4.
ARTHUR SEYMOUR SULLIVAN.

1. I'm but a stranger here, Heaven is my home; Earth is a desert drear, Heaven is my home.
Danger and sorrow stand Round me on every hand, Heaven is my father-land, Heaven is my home.

261 *The Christian's Fatherland.*

1 I'M but a stranger here,
Heaven is my home;
Earth is a desert drear,
Heaven is my home.
Danger and sorrow stand,
Round me on every hand,
Heaven is my fatherland,
Heaven is my home.

2 What though the tempest rage,
Heaven is my home;
Short is my pilgrimage,
Heaven is my home.

Time's cold and wintry blast,
Soon will be overpast,
I shall reach home at last,
Heaven is my home.

3 There at my Saviour's side,
Heaven is my home;
I shall be glorified,
Heaven is my home.
There are the good and blest,
Those I loved most and best,
There, too, I soon shall rest,
Heaven is my home.

Thos. R. Taylor, alt.

[SECOND TUNE.]

OAK. 6, 4.
LOWELL MASON.

1. I'm but a stranger here, Heaven is my home; Earth is a des-ert drear, Heaven is my home.
Danger and sorrow stand Round me on every hand, Heaven is my father-land, Heaven is my home.

Copyright. Used by per. of O. Ditson & Co.

SONGS OF HEAVEN.

SHINING SHORE.
Geo. F. Root.

1. My days are gliding swiftly by, And I, a pilgrim stranger,
Would not detain them as they fly, Those hours of toil and danger.

REFRAIN.
For, oh, we stand on Jordan's strand, Our friends are passing over;
And, just before the shining shore We may almost discover!

Copyright by O. Ditson & Co.

262 *The rest of Heaven.*

2 We'll gird our loins, my brethren dear,
Our heavenly home discerning;
Our absent Lord has sent us word,
Let every lamp be burning.—Ref.

3 Should coming days be cold and dark,
We need not cease our singing;
That perfect rest naught can molest,
Where golden harps are ringing.—Ref.

4 Let sorrow's rudest tempest blow,
Each cord on earth to sever;
Our King says, "Come," and there's our [home
Forever, oh, forever.—Ref.

David Nelson.

I'M A PILGRIM.
"Buona Notte," Italian Melody.

1. I'm a pilgrim, and I'm a stranger: I can tarry, I can tarry but a night.

SONGS OF HEAVEN.

263 *Longing for Heaven.*

2 There the sunbeams are ever shining,
Oh, my longing heart, my longing heart is there.
Here in this country so dark and dreary,
I long have wandered forlorn and weary.
  CHO.—I'm a pilgrim.

3 Of that country to which I'm going,
My Redeemer, my Redeemer is the light:
There is no sorrow, nor any sighing,
Nor any sin there, nor any dying.
  CHO.—I'm a pilgrim.
    Mrs. Mary S. B. D. Shindler.

264 *Heavenly rest anticipated.*

2 Should earth against my soul engage,
  And fiery darts be hurled,
Then I can smile at Satan's rage,
  And face a frowning world.

3 Let cares like a wild deluge come,
  Let storms of sorrow fall,
So I but safely reach my home,
  My God, my heaven, my all.

4 There I shall bathe my weary soul
  In seas of heavenly rest,
And not a wave of trouble roll
  Across my peaceful breast.
    Isaac Watts.

SONGS OF HEAVEN.

ALIDA. C. M. Double. — D. B. THOMPSON.

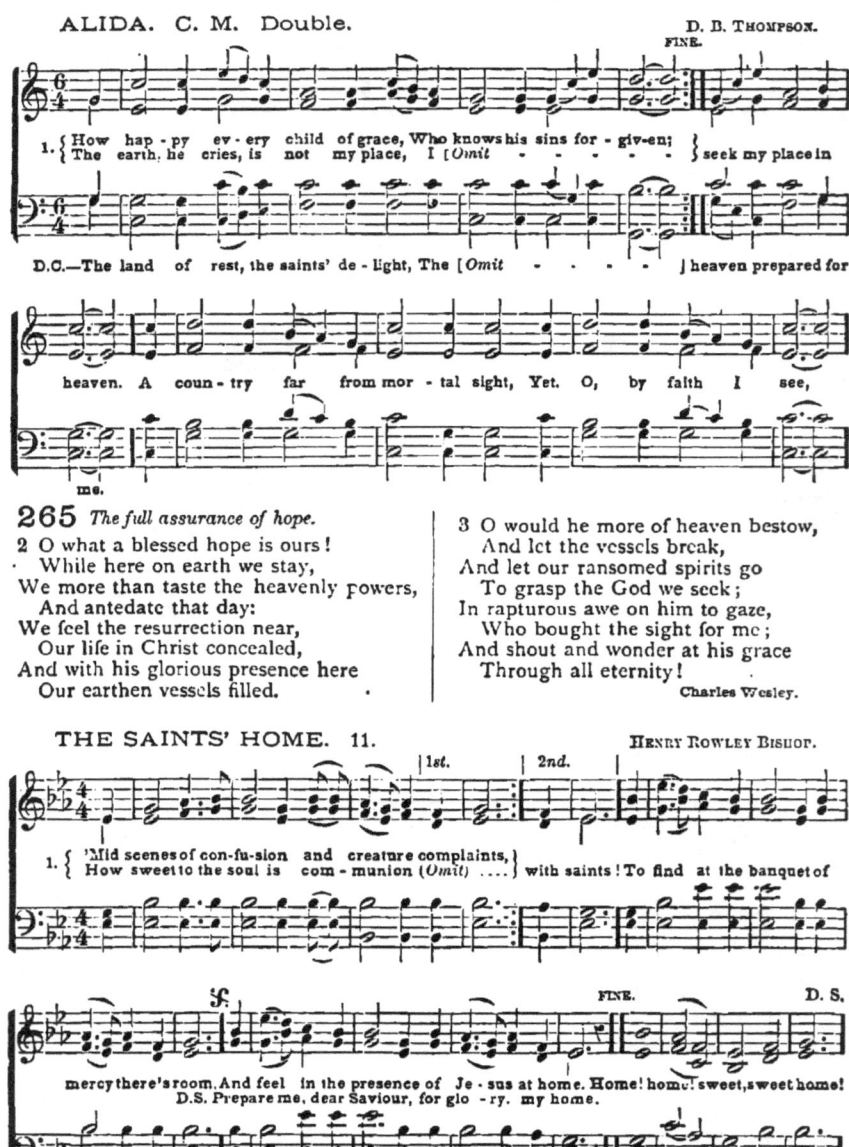

1. { How hap-py ev-ery child of grace, Who knows his sins for-giv-en;
     The earth, he cries, is not my place, I [Omit ......] seek my place in

D.C.—The land of rest, the saints' de-light, The [Omit ......] heaven prepared for

heaven. A coun-try far from mor-tal sight, Yet, O, by faith I see,

me.

265 *The full assurance of hope.*

2 O what a blessed hope is ours!
   While here on earth we stay,
We more than taste the heavenly powers,
   And antedate that day:
We feel the resurrection near,
   Our life in Christ concealed,
And with his glorious presence here
   Our earthen vessels filled.

3 O would he more of heaven bestow,
   And let the vessels break,
And let our ransomed spirits go
   To grasp the God we seek;
In rapturous awe on him to gaze,
   Who bought the sight for me;
And shout and wonder at his grace
   Through all eternity!

— Charles Wesley.

THE SAINTS' HOME. 11. — HENRY ROWLEY BISHOP.

1. { 'Mid scenes of con-fu-sion and creature complaints,
     How sweet to the soul is com-munion (Omit) .... with saints! To find at the banquet of

mercy there's room, And feel in the presence of Je-sus at home. Home! home! sweet, sweet home!
D.S. Prepare me, dear Saviour, for glo-ry. my home.

SONGS OF HEAVEN.

THE SAINTS HOME.—*Continued.*

266 *Home! home! sweet, sweet home.*
2 Sweet bonds that unite all the children of peace!
And, thrice precious Jesus, whose love can-[not cease,
Though oft from thy presence in sadness I roam,
I long to behold thee in glory, at home.
3 I sigh from this body of sin to be free,
Which hinders my joy and communion with thee;
Though now my temptation like billows [may foam,
All, all will be peace, when I'm with thee at home.

4 While here in the valley of conflict I stay,
O give me submission, and strength as my day;
In all my afflictions to thee would I come,
Rejoicing in hope of my glorious home.
5 I long, dearest Lord, in thy beauties to shine;
No more as an exile in sorrow to pine;
And in thy dear image arise from the tomb,
With glorified millions to praise thee at home.
David Denham.

WELCOME TO GLORY. — Mrs. Joseph F. Knapp.

1. O, when I shall sweep thro' the gates! The scenes of mor-tal-i-ty o'er,
   What then for my spir-it a-waits? Will they sing on the glo-ri-fied shore?

CHORUS.
Wel-come home! wel-come home! A wel-come in glo-ry for me;
Welcome home! welcome home!
Welcome home! welcome home! A welcome for me!
Welcome home! welcome home! welcome home!
Copyright, 1872, by Joseph F. Knapp.

267 *Welcome to glory.*
2 And when from earth's cares I arise,
And pass through the portals above,
Will shouts, Welcome home to the skies!
Resound through the regions of love?
Welcome home! etc.

3 Yes! loved ones who knew me below,
Who learned the new song with me here,
In chorus will hail me, I know,
And welcome me home with good cheer!
Welcome home! etc.

4 The beautiful gates will unfold,
The home of the blood-washed I'll see;
The city of saints I'll behold!
For, O! there's a welcome for me!
Welcome home! etc.

5 A sinner made whiter than snow,
I'll join in the mighty acclaim,
And shout through the gates as I go,
Salvation to God and the Lamb!
Welcome home! etc.
Phœbe Palmer.

SONGS OF HEAVEN.

FREDERICK. 11, or 13, 11, 12. GEORGE KINGSLEY.

268 *I would not live always.*

1 I WOULD not live alway; I ask not to stay
Where storm after storm rises dark o'er the way:
The few lurid mornings that dawn on us here
Are enough for life's woes, full enough for its cheer.

2 I would not live alway; no, welcome the tomb!
Since Jesus hath lain there, I dread not its gloom;
There sweet be my rest till he bid me arise,
To hail him in triumph descending the skies.

3 Who, who would live alway, away from his God;
Away from yon heaven, that blissful abode,
Where the rivers of pleasure flow o'er the bright plains,
And the noontide of glory eternally reigns?

4 Where the saints of all ages in harmony meet,
Their Saviour and brethren transported to greet;
While the anthems of rapture unceasingly roll,
And the smile of the Lord is the feast of the soul.

William A. Muhlenberg.

EXHORTATION. C. M. S. HIBBARD, 1803.

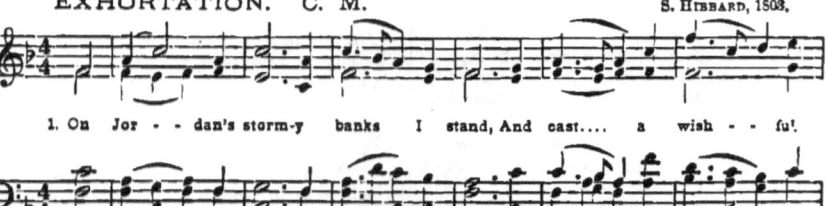

SONGS OF HEAVEN.

EXHORTATION.—*Concluded.*

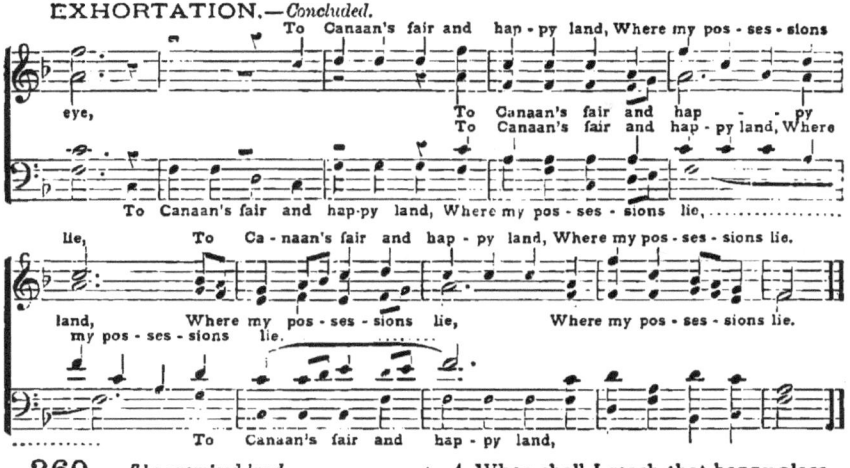

269 *The promised land.*

2 O the transporting, rapturous scene,
  That rises to my sight!
Sweet fields arrayed in living green,
  And rivers of delight.

3 O'er all those wide extended plains
  Shines one eternal day;
There God the Son forever reigns,
  And scatters night away.

4 When shall I reach that happy place,
  And be forever blest?
When shall I see my Father's face,
  And in his bosom rest?

5 Filled with delight, my raptured soul
  Would here no longer stay:
Though Jordan's waves around me roll,
  Fearless I'd launch away.
      Samuel Stennett.

VARINA. C. M.   Geo. F. Root. (1849.)

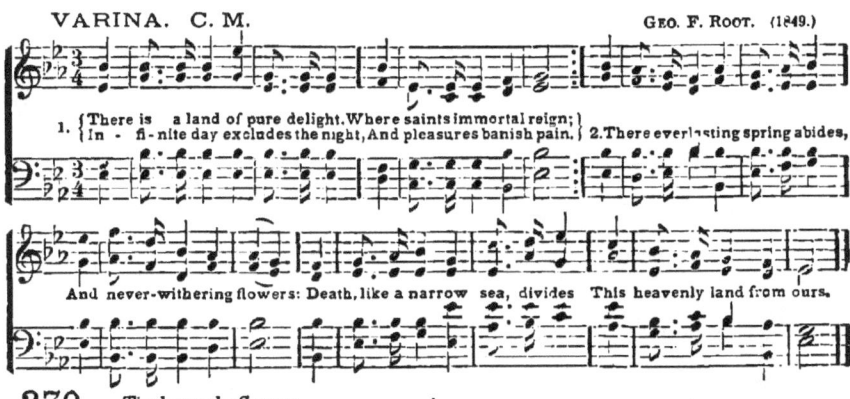

270 *The heavenly Canaan.*

3 Sweet fields beyond the swelling flood,
  Stand dressed in living green;
So to the Jews old Canaan stood,
  While Jordan rolled between.

4 Could we but climb where Moses stood,
  And view the landscape o'er,
Not Jordan's stream, nor death's cold flood,
  Should fright us from the shore.
      Isaac Watts.

SONGS OF HEAVEN.

JERUSALEM THE GOLDEN. 7, 6. — Alexander Ewing

271 *The home of God's elect.*

1 JERUSALEM the golden,
  With milk and honey blest,
Beneath thy contemplation
  Sink heart and voice opprest:
I know not, O I know not
  What joys await us there;
What radiancy of glory,
  What light beyond compare.

2 They stand, those halls of Zion,
  All jubilant with song,
And bright with many an angel,
  And all the martyr throng:
The Prince is ever in them,
  The daylight is serene,
The pastures of the blessed
  Are decked in glorious sheen.

3 There is the throne of David;
  And there, from care released,
The song of them that triumph,
  The shout of them that feast;
And they who, with their Leader,
  Have conquered in the fight,
Forever and forever
  Are clad in robes of white.

4 O sweet and blessed country,
  The home of God's elect!
O sweet and blessed country
  That eager hearts expect!
Jesus, in mercy bring us
  To that dear land of rest;
Who art, with God the Father,
  And Spirit, ever blest.

Bernard of Cluny. Tr. by J. M. Neale.

SONGS OF HEAVEN.

SHALL WE GATHER AT THE RIVER? Rev. R. Lowry, by per.

272 *The river of salvation.*

2 On the margin of the river,
   Washing up its silver spray,
We will walk and worship ever,
   All the happy golden day.
CHO.—Yes, we'll gather at the river, &c.

3 Ere we reach the shining river,
   Lay we every burden down;
Grace our spirits will deliver,
   And provide a robe and crown.
CHO.—Yes, we'll gather at the river, &c.

4 At the smiling of the river,
   Mirror of the Saviour's face,
Saints whom death will never sever
   Lift their songs of saving grace.
CHO.—Yes, we'll gather at the river, &c.

5 Soon we'll reach the silver river,
   Soon our pilgrimage will cease;
Soon our happy hearts will quiver
   With the melody of peace.
CHO.—Yes, we'll gather at the river, &c.
                            Robert Lowry.

SONGS OF HEAVEN.

WE SHALL MEET.

HUBERT P. MAIN, by per.

1. We shall meet be-yond the riv-er, By and by, by and by;
And the dark-ness shall be o-ver, By and by, by and by;
With the toil-some jour-ney done, And the glo-rious bat-tle won,
We shall shine forth as the sun, By and by, by and by.

Copyright, 1869, by Hubert P. Main.

273   *By and by.*

2 We shall strike the harps of glory,
  By and by, by and by;
We shall sing redemption's story,
  By and by, by and by;
And the strains for evermore
Shall resound in sweetness o'er
Yonder everlasting shore,
  By and by, by and by.

3 We shall see and be like Jesus,
  By and by, by and by;
Who a crown of life will give us,
  By and by, by and by;

And the angels who fulfil
All the mandates of his will
Shall attend, and love us still,
  By and by, by and by.

4 Wearing robes of snowy whiteness,
  By and by, by and by;
And with crowns of dazzling brightness,
  By and by, by and by;
Then, our storms and perils passed,
And with glory ours at last,
We'll possess the kingdom vast,
  By and by, by and by.

Rev. John Atkinson D. D., alt.

SONGS OF HEAVEN.

WHAT A MEETING THAT WILL BE!
THEODORE WOOD.

274 *The reunion of heaven.*

2 When we all meet at home in the morning,
And from sorrow forever be free;
When we join in the song of the ransom'd,
What a gath'ring indeed that will be!
CHO.—Gather'd home, gather'd home,
  On the shore of that bright crystal sea;
  Gather'd home, gather'd home,
  With our lov'd ones forever to be.

3 When we all meet at home in the morning,
With our blessed Redeemer to be;
When we know and are known by our lov'd
What a meeting indeed that will be! [ones,
CHO.—Gather'd home, gather'd home,
  On the shore of that bright crystal sea;
  Gather'd home, gather'd home,
  With our lov'd ones forever to be.
                        T. Wood.

SONGS OF HEAVEN.

SHALL WE KNOW EACH OTHER?—*Concluded.*

275 *"Then shall I know."*

2 When the holy angels meet us,
 As we go to join their band,
Shall we know the friends that greet us,
 In the glorious spirit land?
Shall we see the same eyes shining,
 On us, as in days of yore?
Shall we feel their dear arms twining
 Fondly round us as before?—CHO.

3 O ye weary, sad, and toss'd ones,
 Droop not, faint not by the way;
Ye shall join the loved and just ones
 In the land of perfect day!
Harp-strings touched by angel fingers,
 Murmured in my raptured ear,
Evermore their sweet song lingers,
 "We shall know each other there."—CHO.
   —Anon.

BEULAH LAND. JNO. R. SWENEY, by per.

1. I've reach'd the land of corn and wine, And all its rich-es freely mine; Here shines undimm'd one
2. The Saviour comes and walks with me, And sweet communion here have we; He gently leads me

bliss-ful day, For all my night has pass'd a-way. O Beu-lah land, sweet Beu-lah land, As
with his hand, For this is heaven's bor-der land.

on thy high-est mount I stand, I look a-way across the sea, Where mansions are prepared for me,

And view the shining glo ry shore, My heav'n, my home for-ev-er-more.

276 *"Sorrow and sighing shall flee away."*

3 A sweet perfume upon the breeze,
 Is borne from ever vernal trees,
 And flow'rs that never fading grow
 Where streams of life forever flow.—CHO.

4 The zephyrs seem to float to me,
 Sweet sounds of heaven's melody,
 As angels, with the white-robed throng,
 Join in the sweet redemption song.—CHO.
   —Edgar Page Stites.

SONGS OF HEAVEN.

SWEET BY-AND-BY.

Jos. P. Webster.

1. There's a land that is fair-er than day, And by faith we can see it a-far; For the Fa-ther waits o-ver the way, To pre-pare us a dwell-ing place there.

CHORUS.
In the sweet by-and-by, We shall meet on that beau-ti-ful shore, In the sweet by-and-by, We shall meet on that beau-ti-ful shore.

277 *The Christian's home.*

2 We shall sing on that beautiful shore
  The melodious songs of the blest,
And our spirits shall sorrow no more,
  Not a sigh for the blessing of rest.
    Cho.—In the sweet, &c.

3 To our bountiful Father above,
  We will offer our tribute of praise.
For the glorious gift of his love,
  And the blessings that hallow our days
    Cho.—In the sweet, &c.

S. Fillmore Bennett.

SONGS OF HEAVEN.

ANGELS' SONG. 11, 10. JOHN BACCHUS DYKES.

1. Hark, hark, my soul! angelic songs are swelling O'er earth's green fields and ocean's wave-beat shore:
How sweet the truth those blessed strains are telling Of that new life when sin shall be no more!

CHORUS.
Angels of Jesus, angels of light, Singing to welcome the pilgrims of the night! Singing to welcome the pilgrims, the pilgrims of the night!

278 *The night is far spent, the day is at hand.*
Rom. 13: 12.

2 Onward we go, for still we hear them singing,
"Come, weary souls, for Jesus bids you come;"
And through the dark, its echoes sweetly ringing,
The music of the gospel leads us home.

3 Far, far away, like bells at evening pealing,
The voice of Jesus sounds o'er land and sea,
And laden souls by thousands, meekly stealing,
Kind Shepherd, turn their weary steps to thee.

4 Rest comes at length, though life be long and dreary;
The day must dawn, and darksome night be past;
All journeys end in welcome to the weary,
And heaven, the heart's true home, will come at last.

5 Angels, sing on! your faithful watches keeping;
Sing us sweet fragments of the songs above;
Till morning's joy shall end the night of weeping,
And life's long shadows break in cloudless love.

Frederick W. Faber.

SONGS FOR THE LITTLE ONES.

FATHER, LEAD THY LITTLE CHILDREN.
W. H. Doane.

1. Father, lead thy lit-tle children Ver-y ear-ly to thy throne; We will have no gods before thee;
D. S. We will have no gods before thee;

Thou art God, and thou a-lone.
Thou art God, and thou a-lone. Lead, O lead thy lit-tle chil-dren Ver-y ear-ly to thy throne;

Copyright, 1882, by Biglow & Main.

279 *The first Commandment.*

2 In the Bible thou hast taught us
All our thoughts to thee are known;
Thou canst see us in the darkness;
Thou art God, and thou alone.—REF.

3 Though the heathen bow to idols
They have made of wood and stone,
We have Christian friends to tell us
Thou art God, and thou alone.—REF.

4 Thou dost give us all our comforts,
Everything we call our own
Comes from thee, our Heavenly Father;
Thou art God, and thou alone.—REF.

Fanny J. Crosby.

JESUS LOVES ME.
Wm. B. Bradbury.

1. Jesus loves me! this I know, For the Bible tells me so, Little ones to him belong, They are weak, but

CHORUS.

he is strong, Yes, Jesus loves me, Yes, Jesus loves me, Yes, Jesus loves me, The Bible tells me so.

Copyright, 1862, in Golden Shower, by W. B. Bradbury.

280 *We love him because he first loved us.*

2 Jesus loves me! he who died,
Heaven's gate to open wide;
He will wash away my sin,
Let his little child come in.—CHO.

3 Jesus loves me! loves me still,
Though I'm very weak and ill;
From his shining throne on high,
Comes to watch me where I lie.—CHO.

4 Jesus loves me; he will stay
Close beside me all the way;
If I love him, when I die
He will take me home on high.—CHO.

Anna Bartlett Warner.

SONGS FOR THE LITTLE ONES.

"JESUS BIDS US SHINE."
WM. J. KIRKPATRICK, by per.

Copyright, 1885, by W. J. Kirkpatrick.

281 *Every one to shine.*

2 Jesus bids us shine, first of all for him,
Well he sees and knows it if our lights are dim,
He looks down from Heaven to see us shine, You in, etc.

3 Jesus bids us shine, then, for all around
Many kinds of darkness in this world are found;
Sin, and want, and sorrow: so we may shine, Yon in, etc.
Anna Bartlett Warner.

I THINK, WHEN I READ.
English.

282 *The Children's Friend.*

2 I wish that his hands had been placed on my head,
That his arms had been thrown around me,
And that I might have seen his kind looks when he said,
"Let the little ones come unto me."

3 Yet still to his footstool in prayer I may go,
And ask for a share in his love;
And if I now earnestly seek him below,
I shall see him and hear him above:—

4 In that beautiful place he is gone to prepare
For all who are washed and forgiven:
And many dear children are gathering there,
"For of such is the kingdom of heaven."
Mrs. Jemima Luke.

203

SONGS FOR THE LITTLE ONES.

JESUS LOVES THE CHILDREN.
D. B. PURINTON.

1. Je-sus lov'd the children, Lov'd them so, lov'd them so, That he died to save them From a world of woe.

CHORUS.
I am but a little child, This I know, this I know; But I love the Saviour, Because he loves me so.

283 *"Suffer the little children."*

2 Jesus bids the children
   Come to him, come to him;
   Even they may find him
   Precious to redeem.—CHO.

3 Jesus, blessed Jesus,
   Now I pray, humbly pray,
   Ever love and keep me;
   Take my sins away.—CHO.
   D. B. P.

DEAR JESUS, HEAR ME.
WM. B. BRADBURY.

1. Saviour, bless a little child; Teach my heart the way to thee; Make it gentle, good and mild; Loving Saviour, care for me.

CHORUS.
Dear Je-sus, hear me, Hear thy lit-tle child to-day; Dear, O hear me, Hear me when I pray.

284 *"Hear me when I call."*

2 I am young, but thou hast said,
   All who will may come to thee;
   Feed my soul with living bread;
   Loving Saviour, care for me.—CHO.

3 Jesus, help me, I am weak;
   Let me put my trust in thee;
   Teach me how and what to speak;
   Loving Saviour, care for me.—CHO.

4 I would never go astray,
   Never turn aside from thee;
   Keep me in the heavenly way;
   Loving Saviour, care for me.—CHO.
   Fanny J. Crosby.

SONGS FOR THE LITTLE ONES.

O WHAT CAN YOU TELL.

J. C. Lowry, 1820, arr.

285 *The chorus of praise.*

2 O what can you tell, little flower, little flower,
O what can you tell, little flower on the lea!
The secret of your sweet perfume,
Now whisper it to me.
Ref.—It is the love of God in heav'n,
The God who made both you and me,
And every day I breathe his praise
In fragrance on the lea.

3 O what can you tell, little bird, little bird,
O what can you tell, little bird upon the tree!
The secret of your joyous song,
Now whisper it to me!
Ref.—It is the love of God in heav'n,
The God who made both you and me,
And every day I sing his praise
Upon the summer tree.

4 O what can you tell, little child, little child,
O what can you tell, little child upon my knee!
The secret of your happy smile,
Now whisper it to me!
Ref.—It is the love of God in heav'n,
The God who made both you and me!
And every day I seek his praise
Upon my bended knee!
Full Cho.—Thus to the love of God in heav'n,
The God who made both you and me,
The praise of all things here is giv'n!
And evermore shall be!

Rossiter W. Raymond.

GOD IS IN HEAVEN! (S. AGATHA.)

Rev. A. G. Mortimer.

Copyright, 1879, by Rev. Alfred G. Mortimer.

286 *Thou God see'st me.*

2 God is in heaven, can he see
 When I am doing wrong?
 Yes, that he can, he looks at thee
 All day and all night long.
3 God is in heaven, would he know
 If I should tell a lie?
 Yes, tho' thou saidst it very low,
 He'd hear it in the sky.

4 God is in heaven, does he care
 Or is he kind to me?
 Yes, all thou hast to eat or wear
 'Tis God that gives it thee.
5 God is in heaven, may I pray
 To go there when I die?
 Yes, love him, seek him, and one day
 He'll call thee to the sky.

Mrs. Ann Taylor Gilbert.

SONGS FOR THE LITTLE ONES.

LEAD ME, PRECIOUS SAVIOUR.
Mrs. Jos. F. Knapp.

1. Lead me, lead me, Lead me precious Saviour In-to the narrow way, In-to the narrow way,

CHORUS.
Fold me, fold me, Fold me to thy bo-som, And may I nev-er stray, O nev-er stray, And I will praise thee ev-ermore, yes ev-ermore, And I will praise thee evermore, yes, ev-er-more.

Copyright, 1869, Joseph F. Knapp.

287 *A child's prayer.*

2 I will love thee,
Ever, ever love thee;
May sinful thoughts depart,
O take them from my heart.—Cho.

3 Lead me, fold me,
Guide and ever keep me,
And thanks my heart will give,
Dear Saviour, while I live.—Cho.

Mrs. Jos. F. Knapp.

GROWING UP FOR JESUS.
Wm. J. Kirkpatrick.

1. Growing up for Je-sus, we are tru-ly blest, In his smile is welcome, in his arms our rest,

FINE.
In his truth our treasure, in his love our rule, Growing up for Je-sus in our Sun-day school.

D.S. In his truth our treasure, in his love our rule, Growing up for Je-sus in our Sun-day school.

Copyright, 1885, by Wm. J. Kirkpatrick

SONGS FOR THE LITTLE ONES.

GROWING UP FOR JESUS.—Concluded.

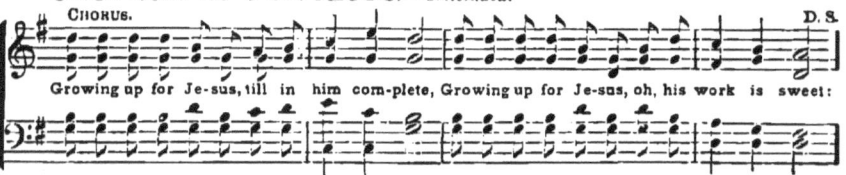

Growing up for Je-sus, till in him com-plete, Growing up for Je-sus, oh, his work is sweet:

288 *Little Branches of the Vine.*

2 Not too young to love him, little hearts beat true,
Not too young to serve him as the dew-drops do,
Not too young to praise him singing as we come,
Not too young to answer when he calls us home.—CHO.

3 Growing up for Jesus, learning day by day
How to follow onward in the narrow way;
Seeking holy treasure, finding precious truth,
Growing up for Jesus in our happy youth.—CHO.

Priscilla J. Owens.

DEAR SAVIOUR, EVER AT MY SIDE. Wm. B. Bradbury.

1. Dear Sav-iour, ev-er at my side, How lov-ing Thou must be, To leave Thy home in heaven to guard A lit-tle child like me! Thy beau-ti-ful and shin-ing face I see not, tho' so near; The sweetness of Thy soft, low voice I am too deaf to hear.

Copyright, 1859, in Oriola, by W. B. Bradbury.

289 *He carries them in his bosom.*

2 I cannot feel thee touch my hand
With pressure light and mild,
To check me, as my mother doth,
While I am but a child;
But I have felt Thee in my thoughts
Fighting with sin for me;
And when my heart loves God, I know
The sweetness is from thee.

3 And when, dear Saviour! I kneel down
Morning and night to prayer,
Something there is within my heart
Which tells me thou art there;
Yes! when I pray, thou prayest too—
Thy prayer is all for me;
But when I sleep, thou sleepest not,
But watchest patiently.

Rev. F. W. Faber.

SONGS OF THE LITTLE ONES.

SUNBEAMS.
Mrs. Jos F. Knapp.

1. We welcome you all and our greeting shall be A song that is mer-ry and gay, and gay; It comes from the heart and it speaks in the eye. O happy are we to-day. Hap-py to-day, yes hap-py to-day,
2. We sing of a tree that will nev-er grow old, But always be vernal and bright, and bright; Pro-tecting a gar-den all blooming with flowers, And sparkling with joy and light.

CHORUS.
Happy dear friends are we, are we; Joy-ful the song now floating a-long, Happy, dear friends are we.

Copyright, 1883, by Joseph F. Knapp.

290   *Happy children.*

3 The Church is the tree—t'was planted by faith,
Our School is the garden so fair, so fair;
And we are the sunbeams, the buds and the flowers,
So lovingly twining there.—CHO.

Fanny J. Crosby.

BEAUTIFUL, THE LITTLE HANDS.
Bishop W. Jones.

1. Beau-ti-ful the lit-tle hands, That ful-fill the Lord's commands; Beauti-ful the lit-tle eyes, Kind-led with light from the skies.

CHORUS
Beau-ti-ful, beau-ti-ful lit-tle hands, That ful-fill the

From "Gospel Bells." By permission of H. A. Sumner & Co., Chicago.

SONGS FOR THE LITTLE ONES.

BEAUTIFUL, THE LITTLE HANDS.—*Concluded.*

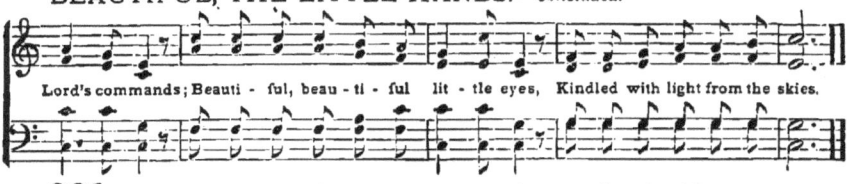

Lord's commands; Beauti - ful, beau - ti - ful lit - tle eyes, Kindled with light from the skies.

291 *Something for each to do.*

2 All the little hands were made,
Jesus' precious cause to aid;
All the little hearts to beat
Warm in his service so sweet.
　Cho.—Beautiful, &c.

3 All the little lips should pray
To the Saviour, ev'ry day;

All the little feet should go
Swift on his errands below,
　Cho.—Beautiful, &c.

4 What your little hands can do,
That the Lord intends for you;
Make that thing your first delight,
Do it to him with your might.
　Cho.—Beautiful, &c.

　　　　　　　　　　T. Corben.

LITTLE BUDS OF PROMISE.
　　　　　　　　　　Mrs. Jos. F. Knapp.

1. Blooming all for Je - sus In a gar-den fair, Fold-ed on his bo-som, Sheltered by his care.

CHORUS.

Lit - tle buds of prom-ise, Hap-py now are we, Saviour, keep us ev - er Ver-y near to thee;

Near to thee, near to thee, Ver - y near to thee, Sav-iour, O Sav-iour, keep us near to thee.

Copyright, 1884, by Joseph F. Knapp.

292 *Suffer them to come.*
2 We would shine for Jesus,
　Don't you think we may,
　Like the pretty sunbeams
　Shining on our way.—Cho.

3 We can work for Jesus,
　He has told us so,
　We can scatter sunshine
　Every-where we go.—Cho.
　　　　　　Mrs. Jos. F. Knapp.

SONGS—MISCELLANEOUS.

COME WITH REJOICING.

Mrs. Joseph F. Knapp.

Copyright, 1882, by Joseph F. Knapp.

293 *Songs of gladness.*

1 COME with rejoicing, come with delight,
  Nature is waking, glad and bright;
  Hearts overflowing gather to-day,
    Fill us with rapture, Lord, we pray.
    Praise our Redeemer, tell of his love,
    Praise our Redeemer, God above.
    Tell of his mercy, boundless and free,
      None can protect us, Lord, like
        thee.

2 Guarded from danger, sheltered and blest,
  Under his banner, calm, we rest,
  Come we before him, come with a song,
  Tell how he leads us all day long.
    Praise our Redeemer, etc.

3 O! what a Saviour, gracious to all,
  O! how his blessings 'round us fall;
  Gently to comfort, kindly to cheer,
  Sleeping or waking, God is near.
    Praise our Redeemer, etc.

4 Still may his mercy tenderly flow,
  Still may he guide us here below;
  Then when our journey safely is past
  May we be gathered home at last.
    Praise our Redeemer, etc.

Fanny J. Crosby.

SONGS—MISCELLANEOUS.

OUR GLAD JUBILEE.
WM. F. SHERWIN.

294 *Thou crownest the year with thy goodness.*

1 WAKE, wake the song! our glad jubilee
Once more we hail with sweet melody,
Bringing our hymns of praise unto thee,
O most holy Lord!
Praise for thy care by day and by night,
Praise for the homes by love made so bright;
Thanks for the pure and the soul-cheering [light
Beaming from thy word.

2 Marching to Zion, dear blessed home!
Lord, by thy mercy hither we come;
Guide us, we pray where'er we may roam,
Keep us in thy fear;
Fill every soul with love all divine,
Now cause thy face upon us to shine:
Grant that our hearts may truly be thine
All the coming year.

3 Yet once again the anthem repeat,
Join every voice the Master to greet;
Love's sacrifice we lay at his feet,
In his temple now;
Jesus, accept the offering we bring,
Blending with songs the odors of spring;
Still of thy wondrous love we will sing,
Till in heaven we bow.
W. F. Sherwin.

295 *His wonderful love.*

3 Praise his great name! let the nations adore;
Redeemer and Saviour, God evermore;
Enthroned with the angels, blessed above;
Praise him, O earth for his wonderful love!
Praise him ye smallest and greatest of all!
Praise him, ye kindred that rise from the fall!
Praise him, ye children of weakness and death!
Praise him! O, praise him, all ye that have breath!

George D. Emerson.

SONGS—MISCELLANEOUS.

HARVEST HOME.
JOHANN A. P. SCHULZ.

296 *God of the harvest.*

1 We plough the fields, and scatter
　The good seed on the land,
But it is fed and watered
　By God's almighty hand;
He sends the snow in winter,
　The warmth to swell the grain,
The breezes, and the sunshine,
　And soft refreshing rain.—CHO.

2 He only is the Maker
　Of all things near and far:
He paints the wayside flower,
　He lights the evening star;
The winds and waves obey him,
　By him the birds are fed;
Much more to us, his children,
　He gives our daily bread.—CHO.

3 We thank thee, then, O Father,
　For all things bright and good,
The seed time and the harvest,
　Our life, our health, our food;
Accept the gifts we offer,
　For all thy love imparts,
And, what thou most desirest
　Our humble, thankful hearts.—CHO.

Jane Montgomery Campbell. (tr. from Ger. of Matthias Claudius.)

SONGS—MISCELLANEOUS.

SUMMER SUNSHINE.
SAMUEL SMITH.

1. Summer suns are glowing O'er land and sea, Happy light is flowing Bountiful and free. Everything rejoices In the mellow rays, All earth's thousand voices Swell the psalm of praise.

297 *The sunshine of God's presence.*

2 God's free mercy streameth
  Over all the world,
And his banner gleameth
  Everywhere unfurled.
Broad and deep and glorious
  As the heaven above,
Shines in might victorious
  His eternal love.

3 Lord, upon our blindness
  Thy pure radiance pour;
For thy loving kindness
  Make us love thee more.
And when clouds are drifting
  Dark across our sky,
Then, the veil uplifting,
  Father, be thou nigh.
    Wm. Walsham How.

AUTUMN LEAVES.
FREDERICK ILIFFE

Quietly.

1. The year is swiftly waning, The summer days are past; And life, brief life, is speeding: The end is nearing fast.

298 *The harvest is passing.*

2 The ever-changing seasons
  In silence come and go;
But thou Eternal Father,
  No time or change canst know.

3 Oh! pour thy grace upon us
  That we may worthier be,
Each year that passes o'er us,
  To dwell in heaven with thee.

4 Our barren hearts make fruitful
  With every goodly grace,
That we thy name may hallow,
  And see at last thy face.
    Wm. Walsham How.

SONGS—MISCELLANEOUS.

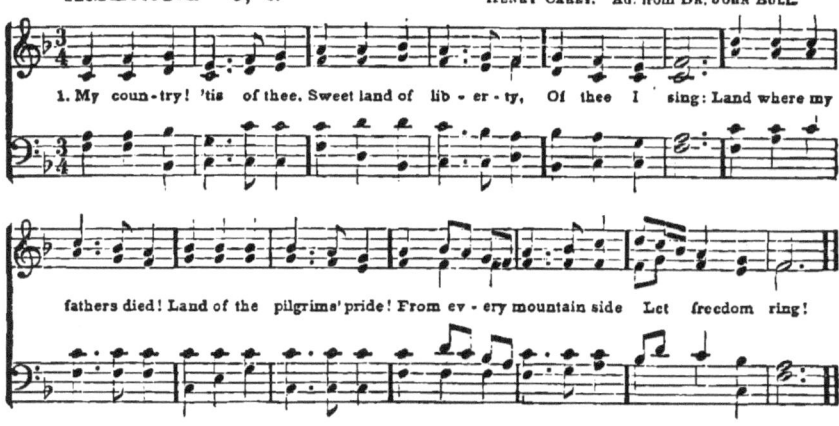

299 *National hymn.*

2 My native country, thee,
Land of the noble, free,
   Thy name I love;
I love thy rocks and rills,
Thy woods and templed hills:
My heart with rapture thrills
   Like that above.

3 Let music swell the breeze,
And ring from all the trees
   Sweet freedom's song:
Let mortal tongues awake;
Let all that breathe partake;
Let rocks their silence break,
   The sound prolong.

4 Our fathers' God! to thee,
Author of liberty,
   To thee we sing:
Long may our land be bright
With freedom's holy light;
Protect us by thy might,
   Great God, our King!
               Samuel F. Smith.

300 *Thanksgiving choral.*

1 SWELL the anthem, raise the song;
Praises to our God belong;
Saints and angels join to sing
Praises to the heavenly King.

2 Blessings from his liberal hand
Flow around this happy land:
Kept by him, no foes annoy;
Peace and freedom we enjoy.

3 Here, beneath a virtuous sway
May we cheerfully obey;
Never feel oppression's rod,
Ever own and worship God.

4 Hark! the voice of nature sings
Praises to the King of kings;
Let us join the choral song,
And the grateful notes prolong.
               Nathan Strong.

SONGS—MISCELLANEOUS.

NO COMPROMISE.
W. H. Doane.

1. Lo! a mighty host is rising now, See! their banner is unfurled! Its fair legend, Truth and Righteousness; Spread the tidings thro' the world.

CHORUS.
No compromise! No compromise! No more yielding to the foe; No compromise! no compromise! No, no, no, no, no, no, NO!

Copyright, 1874, by W. H. Doane.

301 *Firmness for the right.*

2 See the mighty host advancing now!
Look! the proud oppressors flee!
So our country breaks its fetters off,
And her captive sons are free.
CHO.—No compromise! etc.

3 Weary watchers, cease your vigils now,
For the morning surely comes;
Night is fleeing, joy is dawning now
On your hearts and on your homes.
CHO.—No compromise! etc.

4 Sing, O Zion! no more desolate,
Lift thine eyes, the brightness see!
Thy Redeemer makes thee glorious,
Thine oppressors bend to thee.
CHO.—No compromise! etc.

Mrs. M. A. Collins.

SONGS—MISCELLANEOUS.

WE'LL HELP THE CAUSE ALONG.
W. H. DOANE, by per.

1. We must work and pray together, Working, praying for the right; We must fight against the e-vil,
2. In defence of truth and justice, Like a bulwark we must stand, And the soul that's full of courage
3. We must work and not be weary, Tho' we conquer not to-day; For the rescue of our brothers,

CHORUS.

Till we conquer by our might.
Will give courage to the hand.
We must work as well as play.

We're strong to do, we're strong to dare, In faith and hope we're strong; U-nited thus in strength and pray'r, We'll help the cause along.

Copyright, 1874, by W. H. Doane.

302 *Strength and prayer.*

4 Hark! the crystal streams and fountains
Swell the chorus of our song;
And they seem to be rejoicing
As they help the cause along.
CHO.—We're strong to do, &c.
— *Josephine Pollard.*

GOD SPEED THE RIGHT.
WM. B. BRADBURY, by per.

|1st. |2d.

1. { Now to heav'n our pray'r ascending, God speed the right { Be their zeal in heav'n recorded,
   { In a noble cause contending, God speed the.... right! { With success on earth rewarded, } God speed the right, God speed the right!

303 *God speed the right.*

2 Be that prayer again repeated,
  God speed the right!
Ne'er despairing though defeated,
  God speed the right!
Like the good and great in story,
If they fail, they fail with glory,
  God speed the right!

3 Patient, firm, and persevering,
  God speed the right!
Ne'er the event our danger fearing,
  God speed the right!

Pains, nor toils, nor trials heeding,
And in heaven's own time succeeding,
  God speed the right!

4 Still their outward course pursuing,
  God speed the right!
Every foe at length subduing,
  God speed the right!
Truth, thy cause, whate'er delay it,
There's no power on earth can stay it,
  God speed the right!
— W. E. Hickson.

SONGS—MISCELLANEOUS.

THE SPARKLING RILL.

JAMES B. TAYLOR.

1. Gushing so bright in the morning light, Gleams the wa-ter in yon foun-tain; And as pure-ly, too, as the ear-ly dew That gems the distant moun-tain.

CHORUS.
Then drink your fill of the gush-ing rill, And leave the cup of sor-row; Tho' it shine to-night in the gleaming light, 'Twill sting thee on the mor-row.

304   *Pure water.*

2 Quietly glide in their silvery tide,
   Pearly brooks from rocks to valley;
And the flashing streams in the strong sunbeams
   Like bannered armies rally.—CHO.

3 Touch not the wine, though it brightly shine,
   When a purer draught is given;
A gift so sweet all our wants to meet,
   A beverage bright from heaven.—CHO.

4 O fountain clear, with a heart sincere
   We will praise thy glorious Giver;
And when we rise to our native skies,
   We'll drink of life's bright river.—CHO.

Anon.

SONGS—MISCELLANEOUS.

BENEVENTO. 7. D. — Samuel Webbe

1. While, with ceaseless course, the sun Hasted through the former year, Many souls their race have run, Never more to meet us here: Fixed in an e-ter-nal state, They have done with all below; We a lit-tle longer wait, But how little—none can know.

305 *Retrospect of the year.*

2 As the wingéd arrow flies
  Speedily the mark to find;
As the lightning from the skies
  Darts, and leaves no trace behind;
Swiftly thus our fleeting days
  Bear us down life's rapid stream;
Upward, Lord, our spirits raise;
  All below is but a dream.

3 Thanks for mercies past receive;
  Pardon of our sins renew;
Teach us henceforth how to live
  With eternity in view:
Bless thy word to young and old;
  Fill us with a Saviour's love;
And when life's short tale is told,
  May we dwell with him above.
John Newton.

ERNAN. L. M. — Lowell Mason.

1. The morn-ing flowers display their sweets, And gay their silk-en leaves un-fold, As care-less of the noon-tide heats, As fear-less of the even-ing cold.

306 *Sown in dishonor—raised in glory.*

2 Nipped by the wind's unkindly blast,
  Parched by the sun's directer ray,
The momentary glories waste,
  The short-lived beauties die away.

3 Yet these, new rising from the tomb,
  With luster brighter far shall shine,
Revive with ever-during bloom,
  Safe from diseases and decline.

4 Let sickness blast, let death devour,
  If heaven must recompense our pains;
Perish the grass, and fade the flower,
  If firm the word of God remains.
Samuel Wesley, Jr.

CHANTS.

307 VENITE, EXULTIMUS DOMINO.   William Boyce.

1. O come, let us sing un-| to the | Lord ; || let us heartily rejoice in the | strength of | our sal-| vation.
2. Let us come before his presence | with thanks-| giving, || and show ourselves | glad in | him with | psalms.
3. For the Lord is a | great—| God, || and a great | King a-| bove all | gods.
4. In his hands are all the corners | of the | earth ; || and the strength of the | hills is | his—| also.
5. The sea is his, | and he | made it; || and his hands pre-| pared the | dry—| land.
6. O come, let us worship | and fall | down, || and kneel be-| fore the | Lord our | Maker.
7. For he is the | Lord our | God, || and we are the people of his pasture, and the | sheep of | his—| hand.
8. O worship the Lord in the | beauty " of | holiness;— || let the whole earth | stand in | awe of | him. .
*9. For he cometh, for he cometh to | judge the | earth, || and with righteousness to judge the world, and the | people | with his | truth.
10. Glory be to the Father, and | to the | Son, || and | to the | Holy | Ghost;
11. As it was in the beginning, is now, and | ever | shall be, || world | without | end. A-| men.

Begin at middle of Chant.

308 JUBILATE DEO.   Mornington.

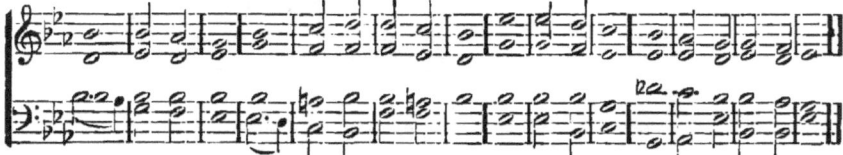

1. O be joyful in the Lord, | all ye | lands ; || serve the Lord with gladness, and come before his | presence | with a | song.
2. Be ye sure that the Lord | he is | God; || it is he that hath made us, and not we ourselves : we are his people, | and the | sheep of " his | pasture.
3. O go your way into his gates with thanksgiving, and into his | courts with | praise; || be thankful unto him, and | speak good | of his | name.
4. For the Lord is gracious, his mercy is | ever-| lasting; || and his truth endureth from gener-| ation " to | gener-| ation.
5. Glory be to the Father, and | to the | Son, || and | to the | Holy | Ghost;
6. As it was in the beginning, is now, and | ever | shall be, || world | without | end. A- | men.

CHANTS.

309 BENEDICTUS. R. Langdon.

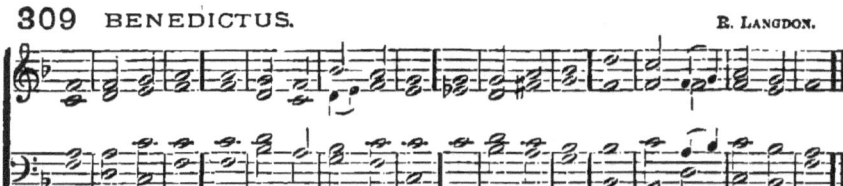

1 Blessed be the Lord | God of | Israel, || for he hath visited | and re- | deemed his | people;
2 And hath raised up a mighty sal- | vation | for us, || in the | house ·· of his|servant | David;
3 As he spake by the mouth of his | holy | prophets, || which have been | since the | world be- | gan;
4 That we should be saved | from our | enemies, || and from the | hand of | all that | hate us.
5 Glory be to the Father, and | to the | Son, || and | to the | Holy | Ghost;
6 As it was in the beginning, is now, and | ever | shall be, || world | without | end. A- | men.

BENEDICTUS. Richard Farrant. Rev. Wm. Felton.

310 DEUS MISEREATUR. Richard Farrant.

1 God be merciful unto | us, and | bless us; || and show us the light of his countenance, and be | merci ·· ful | unto | us.
2 That thy way may be | known up ·· on | earth ; | thy saving | health a- | mong all | nations.
3 Let the people praise | thee, O | God; || yea, let | all the | people | praise thee.
4 O let the nations rejoice | and be | glad; || for thou shalt judge the folk righteously, and govern the | nations | upon | earth.
5 Let the people praise | thee, O | God; || yea, let | all the | people | praise thee.
6 Then shall the earth bring | forth her | increase; || and God, even our own | God, shall | give us ·· his | blessing.
7 God | shall— | bless us; || and all the ends of the | world shall | fear— | him.
8 Glory be to the Father. and | to the | Son, || and | to the | Holy | Ghost;
9 As it was in the beginning, is now, and | ever | shall be, || world | without | end. A- | men.

CHANTS.

311 BONUM EST CONFITERI.
GREGORIAN.
JOHN ALCOCK.

1. It is a good thing to give thanks un-| to ·the | Lord: and to sing praises unto thy Name| O ·—| Most ·—| Highest.
2. To tell of thy loving-kindness early | in ·the | morning: and of thy truth | in ·the | night ·—| season.
3. Upon an instrument of ten strings, and up-|on ·the |lute: upon a loud instrument |and· up-| on ·the | harp.
4. For thou, Lord, hast made me glad | through · thy | works : and I will rejoice in giving praise, for the operations | of ·—| thy ·—| hands.
5. Glory be to the Father, | and · to the | Son, and | to ·the | Holy | Ghost;
6. As it was in the beginning, is now, and | ev-er |shall be, world | with-out | end. A-| men.

312 DOMINUS REGIT ME.
LOWELL MASON.

1. THE Lord is my Shepherd; I | shall not | want; || he maketh me to lie down in green pastures, he leadeth me beside the | still—| waters.
2. He restoreth my soul; he leadeth me in the paths of righteousness for his | name's—| sake. || Yea, though I walk through the valley of the shadow of death, I will fear no evil, for thou art with me; thy rod and thy staff | they—| comfort me.
3. Thou preparest a table before me, in the presence of mine enemies, thou anointest my head with oil; my | cup ·· runneth | over. || Surely goodness and mercy shall follow me all the days of my life; and I will dwell in the house of the | Lord for-| ever. || A- | men.

313 VENITE AD ME.
UNKNOWN.

1. COME unto me all ye that labor and are | heavy-| laden, || and | I will | give you | rest.
2. Take my yoke upon you, and learn of me : for I am meek and | lowly ·· |in | heart : || and ye shall find | rest ·· unto | your—| souls.
3. For my yoke is easy, and my | burden ·· is | light, || for my yoke is easy, | and my | burden ·· is | light.
4. And the Spirit and the Bride say, Come. And let him that | heareth, ·· say,| Come. || And let him that is athirst come; and whosoever will, let him take the | water ·· of | life—| freely. A—| men.

CHANTS.

314 GLORIA IN EXCELSIS.
Unknown.

PART I.

GLORY be to | God on | high, || and on earth | peace, good-| will⋅⋅toward | men.
We praise thee, we bless thee, we | worship | thee, || we glorify thee, we give thanks to | thee for | thy great | glory.

PART II.

O Lord God, | heavenly | King, || God the | Father | Al-⋅⋅-| mighty!
O Lord, the only-begotten Son, | Jesus | Christ, || O Lord God, Lamb of | God, Son | of the | Father,

PART III.

That takest away the | sins⋅⋅of the | world, || have mercy | upon | us.
Thou that takest away the | sins⋅⋅of the | world, || have mercy | upon | us.
Thou that takest away the | sins⋅⋅of the | world, || re- | ceive our | prayer.
Thou that sittest at the right hand of | God the | Father, || have mercy | upon | us.
Return to PART I.
For thou | only⋅⋅art | holy, || thou | only | art the | Lord.
Thou only, O Christ, with the | Holy | Ghost, || art most high in the | glory⋅⋅of | God the | Father. || A- | men.

315 Responses to the Commandments.

Lord, have mer-cy up-on us, and in-cline our hearts to keep this law.

After the Tenth Commandment. *Slow.*

Lord, have mercy up-on us, and write all these thy laws in our hearts we beseech thee.

CHANTS.

316 THY WILL BE DONE. — Isaac Baker Woodbury.

"Thy will be done."

1 "THY will be | done!" || In devious way
    The hurrying stream of | life may | run; ||
    Yet still our grateful hearts shall say, |
    "Thy will be | done!"

2 "Thy will be | done!" || If o'er us shine
    A gladdening and a | prosperous | sun, ||
    This prayer will make it more divine: |
    "Thy will be | done!"

3 "Thy will be | done!" || Though shrouded o'er
    Our | path with | gloom, || one comfort, [one
    Is ours: to breathe, while we adore, |
    "Thy will be | done!"

— John Bowring.

317 THE LORD'S PRAYER. — Gregorian.

1 Our Father who art in heaven, | Hallowed | be thy | name. ||
    Thy kingdom come: Thy will be done in | earth, "as it | is in | heaven,

2 Give us this | day our—| daily | bread: ||
    And forgive us our debts, as | we for-| give our | debtors.

3 Lead us not into temptation, but de- | liver | us from | evil ; ||
    For thine is the kingdom, and the power, and the glory, for | ever. | A- —|men.

318 GLORIA PATRI. — Charles Meineke.

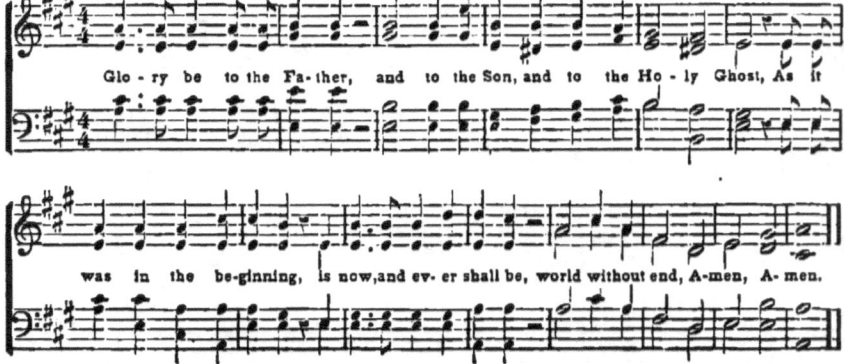

Glo - ry be to the Fa - ther, and to the Son, and to the Ho - ly Ghost, As it was in the be-ginning, is now, and ev - er shall be, world without end, A-men, A-men.

CHANTS.

310 TE DEUM LAUDAMUS.
CROTCH.

PART I.

1. WE praise | thee·O | God ‖ we acknowledge | thee·to | be·the | Lord.
2. All the earth doth | wor - ship | thee ‖ the Father | ev - er- | last- — | ing.
3. To thee all angels | cry·a- | loud ‖ the heavens, and | all·the | powers.there- | in.
4. To thee, Cherubim and | Ser - a- | phim ‖ con- | tin - ual- | ly·do | cry:
5. Holy, | Holy, | Holy ‖ Lord | God·of | Sa - ba- | oth.
6. Heaven and | earth·are | full ‖ of the | majes - ty | of·thy | glory.
7. The glorious company | of·the A- | postles ‖ praise | — — | — — | thee.
8. The goodly fellowship | of·the | Prophets ‖ praise | — — | — — | thee.
9. The noble | army·of | Martyrs ‖ praise | — — | — — | thee.
10. The Holy Church throughout | all·the | world ‖ doth | — ac- | knowl - edge | thee.
11. The Fa- | — — | ther | of an | infi - nite | Ma - jes- | ty;
12. Thine adorable, true, and | on - ly | Son ‖ also the Holy | Ghost·the | Com - fort-| er.
13. Thou | art·the | King ‖ of | glo - ry | O — | Christ.
14. Thou art the ever- | last - ing | Son ‖ of | —the | Fa- — | ther.

PART II.   From BEETHOVEN, by J. GOSS.

15. When thou tookest upon thee to de- | liv - er | man ‖ thou didst humble thyself to be | born — | of·a | Virgin.
16. When thou hadst overcome the | sharpness·of | death ‖ thou didst open the kingdom of | heaven·to | all·be- lievers.
17. Thou sittest at the right | hand·of | God ‖ in the | glo - ry | of·the | Father.
18. We believe that | thou·shalt | come ‖ to | be —| our —| Judge.
19. We therefore pray thee, | help·thy | servants ‖ whom thou hast redeemed | with· thy | pre - cious | blood.
20. Make them to be numbered | with·thy | saints ‖ in | glo - ry | ev - er- | lasting.
21. O Lord, | save·thy | people ‖ and | bless·thine | her - it- | age.
22. Gov- | ern | them ‖ and | lift·them | up·for | ever.

Return to PART I.

23. Day | — by | day ‖ we | mag - ni- | fy | — | thee.
24. And we worship | thy·name | ever ‖ world | — with- | out — | end.
25. Vouchsafe, | O — | Lord ‖ to keep us this | day·with- | out — | sin.
26. O Lord, have mercy up- | on — | us ‖ have | mercy·up- | on — | us.
27. O Lord, let thy mercy | be·up- | on us ‖ as our | trust -- | is·in | thee.
28. O Lord, in thee | have·I | trusted ‖ let me | nev - er | be·con- | founded.

The figures refer to the hymns.

Affliction, 69, 137, 142, 153, 162, 163, 165, 171, 192, 194, 202.
Anniversary, 293, 294.
Assurance, 150, 169, 177. See also "Trust."
Childhood: Christ's love for, 280, 282, 283, 289.
  Consecrated, 116, 149, 216, 232, 250, 281, 287, 288, 291, 302, 303.
  Death in, 306.
  Giving praise, 54, 64, 73, 76, 78, 290.
  God's love for, 285, 286.
  Home in heaven, 64, 79, 129.
  In temptation, 205.
  Seeking help, 12, 14, 82, 83, 145, 191, 279, 284.
Christ: Advent, 48–55.
  Ascension, 64.
  Calling, 104–106, 108, 110, 111, 114, 115.
  Character and Attributes, 68, 74, 77, 94, 134, 167.
  Friend of children, 79, 82, 83.
  His reign, 249, 257.
  Redeemer and Saviour, 2, 3, 38, 67, 70–72, 74, 75, 96, 102, 109, 117, 132.
  Risen, 60–63.
  Songs of, 48–84.
  Source of comfort, 8, 11, 23, 24, 58, 69, 70–72, 84, 91, 94, 119, 154, 155, 160, 168, 171, 178, 179.
  Suffering and death, 56, 57, 59.
  Worshiped, 2, 3, 6, 37, 65–67, 73–77, 80, 81.
Christian life: Songs of, 133–239. See also "Affliction," "Consecration," "Trust," "Providence," "Work."
Church: Fellowship, 259, 260.
  Foundation, 243.
  Glorious, 240, 301.
  God in midst of, 242, 244.
  Songs of the, 240–260.
  Spreading the gospel, 245–248, 250–257, 301.
  Toil for, 241.
  Triumphant, 241, 249, 258.
Consecration, 59, 77, 81, 102, 113, 116, 122, 135, 136, 147–152, 163, 164, 166, 171, 177, 193, 206, 218.
Death, 305, 306.
God: Calling, 47, 113.
  Creator, 1, 44.
  Goodness of, 1, 39, 40, 41–43, 45, 47, 153, 182.
  Invoked, 8, 9, 26, 126, 147.
  Praised, 1, 8, 27, 30, 33, 37, 38, 44, 46, 95.
  Reconciled, 52.
  Songs of, 37–47.
Gratitude, 38, 42, 56, 57, 91, 101.
Heaven, 10, 79, 159, 210.
  Songs of, 261–278.
Holy Spirit: Inviting, 124.
  Invoked, 8, 37, 85–87, 126.
  Songs of the, 85–88.
  Worshiped, 33, 88.

Invitation, 47, 96, 103–106, 108, 110–115, 118, 120, 121, 124, 159, 168, 194.
Joy, 70, 71, 80, 143, 158, 160, 179, 183, 227.
Little ones: Songs for, 279–292.
Missionary, 244–249, 251, 252, 256, 257.
Miscellaneous, 293–306.
Mercy, 47, 72, 109, 119, 126.
Obedience, 92, 185, 203.
Peace, 29, 48, 55, 58, 90, 106, 161, 175.
Patriotic, 299, 300.
Praise, 1–5, 8, 10, 12, 15, 16, 33, 37, 38, 42, 44, 70, 73, 166, 177, 207, 212, 219, 293.
Prayer, 13, 36, 164, 165, 198, 199.
Providence, 1, 10, 14, 20, 42, 43, 45, 133, 146, 147, 156, 176, 180, 182, 183, 186, 188, 201, 204.
Revival, 9, 126, 219, 242.
Reward, 22, 41, 79, 214, 215, 226, 229, 232–234, 238, 252, 258.
Sabbath, Songs of the, 31–36.
Salvation: Offered, 96, 97, 103, 106, 127.
  Provided, 2, 3, 56, 65, 67, 74, 75, 93, 95, 98, 100–102, 108, 112, 117, 123, 124, 129, 132, 169, 254.
  Sought, 99, 104, 105, 109, 125, 128–130, 138, 168, 174.
  Songs of, 93–132.
Scriptures, 5, 8, 9, 89, 90, 97.
  Songs of the, 89–92.
Seasons: Autumn, 298.
  Harvest, 296.
  Summer, 297.
  Watch-night, 305.
Supplication: For blessing, 9, 25, 28, 86, 181, 196, 200.
  For guidance, 14, 21, 28, 87, 140, 141, 144–146, 156, 157, 187–189, 197, 202, 203.
  For help, 8, 134, 173.
  For peace, 34.
  For revival, 9, 126, 219, 242.
  For salvation, 125, 126, 197.
Temperance, 301–304.
Thanksgiving, 295.
Trust: For guidance, 170–172, 176, 180, 182, 186, 187, 201, 204, 211.
  For salvation, 119, 123, 130, 131, 155, 174, 178, 190, 200.
  In trial, 13, 133, 139, 144, 157, 161, 163, 184, 192, 193, 202.
Warning, 107, 114, 117, 118, 120, 122, 127.
Witnessing, 174, 195, 212, 213–215, 221, 223, 239, 245.
Work, 187, 205, 208, 209, 214, 215, 217, 220, 223, 224–239, 250–256, 302, 303.
Worship: Morning, 1–3, 5–7, 11, 12, 35, 46.
  Evening, 7, 17–29, 188, 278.
  Opening, 1–3, 5–15, 31–36, 260.
  Closing, 16, 19–29, 156, 188, 196, 259.
  Songs of, 1–30.

INDEX.

TITLES AND FIRST LINES.

To facilitate the finding of Hymns the *Titles* are set in CAPS on the margin, and *First Lines* in Roman, slightly to the right.

	Hymn
Abide with me! Fast falls the eventide.	21
A BROTHER'S CARE. 8, 7	183
Again as evening's shadow falls	17
Alas! and did my Saviour bleed	56
ALETTA. 7	175
ALIDA. C. M. D.	265
Alleluia! Alleluia! Alleluia!	61
ALL FOR THEE	152
All hail the power of Jesus' name	65
All my doubts I give to Jesus	190
All people that on earth do dwell	1
ALL THE WAY	176
All the way my Saviour leads me	176
All things beautiful and fair	40
All unseen the Master walketh	22
Almighty Spirit, we confess	88
ALONE WITH JESUS	154
AMERICA. 6, 4	299
Am I a soldier of the cross	214
ANGELS' SONG. 11, 10	278
ANGEL VOICES	30
Angel voices breathing ever	7
Angel voices ever singing	30
ANTIOCH. C. M	50
ARIEL. C. P. M	167
ARISE, GO FORTH TO CONQUER	250
Arise, my soul, arise	169
ARLINGTON C. M	214
ARMENIA. C. M	89
Art thou saddened? Christ will cheer	162
ASCENSION	64
AURELIA. 7, 6. D	243
AUSTRIA. 8, 7. D	240
AUTUMN. 67
AUTUMN LEAVES. 7, 6	298
AVON. C. M	136
Awake, and sing the song	6
Awake! awake! the Master now, etc.	251
AWAKE, MY SOUL. C. M	238
Awake, my soul, stretch every nerve	238

	Hymn
A WONDERFUL JOY	158
A wonderful joy and salvation	158
AZMON. C. M	2
BALERMA. C. M	135
BATTLING FOR THE LORD	224
BEAUTIFUL, THE LITTLE HANDS	291
Beautiful Saviour, King of creation	77
BENEVENTO 7. D	305
BETHANY. 6, 4, 6	147
BETHLEHEM	55
BEULAH LAND	276
BLESSED ASSURANCE	177
Blessed assurance, Jesus is mine	177
Blest are the hungry, they shall be	110
Blest be the tie that binds	259
BLESSED HOUR OF PRAYER	13
Blooming all for Jesus	292
BLOW THE TRUMPET	245
BLUMENTHAL. 7. D	109
BOYLSTON. S. M	114
BREAD OF LIFE. 10	90
Break thou the bread of life	90
Broken in spirit and laden with care	142
BROWNE. 6, 8, 4	171
CALEDONIA. 7, 7, 7, 6	229
Called to the feast by the King are we	222
Calm on the listening ear of night	49
CAN YE NOT WATCH ONE LITTLE HOUR	217
CHANTS	207
Blessed be the Lord God of	309
Come unto me, all ye	313
Glory be to God on high	314
Glory be to the Father	315
God be merciful unto us	310
It is a good thing to give	311
O be joyful in the Lord	308
O come, let us sing unto	307
Our Father, who art in heaven	317

TITLES AND FIRST LINES.

Title / First line	Hymn
Te Deum Laudamus	319
Responses	315
The Lord is my Shepherd	312
Thy will be done	316
CHILD OF A KING	211
CHRIST IS NEAR THEE	162
CHRISTMAS. C. M.	51
CHURCH RALLYING SONG	251
CLEANSING FOUNTAIN. C. M.	101
CLEANSING WAVE	102
COME AND WORSHIP	7
COME, CHRISTIAN CHILDREN	73
Come, Christian children, come and	73
COME, COME TO JESUS	111
Come, Holy Ghost, in love	86
Come, Holy Ghost, our hearts inspire	85
Come, let us join our cheerful songs	3
Come, my soul, thy suit prepare	164
COMMUNION. C. M.	56
Come, said Jesus' sacred voice	106
Come, thou Almighty King	8
COME TO JESUS	112
Come to Jesus and be saved	112
COME TO THE FOUNTAIN	120
Come, thou Fount of every blessing	166
Come unto me, when shadows darkly	159
Come, ye that love the Lord	212
COME WITH REJOICING	293
Come with rejoicing, come with delight	293
Come with thy sins to the fountain	120
COME, YE DISCONSOLATE. 11, 10	194
COME, YE SINNERS. 8, 7	96
Come, ye sinners, poor and needy	96
CORONATION. C. M.	65
COURAGE. 7	235
COWPER. C. M.	101
CROWN HIM WITH MANY CROWNS	66
CRUSADERS' HYMN	77
DARE TO DO RIGHT	208
Dare to do right, dare to be true	208
Day is dying in the west	27
DEAR JESUS, HEAR ME	284
DEAR SAVIOUR, EVER AT MY SIDE	289
Deep are the wounds which sin has	93
DENNIS. S. M.	259
Depth of mercy! can there be	109
DOVER. S. M.	92
DOWNS. C. M.	94
DUANE STREET. L. M. D.	174
DUKE STREET. L. M.	5
EARNESTLY FIGHTING FOR JESUS	220
EASTER HYMN	62
ELMSWOOD. S. M. D.	237
EMMONS. C. M.	70
ENDLEIGH. 7, 6	244
ERNAN. L. M.	306
EUCHARIST. L. M.	57
EVAN. C. M.	43
EVENING HYMN. L. M.	19
EVENING PRAYER. 8, 7	28
EVEN ME	126
EVENTIDE. 10	21
EVERLASTING LOVE	100
EXHORTATION. C. M.	269
FAITHFUL SHEPHERD. 6, 5	146
Faithful Shepherd, feed me	146
Far and near the fields are teeming	255
Far out on the desolate billow	182
Father, I stretch my hands to thee	99
FATHER, LEAD ME. 7	187
Father, lead me day by day	187
FATHER, LEAD THY LITTLE CHILDREN	279
FATHER, MOST HOLY	37
Father, whate'er of earthly bliss	181
FEAR NOT	139
Fear not! God is thy shield	139
FEAST OF BLESSING	110
FINAL VICTORY	258
FLEMMING. 8, 6	157
Forever here my rest shall be	136
FREDERICK. 11	268
FREE GRACE	95
FREELY FOR ME	132
From all that dwell below the skies	5
From every stormy wind that blows	198
From Greenland's icy mountains	247
GARDEN	242
GATHER' THEM IN	256
Gather them in, for yet there is room	256
Give me some work to do	230
GIVE PRAISE TO GOD	38
GLORIA PATRI	1, 318
Glorious things of thee are spoken	240
Glory be to God above	260
Glory be to the Father	1, 318
Glory to thee, my God, this night	19
GOD BE WITH YOU	26
God be with you till we meet again	26
God calling yet! shall I not hear	113
GOD HATH SENT HIS ANGELS	63
GOD IS GOOD. 7	39
GOD IS IN HEAVEN	286
God is in heaven, can he hear	286
GOD IS LOVE	40
GOD SPEED THE RIGHT	303
GOD'S ANVIL	192
Golden harps are sounding	64
GOTTSCHALK. 7	18
Grace, 'tis a charming sound	98
GRATEFUL PRAISE. 7	12
GREENVILLE. 8, 7, 4	96
GREENWOOD. S. M.	179
GROWING UP FOR JESUS	288
Guide me, O thou great Jehovah	156
Gushing so bright in the morning	304

TITLES AND FIRST LINES.

	Hymn
Hail, thou once despiséd Jesus	67
HALLELUJAH, 'TIS DONE	129
HAPPY DAY. L. M.	150
Hark, hark, my soul	278
Hark! the herald-angels sing	52
HARVEST HOME	296
Hasten, sinner, to be wise	107
HEAVEN IS MY HOME. 6, 4	261
HEAVENLY FATHER, WE ADORE THEE	10
HEBER. C. M.	34
HE IS CALLING. 8, 7	47
HE LEADETH ME. L. M.	180
He leadeth me! O blessed thought	180
HENDON. 7	9
HENLEY. 11, 10	159
HERALD ANGELS	52
HIDE THOU ME	140
HOLY CROSS. C. M.	71
Holy, holy, holy, Lord God Almighty	46
HOLY SPIRIT, FAITHFUL GUIDE	87
HORTON. 7	106
How firm a foundation	133
How good thou art to me	39
How happy every child of grace	265
How precious is the book divine	89
How sweet the name of Jesus sounds	94
HURSLEY	23
I am coming to the cross	131
I AM TRUSTING, LORD, IN THEE	131
I DO BELIEVE. C. M.	99
If my disciple thou wouldst be	223
If on a quiet sea	201
I heard the voice of Jesus say	168
I lay my sins on Jesus	138
I love thy kingdom, Lord	241
I love thy will, O God	193
I LOVE TO SING THE STORY	227
I LOVE TO TELL THE STORY	213
I'M A PILGRIM	263
I'm a pilgrim, and I'm a stranger	263
I'm but a stranger here	261
I'm poor and blind and wretched	104
INGHAM. L. M.	113
I NEED THEE EVERY HOUR	173
In some way or other	186
In the cross of Christ I glory	58
IN THE FIELD WITH THEIR FLOCKS	48
IN THE SECRET OF HIS PRESENCE	161
In thy cleft, O Rock of Ages	140
In thy name, O Lord, assembling	15
INVITATION. C. M. D.	168
INVITATION ACCEPTED	116
I SING OF HIS MERCY	72
IS MY NAME WRITTEN THERE	210
Is this thy time of trouble	137
ITALIAN HYMN. 6, 4	8
I THINK, WHEN I READ	282
'I think, when I read that sweet	282
I thirst, thou wounded Lamb of God	151

	Hymn
IT IS WELL WITH MY SOUL	155
I was a wandering sheep	170
I WILL SING FOR JESUS	195
I would not live alway	268
I've found a joy in sorrow	143
I've reached the land of corn and wine	276
JERUSALEM THE GOLDEN. 7, 6	271
JESUS BIDS US SHINE	281
Jesus, high in glory	14
JESUS IS CALLING	108
Jesus is tenderly calling	108
Jesus loved the children	283
Jesus, lover of my soul	202
JESUS LOVES ME	280
Jesus loves me, this I know	280
JESUS LOVES THE CHILDREN	283
JESUS, MY ALL	200
Jesus, my all, to heaven is gone	174
Jesus, my Lord, to thee I cry	128
JESUS, MY PORTION	143
Jesus, my Saviour, thou Lamb of God	132
JESUS SHALL REIGN. L. M.	249
Jesus shall reign where'er the sun	249
Jesus, the very thought of thee	71
Jesus, where'er thy people meet	11
JEWETT. 6	163
Joy to the world, the Lord	50
Just as I am, O Lord	116
"Just as I am," thine own to be	149
Just as I am, without one plea	130
JUST A WORD FOR JESUS	221
Keep me, hide me, O my Father	144
KEEP THOU MY WAY	203
Keep thou my way, O Lord	203
KEEP TO THE RIGHT	232
Lead, kindly light, amid the	188
LEAD ME, PRECIOUS SAVIOUR	287
LEAD THOU ME	141
LEBANON. S. M.	170
Let the love of God, like	41
LENOX. H. M.	109
LITTLE BUDS OF PROMISE	292
LOOK UP	137
Lo! a mighty host is rising	301
Lord, at thy mercy-seat	200
Lord, do not leave me	83
Lord, I care not for riches	210
Lord, dismiss us with thy blessing	16
Lord, I hear of showers of blessing	126
Lord Jesus, I long to be perfectly	205
Lord, this day thy children meet	12
Lord, we come before thee now	9
LOUVAN. L. M.	93
LOVE DIVINE. 8, 7. D.	134
Love divine, all love excelling	134
LUTHER. S. M.	6

TITLES AND FIRST LINES.

	Hymn
Lux Benigna. 10, 4, 10	188
Lyons. 10, 11	45
Maitland. C. M.	215
Majestic sweetness sits enthroned	68
Malvern. L. M.	11
Manoah. C. M.	42
Marching to Zion	212
Martyn. 7. D.	202
March along together	232
Mendebas. 7, 6	33
Mercy. 7.	109
'Mid scenes of confusion and creature	266
Miles' Lane. C. M.	65
Milwaukee. 8, 7	191
Missionary Chant. L. M.	240
Missionary Hymn. 7, 6	247
Monkland. 7	300
More Love to Thee. 6, 4, 6	148
More love to thee, O Christ	148
Morning Red	60
Must Jesus bear the cross alone	215
My country! 'tis of thee	299
My days are gliding swiftly by	262
My faith looks up to thee	172
My father is rich in houses and lands	211
My hope is built on nothing less	178
My Jesus, as thou wilt	163
My Sabbath Song	31
My Shepherd	82
My Shepherd's mighty aid	171
My Times are in Thy Hand	204
My Youth is Thine	216
Naomi. C. M.	181
Nearer, my God, to thee	147
Nettleton. 8, 7. D.	166
Never Alone.	182
New Haven. 6, 4	86
Nicæa. 11, 12, 10	46
No Compromise	301
No Name so Sweet	84
None but Jesus	123
Northfield. C. M.	264
Now All the Bells are Ringing	61
Now is the accepted time	114
Now just a word for Jesus	221
Now let my soul, eternal King	91
Now the daylight goes away	20
Now to heaven our prayer ascending	303
Nuremburg. 7	260
Oak. 6, 4	261
O could I speak the matchless worth	167
O day of rest and gladness	33
O for a heart to praise my God	135
O for a thousand tongues, to sing	2
Oft in danger, oft in woe	235
O, God, my youth is thine	216
O happy day that fixed my choice	150

	Hymn
O Come at Once to Jesus	104
O Let Us be Glad	80
O let us be glad in our Saviour	80
O, holy Saviour, friend unseen	157
Oh scatter seeds of loving deeds	226
Old Hundred. L. M.	1
O little town of Bethlehem	55
Olivet. 6, 4	172
O My Saviour, Hear Me	197
One little hour for watching	217
Once more 'tis eventide and we	24
Once was heard the song of children	76
On Jordan's stormy banks I stand	269
O now I see the crimson wave	102
Onward. 6, 5	236
Onward, Christian soldiers	236
Ortonville. C. M.	68
Over the Ocean Wave	248
Our Glad Jubilee	294
O What can You Tell	285
O when shall I sweep through the gates	267
Pain's furnace heat within me quivers	192
Parting Hymn	29
Pass Me Not	119
Pass me not, O gentle Saviour	119
Peterboro. C. M.	3
Pleading With Thee	118
Pleyel's Hymn. 7	107
Portuguese Hymn. 11	133
Praise for His Greatness	44
Praise for his excellent greatness	44
Praise God, from whom all blessings	1
Praise the Rock of our salvation	4
Precious Name. 8, 7	160
Precious Promise	153
Precious promise God hath given	153
Pressing along the narrow way	220
Prince of peace, control my will	175
Rathbun. 8, 7	58
Refuge. 7. D.	202
Remember Me. C. M.	56
Rescue the Perishing	253
Resting from his work to-day	59
Retreat. L. M.	198
Revive us Again	219
Rise, glorious Conqueror, rise	62
Rockingham. L. M.	151
Rock of ages, cleft for me	125
Sabbath Home	32
Sabbath Morn. 7. 6 l	35
Safe in the Arms of Jesus	184
Safely through another week	55
Saviour, abide with us	25
Saviour, again to thy dear name	29
Saviour, bless a little child	284
Saviour, Blessed Saviour	81

TITLES AND FIRST LINES.

	Hymn
Saviour, breathe an evening blessing...	28
Saviour, let me still abide............	141
SAVIOUR, LIKE A SHEPHERD..............	145
SAVIOUR, LISTEN......................	196
Saviour, listen to our prayer.........	196
SAVIOUR, TEACH ME....................	185
Saviour, teach me day by day..........	185
Saviour, thy dying love...............	218
Saviour, who thy flock art feeding....	191
SEEDS OF PROMISE.....................	226
SELVIN. S. M.........................	201
SETTING SUN. S. M....................	25
SEYMOUR. 7...........................	164
SHALL WE GATHER AT THE RIVER..........	272
SHALL WE KNOW EACH OTHER..............	275
SHINING SHORE........................	262
SICILIAN HYMN. 8, 7, 4................	15
SILVER STREET. S. M..................	98
Since Jesus is my friend..............	179
SING ALWAYS..........................	207
SING OF JESUS, SING FOREVER...........	75
Sing them over again to me............	97
Sing with a tuneful spirit............	207
Softly now the light of day...........	18
Soldiers of Christ, arise.............	237
Soldiers of the cross, arise..........	229
Soldiers of the eternal King..........	239
Soldiers who to Christ belong.........	225
SOMETHING FOR JESUS...................	218
SOME WORK TO DO......................	230
So near to the kingdom................	118
SONG OF THE ANGELS...................	49
SOUND THE BATTLE CRY..................	231
STAND UP FOR JESUS...................	252
Stand up, stand up for Jesus..........	234
ST. HILDA. 7, 6......................	138
ST. MARTIN'S. C. M...................	85
STOCKWELL. 8. 7......................	22
Strains of music often greet me.......	31
STRIKE FOR VICTORY....................	233
Strike, O strike for victory..........	233
ST. THOMAS. S. M.....................	241
SUMMER SUNSHINE......................	297
Summer suns are glowing...............	297
SUNBEAMS.............................	296
Sun of my soul, thou Saviour dear.....	23
SUPPLICATION. 6. 5...................	14
SWABIA. S. M.........................	36
Swell the anthem, raise the song......	300
SWEET BY AND BY......................	277
SWEET HOUR OF PRAYER. L. M. D.........	199
Sweet Sabbath-school, more dear to me.	32
Take the name of Jesus with you.......	160
TAKE ME AS I AM......................	128
Take my life and let it be............	152
TAKE UP THE CROSS....................	223
TELL IT TO JESUS.....................	142
TELL IT OUT..........................	257
Tell it out among the nations.........	257

	Hymn
TELL ME MORE ABOUT JESUS.............	60
Thanks be to God for his wonderful...	295
THANKSGIVING HYMN....................	295
THE CALL FOR REAPERS.................	255
THE CHILDREN'S FRIEND................	79
THE CHRISTIAN'S HIDING PLACE.........	144
The Church's one foundation..........	243
THE GOSPEL BELL......................	103
The Gospel bell is ringing...........	103
THE GOSPEL CALL......................	124
The Lord into his garden comes.......	242
The Lord's my Shepherd, I'll not want.	43
THE LOVE OF GOD......................	41
THE LORD WILL PROVIDE................	186
The morning flowers display their....	306
The morning light is breaking........	246
THE NAME OF OUR SALVATION............	74
THE SAINTS' HOME.....................	266
THE SAVIOUR'S TOMB...................	59
THE SOLID ROCK.......................	178
THE SONG OF THE CHILDREN.............	76
THE SPARKLING RILL...................	304
The Spirit and the Bride say "Come".	124
The voice of free grace..............	95
THE WILL OF GOD......................	193
The year is swiftly waning...........	298
THE YOUNG CHRISTIAN..................	149
There is a fountain filled with blood...	101
THERE IS A FRIEND....................	117
There is a land of pure delight......	270
There is no name so sweet on earth...	84
There's a friend for little children.	79
There's a gentle voice within calls..	122
There's a land that is fairer than day.	277
There's a wideness in God's mercy....	47
THINE FOREVER........................	189
Thine forever!—God of love...........	189
This is the day of light.............	36
THIS IS THE WINTER MORN..............	53
Thou art my shepherd.................	82
Thou dear Redeemer, dying Lamb.......	70
Though troubles assail, and dangers..	45
Thy word, almighty Lord..............	92
'Tis the blessed hour of prayer......	13
'Tis known in earth and heaven, too..	69
'Tis the promise of God full salvation.	129
TO JESUS I WILL GO...................	122
TOPLADY. 7. 6 l......................	125
To the name of our salvation.........	74
TO THE WORK..........................	254
To the work, to the work.............	254
TRUSTING IN HIS WORD.................	190
TWILIGHT.............................	27
UP FOR JESUS STAND...................	239
UXBRIDGE. L. M.......................	91
VARINA. C. M. D......................	270
VESPERS. 7...........................	20
VICTORY. 7...........................	225

TITLES AND FIRST LINES.

	Hymn
Waken, Christian Children	54
Wake the Song	4
Wake, wake the song	294
Watchman, blow the Gospel trumpet	245
Weary Child	115
Weary child, by sin oppressed	115
Weary of Earth and Laden	105
Webb	234, 246
Weeping will not save me	123
Welcome Home	267
We'll Help the Cause Along	302
Wellesley. 8, 7	47
We must work and pray together	302
We plow the fields and scatter	296
We praise thee, O God, for	219
We Shall Meet	273
We shall meet beyond the river	273
We welcome you all	290
We've listed in a holy war	224
What a Friend we have in Jesus. 8, 7, D.	165
What a Meeting That will Be	274
When all thy mercies, O my God	42
When at morn we wake from sleep	154
When, His Salvation Bringing	78
When I can read my title clear	264
When I survey the wondrous cross	57
When Jesus comes to reward his	209
When peace like a river	155
When that glorious morn shall come	258
When the King comes in	222
When we all meet at home in the	274
When we hear the music ringing	275
While, with ceaseless course, the sun	305
While shepherds watched their flocks	51
Whiter than Snow	206
Who'll be the Next	121
Who'll be the next to follow Jesus	121
Why do You Wait	127
Why do you wait, dear brother	127
Will Jesus find us Watching	209
Within God's temple now we meet	38
With hearts in love abounding	244
With joy we hail the sacred day	34
Wonderful Words	97
Wondrous words! how rich in	100
Woodworth. L. M	130
Work, for the night is coming	228
Work Song	228
Yes! for me, for me, he careth	183
Yield not to Temptation	205
Zephyr	17, 88
Zion. 8, 7, 4	154

THE END.

www.ingramcontent.com/pod-product-compliance
Lightning Source LLC
Chambersburg PA
CBHW021818230426
43669CB00008B/792